Great British

Walks

Great British

Walks

First published in the United Kingdom in 2014
by National Trust Books, 1 Gower Street
London W1CE 6HD
An imprint of Pavilion Books Group Ltd

© National Trust 2014
The National Trust is a registered charity, no. 205846

ISBN: 978-1-909881-23-5
A CIP catalogue record for this book is available
from the British Library

Colour reproduction by Rival Colour Ltd, UK
Printed by GPS Group Ltd, Slovenia

Front cover: A view of St David's Head with North
Bishop and the sea beyond, Pembrokeshire, Wales.
See walk 88.

Back cover: Autumn colours along the Mill Trail at
Hardcastle Crags, West Yorkshire. See 69.

Above: St David's Head with North Bishop and the sea
beyond, Pembrokeshire, Wales. See walk 90.

Previous page: The Mourne Mountains from Murlough
National Nature Reserve, County Down, Northern
Ireland. See walk 94.

This book can be ordered direct from the publisher at
the website www.pavilionbooks com, or try your local
bookshop. Also available at National Trust shops and
www.nationaltrust.org.uk/shop

Contents

The South West

The South East

East England

The Midlands

The North West

Yorkshire and the North East

Wales

Northern Ireland

Below: Autumn colours along the Mill Trail at Hardcastle Crags, near Hebden Bridge, West Yorkshire. See walk 50.

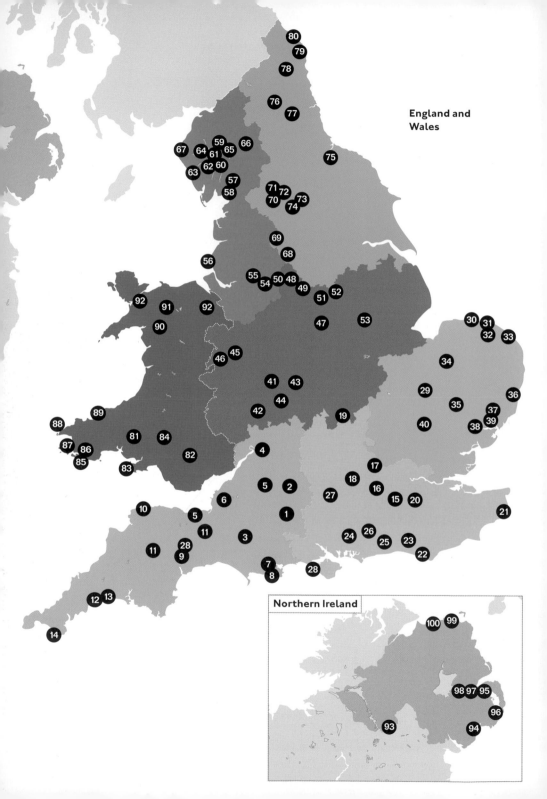

England and
Wales

Northern Ireland

Introduction:
100 Great British Walks

With responsibility for over 600,000 acres of land of outstanding natural beauty, almost 750 miles (1,200km) of coastline, and more than 300 historic buildings, set in glorious parkland and gardens, it is little wonder that the National Trust offers some of the most spectacular walking environments to be found anywhere in England, Wales and Northern Ireland. This beautifully illustrated guide features 100 great walks across some of Britain's most iconic landscapes. Stroll across the Giant's Causeway in County Antrim, around the ancient standing stones at Avebury in Wiltshire, or along the shoreline of Lake Windermere in Cumbria. There's no better way to appreciate the British countryside than to explore it on foot so, whether you're looking for a gentle saunter through rolling parkland or a more strenuous hike across rugged terrain, armed with your copy of *100 Great British Walks* you'll be spoiled for choice when it comes to finding the perfect walk.

A view across Lake Windermere towards fells in the Lake District, Cumbria. See walk 60.

About the Walks

The walks featured cover a wide range of different landscapes and points of interest. Some cross coastal cliff-tops (such as walks 10 and 22) or open fells (61 and 62), affording spectacular views in all directions. Others pass along quiet river valleys (11 and 76), or through ancient woods (40 and 86), nature reserves (30 and 94) and historic parkland (31 and 53). Wildlife features widely, with walks across some of Britain's most precious habitats: limestone grasslands (4 and 25) and heathland (8 and 36), with their associated wild flowers and insect life in spring and summer, and woodland carpeted in bluebells in spring (27 and 52) or ablaze with colour in the autumn (39 and 41). Then there are the special-interest walks, seeking out ancient monuments (1 and 2), medieval churches (33 and 34), and sites of geological interest (6 and 74) or industrial heritage (72 and 90). Discover walks that follow in the footsteps of famous people, such as Victorian prime minister Benjamin Disraeli (18), landscape artist John Constable (38) and Romantic poet William Wordsworth (65).

Nearly all the walks are circular, many with cafés and restaurants along the way. General advice about getting to your starting point is provided, along with postcodes for satellite navigation, and although some areas are too remote to make it a viable option public transport details are avalaible online at www.traveline.org.uk. Also provided are suggestions for local attractions that will help you make the most of your day, such as nearby gardens, castles, country houses and exhibitions, along with information on the all-important availability of toilet facilities.

Many of the walks are suitable for families, with some shorter walks designed specifically with younger children in mind, complete with adventure playgrounds, den-building activities or grassy banks just made for rolling down – look out for the family-friendly symbol against appropriate walks (see key below). To help you judge which walks might best suit your needs, they are graded according to their level of ease, from easy walks with even paths and few inclines, steps and stiles, through moderate walks with more uneven paths and some steeper climbs, to hard walks best suited to more adventurous ramblers. Some walks in particular can become very muddy after rain, so look out for the symbol highlighting the need for wellies or walking boots (see key).

Many more walks are available. Visit: www.nationaltrust.org.uk/walking

Walking Hints and Tips

- Consider taking a mobile phone with you, bearing in mind coverage can be patchy in rural areas.
- If you are walking alone, let someone know where you are and when you expect to return.
- It's advisable to take an Ordnance Survey map with you on country walks to supplement the maps provided.
- Some of the walks take you along small country lanes without pavements. Always walk facing oncoming traffic (except when approaching a right-hand bend when it is advisable to cross the road for a clear view), keep children and dogs under close control, and wear something light or brightly coloured when visibility is poor (e.g. at dusk).
- Take special care of children when walking beside water or along cliff-tops.
- While the authors have taken every care to ensure the accuracy of the walks, be aware that changes to

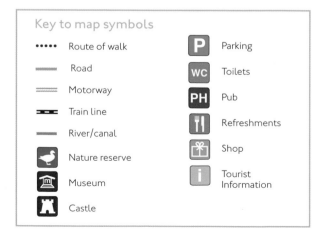

the routes may occur after publication.
- Public transport may also change over time, so, if you're thinking of taking a bus or train to your destination, always check timetables and routes online or with a local tourist information centre before setting out.

Follow the Countryside Code

Here's how to respect, protect and enjoy the countryside:
- Always park sensibly, making sure that your vehicle is not blocking access to drives, fields and farm tracks.
- Leave gates as you find them or follow instructions on signs. If walking in a group, make sure the last person knows how to leave the gate.
- In fields where crops are growing, follow the paths wherever possible.
- Don't leave litter and leftover food – it spoils the beauty of the countryside and can be dangerous

to wildlife and farm animals, too.
- Avoid damaging, destroying or removing flowers, trees or even rocks: they provide homes for wildlife and add to everyone's enjoyment of the countryside.
- Don't get too close to wild animals or farm animals as they can behave unpredictably.
- Be careful not to drop a match or smouldering cigarette at any time of the year, as this can cause fires.
- Keep dogs under control (see special feature on dogs).

Previous page: The Holnicote Estate, Somerset. See walk 5.

Be Dog Wise

Please help the National Trust keep the countryside a safe, healthy and enjoyable place for you and your dog, as well as other visitors, wildlife and livestock:

- Always keep your dog in sight and under control, using a lead if requested. (See 'About this walk' feature on individual walks for specific information regarding the control of dogs.)

- Never let your dog chase wildlife or farm animals.

- Observe local notices when you're out and about. There may be restrictions in woodland or on farmland at sensitive times of year, like in spring, during the lambing season, and between the beginning of March and the end of July when ground-nesting birds are on eggs or raising their young.

- Please always pick up after your dog. We ask that if your dog fouls, particularly in car parks, on paths and by picnic spots, you pick up and remove the mess. At some of our sites we've got dedicated dog-mess bins where you can dispose of it.

50 things to do before you're 11 ¾

To add to the fun of a family walk, check out '50 things to do before you're 11 ¾', which encourage kids to discover their wild side and enjoy the outdoors by building a den, climbing a tree, tracking a wild animal, making a mud pie or skimming a stone, to name but a few. To find out more, visit the National Trust website at www.50things.org.uk where children can register for free.

The South West

1. Exploring the Stonehenge Landscape

Explore Durrington Walls and the link between two of the country's most important henges in this lovely walk that takes you across a less well-known part of the Stonehenge World Heritage Site. Whereas the Stonehenge Stone Circle is known to have been a place of burial in Neolithic times, over 4,500 years ago, Durrington Walls was a place where people lived and held feasts and rituals.

Stonehenge Cottages
King Barrows
Amesbury
Wiltshire SP4 7DD
(NB not start of the walk)
01980 664780
stonehenge@
nationaltrust.org.uk
www.nationaltrust.org.uk/
stonehenge-landscape

About this walk
Area of archaeological interest
A few short, steep slopes
Dogs welcome on a lead

Distance 4 miles (6.4km)

Time 2 hours 30 minutes

Above: King's Barrow Ridge.

Things to see

Henges

Henges are large enclosures with an inner ditch and outer bank, built in the Neolithic period around 4,500 to 5,000 years ago. They're believed to be ceremonial rather than defensive and may contain standing stones, a stone circle or timber posts. Stonehenge actually has its bank and ditch the other way round, so is not technically a henge.

Durrington Walls

The largest complete henge in Britain, Durrington Walls is 1,640ft (500m) in diameter and encloses a natural valley. It may have been built to 'close off' the area once it fell out of use. This area contained timber circles and what seem to have been shrines. The area outside the ditch and bank (and partly under it) was once a settlement, perhaps containing hundreds of houses, making Durrington Walls potentially the largest village in north-west Europe at the time.

The Cuckoo Stone

This former standing stone now lies on its side, beside its original natural site. Over millennia it has been a focus for Bronze Age urn burials, an Iron Age boundary line and Roman remains. It's made of sarsen, a kind of sandstone, the same as the largest stones in the Stonehenge stone circle. The reason for its name remains a mystery but probably refers to the anomaly of finding such a large rock in this area.

The Cuckoo Stone.

How to Get There

By Train Salisbury,
9 miles (14.4km)

By Car Woodhenge car
park is 1.75 miles (2.8km)
north of Amesbury – follow
signs from A345

OS Map Landranger 184;
Explorer 130

Start / End Woodhenge
car park, **OS grid ref:**
SU 151434

Durrington
Walls

Cuckoo
Stone

Woodhenge

New King
Barrows

N

200 m

1. At Woodhenge car park, go through the gate nearest to you and into a field, then walk downhill into Durrington Walls.

2. At the centre of Durrington Walls, you can see how this henge is in an enclosed valley. Next, turn left and walk to the corner of this field. Pass through the gates either side of the road, heading towards a low rock.

3. The Cuckoo Stone is one of very few stones in the area made from sarsen rather than chalk or flint. From here, continue straight ahead to the next gate, keeping the fence line on your right.

4. You're now on the route of the old military railway between Amesbury and Larkhill. Turn right and follow the path

5. When you reach a crossroads and National Trust sign to King Barrow Ridge, turn left and follow the shaded bridleway.

6. On reaching the next junction, turn right through a gate to continue along the ridge, crossing Stonehenge Avenue on your way to a line of 200-year-old beech trees and a fine view of Stonehenge.

7. Continue forwards to New King Barrows, a fine row of early Bronze Age burial mounds, originally capped in white chalk so they would have been visible from a distance. Return to point 6, turn right and follow the stony track to point 8.

8. Bear left through a gap in the hedge to join the old military railway again. This leads back to the gate in the corner of the Cuckoo Stone field.

9. Head across the grassland to Woodhenge and back to Woodhenge car park.

Make the Most of Your Day
Family activities are available throughout the year. A visitor shuttle runs between the stone circle and the nearby English Heritage visitor centre (free to National Trust members).

Food and Facilities
There is a café and toilets at the visitor centre (not National Trust).

2. Avebury Archaeology Walk

Starting at the heart of the Avebury World Heritage Site, this walk takes you through the remains of the largest stone circle in the world and along the West Kennet Avenue into beautiful, rolling chalk downland. You'll catch glimpses of mysterious Silbury Hill, pass Bronze Age burial mounds and walk along ancient roads with fabulous views.

Avebury
Near Marlborough
Wiltshire SN8 1RD
01672 539250
avebury@
nationaltrust.org.uk
www.nationaltrust.org.uk/
avebury

About this walk
Area of archaeological interest

Extensive views

Dogs welcome on a lead

Distance 6 miles (9.6km)

Time 3 to 4 hours

Above: Two of the massive stones forming part of the Avebury Circle Neolithic complex.

Things to see

Neolithic Avebury
Neolithic Avebury dates from around 4,600 years ago. The massive circular bank and ditch (called a henge) surrounding the stone circles is part of a huge ceremonial landscape that took centuries to build. The henge you see today is impressive, especially when you realise the chalk was dug out by hand. Excavation results tell us that originally the ditch was much deeper, with steep sides at least 30ft (9m) deep and the bank over 13ft (4m) high.

Giant standing stones
The stones are made of a hard, grey sandstone called sarsen. Look out for the two remaining stones of the Cove, which originally comprised

three standing stones in the centre of one of the smaller stone circles. The largest of these stones weighs at least 100 tonnes.

West Kennet Avenue
The West Kennet Avenue is a double line of stones that once formed a ceremonial route joining the henge to a timber and stone circle called the Sanctuary.

The henge at Avebury, lined by standing stones.

By Train Pewsey 10 miles (16km); Swindon 11 miles (17.7km)

By Car 6 miles (9.6km) west of Marlborough, 1 mile (1.6km) north of the Bath road (A4) on A4361 and B4003

OS Map Landranger 173; Explorer 157;

Start / End Avebury National Trust car park, **OS grid ref: SU099696**

1. From the car park follow the signs to the henge. Turn right into the High Street and enter the henge via the first gate on your right. Follow the curve of the huge sarsen stones and the ditch. Cross the road and head along the fence line past the bank and trees. Go through the gate and cross the minor road into the West Kennet Avenue.

2. This part of the Avenue was excavated by Alexander Keiller in the 1930s. He re-erected the stones and put markers at holes where stones once stood, the stones having been broken up and taken away for building long ago.

3. At the end of the reconstructed part of the Avenue, cross the road and follow the footpath straight ahead. Look out for the sole remaining stone of Falkner's Circle in the hedgerow on your left. Continue on this footpath until you reach a crossroads.

4. Follow the waymarker pointing right and uphill along the track. As you gain height, looking across the valley you'll be able to see the top of Silbury Hill. Ahead you'll see the 'hedgehogs'. Stay on this path until it meets the well-defined track that is the Ridgeway, an ancient route used since prehistoric times, and now a National Trail.

5. Turn right for a short detour to explore Overton Hill barrow cemetery. The chalk barrows, or burial mounds, found here date from around 4,200 years ago, but nineteenth-century landowners planted trees on top of some of them – you can see why they are known locally as hedgehogs. See if you can spot the grassy remains of a Roman road running across the field. Now retrace your footsteps along the Ridgeway.

6. Continue along the Ridgeway until you meet the junction with Green Street. Turn left along here, heading downhill. Green Street was once the main road from Marlborough to Bath. It's also known as the Herepath, an Anglo-Saxon word meaning 'army road'.

7. Passing through the banks of the henge, go through the gate on your right into the north-east sector of the henge. Cross the road at the gateway behind the giant Cove stones to explore the north-western part of the henge.

8. The steps down from the henge bring you into the farmyard. Turn left for the footpath that takes you back to the car park, or turn right to explore the museum and shop.

Make the Most of Your Day

Talks and guided tours of the landscape and manor house are available, and family activities are held in the holidays. Avebury Manor is well worth a visit, as is the Alexander Keiller Museum, which houses finds from Keiller's excavations, along with interactive displays that bring the landscape to life.

Food and Facilities

Refreshments can be found at the Circles Café or Avebury Manor tea-room. National Trust toilets are also available.

Two giant sarsens stand out against the blue sky at Avebury.

3. Sherborne Estate Family Fun Trail

This fun trail for families takes you through Sherborne Park, a working estate with an abundance of wildlife, from fallow and roe deer to badgers and bats. Along the way, look out for 13 hidden letters that will help you discover the mystery two-part word. Take care to put the letters in the right order as you go along.

Sherborne
Pleasure Grounds
North Cotswolds
Gloucestershire
GL54 3DW
01451 844130
lodgepark@
nationaltrust.org.uk
www.nationaltrust.org.uk/
lodge-park-and-sherborne-
estate

About this walk
A 'Hidden Places' walk
Lots of fun for young children

Distance 1 mile (1.6km)

Time 30 to 40 minutes

Things to see

Sherborne House and Gardens
The first building on the site was probably a hunting lodge for Winchcombe Abbey, which was rebuilt as a house several times over the centuries. What survives today is largely from the 1830s and 1840s. The pleasure grounds also date from the mid-nineteenth century, when winding paths were created through the woodlands and a new ice house built. The house itself is not owned by the National Trust.

The Duttons of Sherborne
The first Dutton at Sherborne was Thomas, a Crown Surveyor from Cheshire born in 1506, who bought the manor in 1551. His son William was prominent in local society; High Sheriff and Deputy Lieutenant

for Gloucestershire, he married the daughter of a Lord Mayor of London, which brought great wealth into the family. This was enjoyed by his son John 'Crump' Dutton – nicknamed after his hunchback – who built Lodge Park and the deer course on the estate.

Bats at Sherborne
Seventeen of the world's 1,000 species of bat breed in the United Kingdom, ranging from the tiny pipistrelle, weighing less than a one pound coin, to Britain's biggest woodland bat, the noctule, which is still smaller than the palm of your hand. Sherborne is home to ten species, which use the woodlands, hedgerows, rivers, gardens and buildings as roosting sites and feeding areas.

Top: The gates at Sherborne Estate, Gloucestershire.
Above: A juvenile male pipistrelle bat.

How to Get There

By Train Cheltenham, 13 miles (20.9km), with bus links to Sherborne

By Car Approach from A40 following Sherborne directions

OS Map Landranger 163

Start / End Ewe Pen Barn car park, **OS grid ref: SP 166140**

---

1. The walk starts in the Ewe Pen Barn car park. Look out for the buildings where sheep used to shelter in the winter. Here is where you'll find your first letter.

2. Turn right as you leave the car park and follow the track. Bear right at the gate to walk along the stone wall. Look out for an elder bush against the wall at the end of the tree line, where you'll find your second letter.

3. Keep on the track and pass the football pitch until you come to the avenue of beech trees. The beech trees lined the original driveway to Sherborne House. One of the first four trees has letter number three hidden among its branches.

4. Go back to the track and follow the edge of Quarry Wood. This area used to be quarried for stone until the First World War, hence the name. The wood is bordered by a young plantation of trees. At the end of the plantation, just before another wall starts, you'll find the fourth letter.

5. You soon reach a metal gate on your left. Go through the gate to enter the pleasure grounds and follow the path down. Before the path goes up again, you'll see a gap looking like a 'valley' on your left. The fifth letter is hidden in this area.

6. Continue on the same path to a beech tree, just before the metal gate. Look up and you'll see a flying bat sculpture. Somewhere around the tree is the sixth letter.

7. Walk through the gate and find the ice house for the seventh letter.

8. The path leads you to another metal gate. Follow the track and keep bearing right to follow the edge of the parkland. At the point where the two fields separate is a fence. Letter number eight can be found on a conifer tree on the woodland side of the fence.

9. Stay on the path until you reach the sculpture with the life cycle of the beetle on it. Somewhere on the tree is the ninth letter.

The Beech Avenue in autumn on the Sherborne Estate.

10. Go back towards the bench and keep bearing right whilst following the path. In the bend there are two Austrian pines – you may find pine cones on the ground here. Look up to find letter number ten.

11. Look out for letter II on an ash tree in the wooded area, just before the waymark post.

12. Follow the path straight on and climb up the hill where a yew tree surrounded by the circular seat stands. You'll find letter 12 on the tree.

13. Run down the hill to the right to find a rock standing on its own. You'll find the last letter here. Now you've found all the letters, you need to put them in the right order to make a two-part word. Have you worked out what it is? From here, follow the track back in reverse to get back to the car park.

Make the Most of Your Day

Make sure to leave time to visit the eighteenth-century water meadows, home to otters, water voles and dragonflies (parking available at Northfield Barn car park). At nearby Lodge Park, you'll find England's only surviving seventeenth-century deer course and grandstand, created in 1634 by John 'Crump' Dutton.

Food and Facilities

A courtyard café can be found at Park Lodge, where award-winning cakes, along with ice creams and snacks, will tempt your taste buds. Toilets are available at Lodge Park (only when property is open). The nearest public toilets are located in Northleach.

4. Rodborough Common Butterfly Walk

The steep grassland slopes of Rodborough Common offer superb opportunities for butterfly spotting and walking, and afford wonderful views over the Severn Estuary. Look out for over 30 varieties of butterfly, including rare species such as the Duke of Burgundy and the Adonis blue, which breed and feed here each summer among the amazing variety of wildflowers.

Rodborough Common
Stroud
Gloucestershire
01452 814213
minchandrod@
nationaltrust.org.uk
www.nationaltrust.org.uk/
minchinhampton-and-
rodborough-commons

About this walk
Wildlife walk

Butterflies in spring and summer

Fine views

Distance 2.75 miles
(4.4km)

Time I hour 30 minutes

Above: Rodborough Common.

Things to see

Adonis blue and other butterflies
Look out for the vivid, iridescent blue and black vein ends of the Adonis blue. These butterflies have

Adonis blue butterfly.

recently recolonised the southern Cotswolds after an absence of 40 years, and Rodborough is now home to several colonies. The best is to be found at Swellshill Bank. Chalkhill blue and small blue also live here. If you're lucky you may spot the green hairstreak and dingy skipper in spring. The marbled white is abundant in July.

Duke of Burgundy
Rodborough Common is one of the best places in the United Kingdom for spotting the Duke of Burgundy butterfly, with five separate colonies along the lower slopes. These butterflies usually fly from the third week in April until late May.

Wildflowers
Keep an eye out for early purple orchids and the striking pasque flower. Pasque flowers bloom in spring, hence their name, which means Easter in French. They are extremely scarce and only found in a small area in southern England. Thirteen types of orchid can be found in the limestone grassland on the top and slopes of the plateau. Early purple orchids blossom in spring, followed by blooming pyramidal orchids and autumn lady's-tresses in late summer.

1. From the car park, head south-west on a path skirting round the houses on the summit of the plateau. Keep the houses on your left.

2. When you reach the grassy outcrop of Rodborough Manor Spur, turn right, away from the houses. Head down the slope of the spur. Pasque flowers grow above the road here. Duke of Burgundy and small blue butterflies can also be found on the lower slopes. Follow the cattle tracks north, traversing the bottom of the slope. A variety of butterflies can be spotted here.

3. North of Little London, between the houses and the larch grove, there is a good colony of Duke of Burgundy butterfly – best seen mid-May.

4. Continue north, still walking across the steep lower slopes. Before you reach Rodborough Fort, head uphill towards the plateau road.

5. Cross the road and explore the slopes of Butterrow Hill, looking for all three species of blue butterfly, before returning south to the car park. You can either continue by car or on foot from here. Turn right out of the car park, taking the first left off the

plateau road and heading straight over a crossroads; carry on until you reach Winstone's Ice Cream Factory.

6. Continue along this lane until you reach more open common. Keep on this route (don't turn left downhill) and look out for a cattle trough on the left.

7. If you took your car, park here and walk downhill to Swellshill Bank; this is the best place to see both Duke of Burgundy and Adonis blue. Afterwards, if you're on foot, retrace your steps to the car park at point 1.

Make the Most of Your Day
Visit Chedworth Roman Villa and walk in the footsteps of the Romans. The villa was home to some of the richest people in the country during its heyday in the fourth century.

Food and Facilities
The historic Winstone's Ice Cream Factory is open all year. There are also several pubs on the edge of the common. Toilets are available in nearby Minchinhampton.

5. Holnicote Estate Wander

Situated in the heart of one of the National Trust's largest countryside properties, this short walk provides wonderful panoramic views across the 20 square miles (52km²) of the Holnicote Estate, encompassing some of the most stunning landscape within Exmoor National Park. It passes through Horner Wood, a haven for wildlife and one of the country's top sites for ancient oaks, some of which are 500 years old or more.

Webbers Post
Holnicote Estate, west of Minehead
West Somerset
01823 451587
holnicote@
nationaltrust.org.uk
www.nationaltrust.org.uk/
holnicote-estate

About this walk
Wildlife walk

Panoramic views

Suitable for off-road buggies

Dogs welcome on a lead

Distance 1 mile (1.6km)

Time 30 to 40 minutes

Above: The view from Selworthy Beacon towards Horner Wood and Dunkery Beacon.

Things to see

Temperate rainforest
Horner is a rainforest owned and managed by the National Trust. An ancient semi-natural woodland,

Horner Wood.

it is one of the largest wooded National Nature Reserves in England, covering some 900 acres (360ha). Horner is classified as an Atlantic Oakwood with a warm and moist oceanic climate, with over 80in (200cm) of rain a year. The rainforest climate is characterised by wet-loving plants such as mosses, ferns and lichens.

The heath fritillary
This striking brown and orange insect is one of Britain's rarest butterflies. It has been in serious decline over the last 30 years and now survives in only four areas of the country. On Exmoor it can be found from late May to July,

in sunny, sheltered, heathland combes, where, following several years of careful management, the species appears to be stable.

Fungi
More than 440 species of fungi have been recorded in Horner Wood and the surrounding area. Although there are many edible fungi to be found, there are also some extremely dangerous varieties such as the most famous and deadly of all poisonous mushrooms, the death cap. The death cap (*Amanita phalloides*) is suspected of having caused more mushroom poisoning deaths than any other species.

How to Get There

By Car 4 miles (6.4km) west of Minehead along A39. Turn off for Luccombe and continue out of village towards Horner. After a mile (1.6km), turn left at Chapel Cross crossroads and climb up hill to Webbers Post

OS Map Landranger 181; Explorer OL9

Start / End Main Webbers Post car park, **OS grid ref: SS903438**

---

1. Leave the main Webbers Post car park by the wooden information panel, at the start of the Webbers Post Easy Access Trail.

2. After a short distance, where the Easy Access Trail forks, take the left-hand fork.

3. As you emerge from the woods you will see the first of several wooden sculptures dotted along the trail. The sculptures were created during Wood 2004, an international wood-carving festival that was hosted on the estate.

4. Continue along the Easy Access Trail. Ignoring the signpost for the Priestway bridleway, follow the trail until you reach the next wooden signpost marked 'Permitted Bridleway to Horner' – the Easy Access Trail begins to turn abruptly to the right here.

5. Leave the Easy Access Trail and follow the permitted bridleway. This is a great spot for finding the nests of wood ants, which are extremely active on warm, sunny days.

6. As you emerge from the woods you will see the wooden Jubilee Hut in front of you. It was originally constructed in 1897 to mark the diamond jubilee

of Queen Victoria. This is a beautiful spot to stop and take in the panoramic views over the ancient Horner Wood, part of the Dunkery and Horner Wood National Nature Reserve.

7. Now retrace your route back to the Easy Access Trail.

8. Once you have rejoined the Easy Access Trail, turn left. Continue along the trail through the conifer plantation and past several more wooden sculptures back to the car park.

Make the Most of Your Day
The Holnicote Estate has more than 170 picturesque cottages and many other vernacular buildings and historical structures to explore. Or visit nearby Watersmeet, a dramatic river gorge set among ancient woodlands, and a haven for wildlife with breath-taking views.

Food and Facilities
There are picnic areas at Horner car park and Selworthy Green, and a tea garden at Watersmeet. Toilets are available at Bossington and Horner.

6. Cheddar Gorge Circuit

The Cliffs
Cheddar
Somerset
01643 862452
cheddargorge@
nationaltrust.org.uk
www.nationaltrust.org.uk/
cheddar-gorge

About this walk
Area of geological interest

Some stiles and steep climbs

Avoid in foggy or very windy weather

Dogs welcome on a lead

Distance 4 miles (6.4km)

Time 1 hour 40 minutes

At almost 400ft (122m) deep and 3 miles (4.8km) long, this is England's largest gorge, and with its weathered crags and pinnacles, one of our most spectacular natural sights. It plays host to a varied community of specialised plants and wildlife, many of which you'll get the chance to spot on this exhilarating circular walk.

Things to see

Cheddar Gorge
Cheddar Gorge is a great, deep fissure cutting through the Mendip Hills. It developed during successive Ice Ages, when water from melting glaciers formed a river that carved into the limestone rock, creating the steep cliffs you see today. The Cheddar Yeo River gradually made its way underground, creating the famous Cheddar caves where cheese is still made, using the milk from cows that graze in the pastures.

Peregrine falcon
Peregrine falcons are just one of the many birds that call the cliffs home and which, if you're lucky, you may spot soaring overhead. Buzzards, ravens and jackdaws also nest in the gorge.

Wildflowers
The famous Cheddar pink and other rare plants such as rock stonecrop grow on the cliff edges. Look out for rock rose and herbs including thyme, wild basil and marjoram on the lower slopes.

Stay Safe Please do not stand under the cliffs as small rocks may fall at any time. Use only the footpaths signed for the gorge walks: it is dangerous to depart from these footpaths.

Above: The spectacular geology at Cheddar Gorge.

How to Get There

By Train Weston-super-Mare 9 miles (14.4km)

By Car 8 miles (12.8km) north-west of Wells, just off A371 to Axbridge on B3135

OS Map Landranger 182; Explorer 141

Start / End National Trust shop and information centre, **OS grid ref: ST468543**

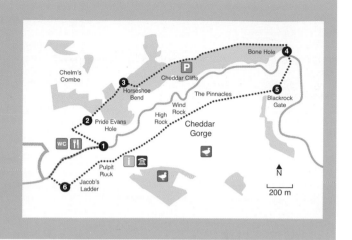

View from the top of the gorge, looking out over the town of Cheddar.

1. Take the track called Cufic Lane, which is off Cheddar High Street, next to the toy shop and opposite the National Trust information centre. A short way up this track you'll come to a National Trust omega sign and a gate leading up a steep path.

2. Go through the gate and follow the path up through the woods. This is a very steep path and the most strenuous part of the route, but it's well worth the climb. Continue uphill until you get to the top of the path and go through the gate at the top.

3. Head towards the stone wall diagonally to your right. Keep the wall/fencing to your right at all times – the cliff edge is just below this area. Continue up the path until you reach a kissing gate. Go through and follow this path. At the bottom of the hill, turn right and follow the track to reach the main road.

4. Turn left and continue up the road for a short distance until you see a footpath on the right side of the road, heading steeply uphill through the woods. Follow this and, on reaching the top of the hill, continue walking until the path divides. (For a shorter walk, turn right instead of left upon reaching the main road, and follow the road back to the information centre. Take care, though, as there are no pavements and the road is busy with some sharp bends.)

5. Bear right rather than taking the route marked to Draycott, and continue until you see a very tall gate. You are now going onto land owned by Cheddar Gorge; this part of the site is free and open to the public. You'll quickly reach the highest point of the gorge and can look across to the other side you've just walked along. Follow the path leading downwards until you get to Jacob's Ladder and Pavey's Lookout Tower. Don't go down Jacob's Ladder but instead take the quieter path to the left, through the trees, which brings you out onto Lippiatt Lane.

6. Turn right down the hill and right again at Shahnaz Restaurant, onto the High Street. Walk back up this road to arrive back at the National Trust information centre.

Make the Most of Your Day

King John's Hunting Lodge in nearby Axbridge is an early Tudor timber-framed wool merchant's house from about 1500, which provides a fascinating insight into local history. Further afield lies Tyntesfield, a spectacular Victorian Gothic Revival house with an air of mystery like something out of a fairytale.

Food and Facilities

There is a range of independent cafés in Cheddar village, as well as public toilets.

7. Purbeck Ramble

This short circular walk takes you across grassland meadows to quiet woodland where you'll find a beautiful landscape and lots of adventure for the kids. Along the way you can explore relics of the Second World War and quarry industry, and enjoy glorious views of Corfe Castle. The walk lies at the heart of the Purbeck countryside, a stunning area of heaths, hills, cliffs and coasts.

Acton
Purbeck
Dorset BH19 3LD
01929 450002
purbeck@
nationaltrust.org.uk
www.nationaltrust.org.uk/
purbeck-countryside

About this walk
A 'Hidden Places' walk
Bluebells in spring
Some stiles

Distance 1 mile (1.6km)

Time 30 to 40 minutes

Things to see

Nissen huts
Nissen huts were invented by British mining engineer Lieutenant Colonel Peter Nissen, and were first employed in the Second World War. They were a cheap, practical military shelter, often used for storage and accommodation. The Nissen hut on this walk was relocated to this site and is affectionately known as Albie's Barn after a warden on the Purbeck Estate.

Langton West Wood
Langton West Wood is ancient woodland, where the wood is harvested for making pea sticks, charcoal and many green woodworking products. In spring the clearings are carpeted in English bluebells. Orchids add variety, and indicate that this area has remained uncultivated and unaffected by

intensive farming practices. Many of the rides or tracks found here were first formed by deer, still common throughout the Purbeck area, in particular sika deer, introduced from the Far East in the nineteenth century.

Corfe Castle
Corfe Castle is one of Britain's most majestic ruins. The demolition of the castle in 1646 by the Parliamentarians marked the end of a rich history as both a fortress and a royal residence. The crumbling ruin, its outline softened by plants, and the building's almost ethereal quality as light and weather change, all contribute to the unique atmosphere of Corfe Castle. From point 5 on the walk you can see how the castle ruins dominate a gap in the Purbeck Hills.

Top: Corfe Castle.
Above: 'Albie's Barn', a Nissen hut on the Purbeck Estate.

How to Get There

By Train Branksome or Poole, both 6.5 miles (10.4km) via ferry; Wareham 12 miles (19.3km)

By Car A351 to Langton Matravers, then west on B3069, turning into Acton opposite red telephone box

OS Map Landranger 15

Start / End Acton car park, **OS grid ref: SY988787**

1. Start from Acton car park and cross the B3069 towards the red phone box and pedestrian gate. Go through this gate and head diagonally right across the grassland to the remains of a stone building and another pedestrian gate. Ahead you'll see a Nissen hut.

2. Go through the gate and head in a diagonal direction towards the water trough and stile. Head over the stile and follow the path between the wall and a hedge to a vehicle track. Turn right here and follow the track in front of the houses until you reach a stile on the bend at the site of Norman's Quarry.

3. Explore the history of this quarry before heading over the stile into the field. Bearing left, follow the wall line to the next field gate on the left. Enter this field, keeping to the right along the wall line and heading towards the woodland gate in front of you.

4. Enter Langton West Wood, bearing left at a fork in the track. Keep going along this woodland track until you meet a vehicle track on the left. Turn left here and head out of the wood to the field gate. Dead wood is left in the woods to provide food and shelter for insects. You may see sika or roe deer here, or hear the loud whistling call of the sika stags in the autumn breeding season.

5. Walk straight back up the field, enjoying the views to the right of Corfe Castle, and heading towards the gate and stile in the fence. Keep going up this field and bear right around the remains of a stone building. Keep left until you get to the stone shelter and the pedestrian gate you used earlier in the walk.

6. Go back to the pedestrian gate by the telephone box that you passed through earlier, and cross the road back to the car park.

Make the Most of Your Day

There's lots to see and do in beautiful Purbeck. While you're here, visit the ruins of Corfe Castle or go to the coast to see the chalk stacks called Old Harry Rocks, one of the most famous landmarks on the South Coast. From here you will get stunning views across Poole Harbour and beyond to the Isle of Wight.

Food and Facilities

Head for the tea-rooms at Corfe Castle where the food is locally sourced wherever possible, and freshly prepared to your order. From here you can enjoy heady views of the castle ruins. Toilets are available at the visitor centre.

After your walk, there's lots of fun to be found at Corfe Castle.

8. Old Harry Rocks and the Agglestone Rock

South Beach car park
Studland
Dorset BH19 3AU
01929 450002
studlandbeach@
nationaltrust.org.uk
www.nationaltrust.org.uk/
studland-beach

About this walk
Spectacular views

Area of geological interest

Some stiles and steep
sections

Dogs welcome under
close control

Distance 5 miles (8km)

Time 3 hours

This delightful 5-mile (8km) coastal walk from the National Trust car park at South Beach, Studland, takes in Old Harry, one of the most famous landmarks on the South Coast, and affords spectacular views over Poole Harbour and as far as the Isle of Wight. Along the way, discover a hidden heathland valley and the Agglestone, a striking rock formation with a place in local legend.

Above: Views across Godlingston Heath.

Things to see

Old Harry
Old Harry is the best known of the chalk stacks formed by the action of the waves in this stunning section of the Jurassic Coast. Others include the sharply pointed Pinnacle. Another stack called Old Harry's Wife once stood just to seaward of her husband, but she toppled over into the sea in 1896, leaving just a stump as a relic of her existence. Her fall is a reminder that the processes that formed these distinctive landmarks continue to work, and further changes are inevitable.

Views of Poole Harbour
Poole Harbour covers around 14 square miles (36km²) and is arguably the second largest natural harbour in the world. It's famous for its islands, the largest of which is Brownsea, owned by the National Trust and accessible by ferry from Poole Quay or Sandbanks. The harbour's northern shores are home to the port of Poole and exclusive residential areas such as Sandbanks. To the south are large areas of unspoiled heathland and marsh, much of which is looked after by the National Trust.

The Agglestone
The Agglestone Rock is a 400-tonne ironstone boulder that rises dramatically from the surrounding heath on the top of a low hill. In legend, it was once a cap worn by the Devil as he sat atop the Needles across the bay on the Isle of Wight. When the Devil spied Corfe Castle, he was so jealous of the beautiful white towers that he tore off his cap and flung it at them, but it fell short and stands to this day where it landed.

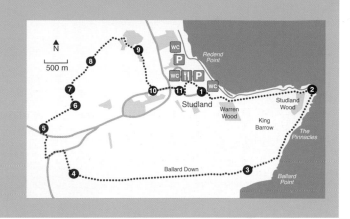

Agglestone Rock, near Studland.

1. Turn right from South Beach car park past the Bankes Arms pub. At the bottom of the hill (by the public toilets) turn left and follow the signs for Old Harry Rocks.

2. Continue straight on past a hazel coppice called Warren Wood and a fallen tree on your right, onto the field known as Old Nick's Ground. On your left you will see Studland Bay, Sandbanks and Bournemouth. On your right is a traditionally laid hedge of hawthorn. (Please keep dogs on a lead here due to the crumbling cliffs.) Continue straight on past Studland Wood on your right out onto open grassland with Old Harry Rocks ahead. Stunning views can be had of Poole, Sandbanks, Bournemouth and the Isle of Wight from here.

3. Turn right up the gentle grass hill and follow the South West Coast Path with the English Channel on your left. Views of Poole Harbour with its four islands will gradually unfold on your right.

4. On reaching the fence line, carry on through the foot gate onto Purbeck Way and Ballard Down. Stunning views unfold on both sides. On reaching a copse, walk past a trig point and views of Swanage and the rugged South Coast appear. Turn around to see the beautiful chalk cliffs of the Isle of Wight reflect the sunlight. Proceed along the footpath through the foot gate. On your left are two small Bronze Age round barrow ceremonial mounds. Follow the (blue arrow) sign for the obelisk on the stone signpost. On your right-hand side is the famous 'stone seat'. Carry

straight on, following the sign for Ulwell. The views unfold further as you gain height. On passing through a further foot gate at the top of Ballard Down, carry on down the track to the obelisk.

5. The obelisk was erected in 1883 to commemorate a new drinking water supply for Swanage, then growing rapidly into a fashionable resort. In 1941 it was hastily taken down on the orders of the Air Ministry, who were concerned German bombers might use it as a landmark for raids on the nearby port of Poole. A plaque on the plinth records its replacement in 1952 by men of the Royal Engineers. On leaving the obelisk, follow the path bearing steeply down to your right towards Ulwell Road. On reaching the road, carefully cross and turn left, following the path for 300 yards (275m). Look out for a stile which may be partially hidden by bushes during the summer. Turn right over the stile.

6. Follow the path over the field and up the hill through the woodland and onto the golf course. Continue across the golf course to the stile, carefully cross over the B3351 Swanage Road and turn left. Walk 10 yards (9m) and turn right through the foot gate. After 5 yards (4.5m), there is a further foot gate onto Godlingston Heath and Harmony Valley, a quiet spot full of reptiles and birds. If you are lucky you may also see some of the resident sika deer. Follow the footpath, and on reaching the barbed wire fence beside the Purbeck Golf Club follow the path to your right along the brow of the hill. You will see views of Bournemouth and Poole Harbour on your left.

7. After 300 yards (275m) turn left through a foot gate, then carry straight on along a bridleway.

8. On reaching the stone sign, with an access gate to the golf course on your left, turn right and walk for 150 yards (140m). At the top of the hill, admire the sweeping views, taking in Old Harry Rocks, the Isle of Wight, Bournemouth, Poole Harbour, the Agglestone, and Godlingston and Studland Heaths.

9. When you have taken in the views, walk down the hill towards the Agglestone, an ironstone rock which split in the early nineteenth century. After a walk around the rock take the steps on the public footpath down the hill towards the rare wet woodland and Wadmore Lane. At the top of the next set of steps, turn right along the footpath and join a bridleway through the woods.

10. Walking along the woodland bridleway, turn right over the footbridge and proceed through the foot gate, still following the bridleway. On reaching a field on the left, turn right along the signposted tree-lined footpath heading towards Heath Green Road and Studland village, past the horses from Studland Stables.

11. On reaching Heath Green Road, cross over onto the pavement and turn left. At Swanage Road, cross over into School Lane past Studland Village Stores. Turn left at the war memorial and walk through the churchyard on your right. Here you will find the memorial stones to the Bankes family, who gifted Studland to the National Trust in 1982. Follow the path to your starting point at South Beach car park.

Make the Most of Your Day

The National Trust hosts year-round events, including children's trails, slacklining, beach volleyball and food events. A coastal change interpretation hut is open all year. A trip to Brownsea Island is always fascinating; a Site of Special Scientific Interest (SSSI), it is a haven for wildlife, with the rare red squirrel and a wide variety of birds.

Food and Facilities

Knoll Beach Café serves fresh, locally sourced food, and has seating inside and out, affording spectacular views of Old Harry Rocks. Toilets can be found in Watery Lane and Rectory Lane in Studland.

Opposite: Sunset over the cliffs at Old Harry Rocks.

9. Ashclyst Forest Butterfly Walk

This leisurely walk, which takes you along sunken lanes and woodland rides, and through broadleaved and coniferous woodland, is ideal for spotting fritillary butterflies, white admiral and other butterflies. It starts at the bus stop on the Killerton road junction, but, for a shorter walk, park in the main Ashclyst Forest car park and join the route clockwise at point 5 on the route map.

Killerton
Broadclyst
Exeter
Devon EX5 3LE
01392 881345
killerton@
nationaltrust.org.uk
www.nationaltrust.org.uk/
killerton

About this walk
Across open fields and woodland

Abundant butterflies in spring and summer

Distance 4 miles (6.4km)

Time 3 to 4 hours

Above: Ashclyst Forest.

Things to see

Fritillaries and nightjars
In the area of birch and bracken beyond point 2, look for small pearl-bordered fritillaries from May to mid-June, along with small numbers of pearl-bordered fritillary (late April to May) and the occasional dark-green fritillary (mid-June to August). The birch is cut on rotation to provide jumps for Exeter Race Course; this creates a good habitat for the nightjar: three or four pairs breed here annually.

Marbled whites and white admirals
The grassy areas around point 4 are good for marbled white, ringlet and common blue, along with pearl-bordered and small pearl-bordered fritillaries. In fact, all of Ashclyst's butterflies visit this broad flowery

ride, including the white admiral. This species is also common in high summer near the stream and brambles beyond point 5. Also look here for purple hairstreak on the tops of the lane oaks, though they are most active after 5pm.

Silver-washed fritillaries and purple emperors
The broad, straight ride down to the Douglas fir plantation beyond point 6 is very good for silver-washed fritillaries. You then enter a long section of white admiral, and possibly purple emperor, country. You may also see dragonflies in the pond. Beyond point 7, Snaffle Park Drive is good for pearl, small pearl and silver-washed fritillaries, and grass-feeding butterflies like the large skipper and ringlet.

A silver-washed fritillary.

How to Get There

By Train Pinhoe (not Sundays)
4.5 miles (7.2km); Exeter
Central 7 miles (11.2km);
Tiverton Parkway 9 miles
(14.4km)

By Car Off B3181 Exeter to
Cullompton road, parking in
the National Trust car park at
Killerton House

OS Map Landranger 192

Start / End Bus stop at
Killerton road junction on
B3181, **OS grid ref: SX983997**,
or Forest Gate car park, **OS
grid ref: SY000995**

1. If you've parked in the Killerton House car park, walk back out onto the approach road, cross it and take the footpath directly opposite the house drive entrance, through New Park and out onto the road. Turn right, cross the motorway bridge and head for the bus stop at Killerton junction. From here, head north (towards Cullompton). At the crest of a low hill, after 275 yards (250m), turn right up the National Trust footpath along a sunken way. Follow this until it ends at a field gate. Turn left into the field and down the slope, following the now grassy footpath. Cross a stream bridge. Follow the waymarked path to the right and then uphill alongside a hedge, turning right by the road corner, and follow the path until it leads into the road through a hunting gate. Turn right onto the road and follow this for about 300 yards (275 metres), then turn right into a bridleway at the start of the forest.

2. The bridleway runs along a short, shady section before rising up and broadening out into an open area of bracken and birch. Keep straight on, along and down, following the broad ride.

3. Follow the straight bridleway down into tall, dense woodland, then follow the bridleway markers uphill. The good surface will soon run out and the way become muddy. Just past the crest of a rise, bear left and then right, following the bridleway (and avoiding two straight-ons and the footpath). This takes you downhill through conifer woodland (which is being thinned out and opened up) to the road.

4. At the road, turn left then immediately right, squeezing under the barrier and proceeding downhill, shortly to turn left at the bend, then walking down to, and crossing, the stream before rising up again. This leads into the broad ride known as the Wayleave (under the electricity cables). Follow the Wayleave path round to the left. The bracken areas here are the best places in Ashclyst for pearl-bordered and small pearl-bordered fritillaries, and are managed for these two scarce butterflies. Carry on along and up the path, turning left into a narrow shady path on the far summit.

5. The often muddy, shady path twists round to meet a lane. At the lane, turn right and walk down towards the cottages. Just before the cottages, by the bench, turn left and take the surfaced path through tall oak and holly woodland. This path is being opened up. It quickly leads to the main Ashclyst car park, which is an oval-shaped design. Turn right to walk along the car park route anticlockwise. As it starts to rise, turn right to follow the Purple Route down and over a little bridge.

6. At the corner by the road, turn right down a long, straight and open section of ride that leads into a Douglas fir plantation. Turn right at the junction here, following the Purple Route down and round. Towards the bottom, in damp woodland, leave the Purple Route (which bears right), carrying straight on along the bridleway, with tall sallows on your right. This path slowly bends to the left and becomes boggy, with tall old oaks on your right. Eventually this muddy path, which runs along the bottom of the Ashclyst slope, opens out, just past a minor stream gully with a small pond.

7. Just after the ride opens and dries out, turn sharp left up a broad open ride called Snaffle Park Drive. Dawdle up this butterfly-rich ride to the road.

8. Walk up a short section of shady lane to a T-junction. This is a classic stretch of Devon lane, carrying one vehicle every 15 minutes.

9. At the minor T-junction, cut diagonally across to enter and walk through Rewe's Cross car park, and then along a shady ride through a developing conifer plantation. Turn left at the minor junction, and head downhill for 275 yards (250m) before turning right at the junction by a red and green-topped post. A short shady stretch between oaks and conifers suddenly opens out, providing views of Killerton House. Carry on straight down to the bottom bridleway that you came along much earlier, then turn right to leave the forest, and left back out onto the approach road. Then follow the route you took up to the forest, heading back down to Killerton junction.

Make the Most of Your Day

Visit nearby Killerton, a fine eighteenth-century house with a renowned historical fashion collection, set in a glorious landscaped garden surrounded by parkland. The garden is beautiful year round, with its rhododendrons, magnolias, unusual trees, flower borders, sweeping lawns and countryside views.

Food and Facilities

The Stables Café at Killerton House serves hot and cold food, or dine at the Killerton Kitchen restaurant, where you can enjoy local, seasonal food made from award-winning produce. Toilets are also available at Killerton House.

A white admiral.

10. Exmoor Cliff-top Ramble

This varied walk takes you through Heddon Valley and along the cliff-tops to Woody Bay, following an historic nineteenth-century carriageway across some of the highest and most dramatic cliffs in England. The views along the coast and across to Wales are breathtaking. Along the way you will pass a Roman fortlet and a waterfall, see plentiful seabirds and walk through ancient sessile oak woodlands.

Heddon Valley
North Devon
01598 763402
heddonvalley@
nationaltrust.org.uk
www.nationaltrust.org.uk/
heddon-valley

About this walk
Coastal walk

Breathtaking views

Some steep sections

Muddy in wet weather;
some parts wet all year

Distance 6 miles (9.6km)

Time 2 hours 30 minutes
to 3 hours

Above: The Carriageway, which runs
from Heddon's Mouth to Woody Bay.

Things to see

The Carriageway
In 1885 'Colonel' Benjamin Lake bought the Martinhoe Manor Estate with grand plans to create a splendid tourist destination. By 1899 he had built a pier in Woody Bay for steamers carrying wealthy passengers. The carriageway you walk along was designed to carry these tourists by carriage from Woody Bay to the Hunter's Inn in the Heddon Valley. But in 1900 the 'Colonel' was declared bankrupt and his grand plans came to nothing.

Martinhoe Roman Fortlet
The small, square fortlet situated on cliffs overlooking Heddon's Mouth is one of several found in Devon. It was manned until AD75, under the command of the Second Augustan legion based at Exeter. With a little imagination you can almost see the barracks, smell the smoke from numerous fires and hear the cries of the soldiers based here.

Seabirds
In spring and summer, a wide variety of seabirds nest and breed on the cliffs between Woody Bay and Heddon's Mouth, most particularly on the rocks of Wringapeak to the east of the vantage point at Great Burland Rocks. Guillemots, razorbills, Manx shearwaters, black-backed gulls, kittiwakes and fulmars are just some of the species you might see.

How to Get There

By Train Barnstaple 16.5 miles (26.4km)

By Car Halfway along A39 between Combe Martin and Lynmouth, turning off for Hunter's Inn

OS Map Landranger 180

Start / End National Trust gift shop, **OS grid ref: SS655480**

Map labels: Highveer Point, Heddon's Mouth, Great Burland Rocks, Waterfall, West Woody Bay, The Beacon Roman Fortlet, Martinhoe, Woody Bay, Waterfall, N, 500 m

1. With the National Trust shop on your right, walk down the road towards the Hunter's Inn public house. At the junction turn right, and then left along the bridleway by the side of the inn. At the fork take the footpath to your right signposted 'Woody Bay 2¾ miles'. You are now walking through Road Wood along a wide track known as the 'Carriageway', which you will follow along its length through Heddon Valley to Woody Bay. This first section along Hill Brook Combe is home to bilberry, common cow–wheat, wild strawberry and wood avens. Also look out for foxgloves in early summer.

2. Carry on straight up and along the Carriageway as it climbs around the headland above Heddon's Mouth and Highveer Rocks. On a clear day there are far-reaching views over the Bristol Channel to Wales.

3. As you follow the track you can see Woody Bay, Valley of the Rocks, Lynmouth Bay and Foreland Point stretching out before you. Look for the signpost on your right that leads up to Beacon Roman Fortlet, taking time to explore this ancient site.

4. Returning to the main track, continue towards Woody Bay. Above Hollow Brook Combe the path is flanked by sessile oaks and rare whitebeams. This is an excellent place to look out for the peregrines and buzzards that breed in this area.

5. Pass through the gate, closing it behind you. You are now walking through West Woody Bay Wood, home to ash, larch and birch, as well as more oaks. Keep an eye out for red deer and woodpeckers.

6. Stay straight on the Carriageway to where it meets the road on a sharp hairpin bend. Turn left and follow the road down the hill, past a small National Trust car park, an alternative starting point for this walk. Just past the car park turn left down a road shown as a dead end that leads to Woody Bay.

7. On a very sharp right-hand bend in the road look for the South West Coast Path on your left, signposted 'Coastpath Hunter's Inn'. Turn onto this path, which you will stay on until you reach your starting point. Follow the steep incline up the side

Visitors walking at Heddon Valley.

of the cliff and pass through the gate into a wood of sessile oaks, sheared by the wind over decades into a myriad of twisted shapes. In the late spring the floor of this woodland is carpeted with bluebells. Hollow Brook Combe waterfall drops in a series of cascades 220 yards (200m) to the sea.

8. Carry on up the side of the combe to Great Burland Rocks. This is an excellent vantage point from which to look for guillemots, razorbills and other seabirds.

9. Carry on along the footpath to the point where it turns back up the Heddon Valley along the side of the combe. This is a good position from which to look down onto the beach and the lime kiln, and across the valley to where the coast path makes its way precipitously around the headland and on to Combe Martin. In autumn the gorse on this section scents the air with the smell of coconuts. You might also see cormorants and ravens here.

10. Carry on down the hill, across some scree, where you will meet a footpath signposted to the right to the beach. Unless you wish to make a short detour to the pebble beach and lime kiln at Heddon's Mouth, turn left along the South West Coast Path signposted '1/2 mile to Hunter's Inn'. Follow the signposts back to the pub and your starting point.

Make the Most of Your Day
Throughout the year the National Trust puts on a great variety of events at Heddon Valley, from coastal cruises, family-friendly fun days, guided walks and even a traditional summer fete. There is also a National Trust shop and information centre at the site. Further afield lies Arlington Court with its impressive Carriage Museum.

Food and Facilities
The Heddon Valley shop sells the best ice creams in the west. Otherwise try Hunter's Inn for something more substantial; toilets are available to customers.

11. Castle Drogo Circuit

Castle Drogo
Drewsteignton
Near Exeter
Devon EX 6PB
01647 433306
castledrogo@
nationaltrust.org.uk
www.nationaltrust.org.uk/
castle-drogo

About this walk

Follows an ancient
wooded gorge

Good for leaping salmon
in autumn

Some steep descents,
moderate climbs and steps

Distance 3.5 miles
(5.6km)

Time 2 hours 30 minutes

This is perhaps the most famous walk on Dartmoor. From the imposing bulk of Castle Drogo it follows the breathtaking Hunter's Path high above the ancient gorge of the River Teign, before descending to cross the river at Fingle Bridge and returning via the riverbank through oak woodland. Look out for the rocky outcrop called Sharp Tor along the way.

Things to see

Castle Drogo
Designed by the great Edwardian architect, Edwin Lutyens, and built between 1910 and 1930, Castle Drogo is renowned as 'the last castle to be built in England'. The beautiful terraced garden is also designed by Lutyens, and is the highest garden in the care of the National Trust, affording dramatic views of Dartmoor.

Fingle Bridge
Fingle Bridge is a thirteenth-century packhorse bridge and a local beauty spot. The meadows nearby are excellent for picnics and the Fingle Bridge Inn sits adjacent to the bridge.

River wildlife
The River Teign plays host to a fine array of wildlife, not least fish, especially salmon and brown trout. When the river is in full spate and the fish are running, it's spectacular to see them leaping up the weirs below Drogo in search of their spawning areas. This mostly happens in September and October after heavy rain.

Fingle Bridge over the River Teign on the estate at Castle Drogo.

Above: View from the roof of Castle Drogo towards Dartmoor and the Teign Valley.

How to Get There

By Train Exeter 19 miles (30.5km)

By Car 5 miles (8km) south of A30 Exeter to Okehampton, off A382, turning off at Sandy Park

OS Map Landranger 191; Explorer 113

Start / End Castle Drogo main car park, **OS grid ref: SX725902**

1. From the car park follow the signs for the Teign Valley estate walks. Turn right, following the sign for Hunter's Path, which takes you down a flight of steps and through a small gate onto Piddledown Common. At the bottom of the steps you join Hunter's Path; turn left and follow signs for Fingle Bridge.

2. As you pass Sharp Tor on your right, pause a moment to enjoy the view. Continue along Hunter's Path, still following signs for Fingle Bridge.

3. Go through Hunter's Gate, a small gate between granite posts, then after about 50 yards (45m) take the right-hand path and go downhill, continuing to follow signs for Fingle Bridge.

4. At the bottom of the path you join the road to Fingle Bridge. Turn right here and walk along the road to the bridge (beware of traffic).

5. At the bridge, cross over to the other side (to the National Trust car park) and immediately turn right, walking through the meadows to the small wooden footbridge at the far end where you join a track (sometimes known as Forester's Track). Alternatively, you could turn right before you cross the bridge and follow Fisherman's Path. Both routes follow the river all the way back through the gorge.

6. If you followed Fisherman's Path, you will ascend and descend the base of Sharp Tor. Please take care here. This route will also take you past the end of Drogo Weir.

7. As you pass the hydroelectric plant, on either path, look up to see Piddledown Common above you; you might just catch a glimpse of the castle above the trees as well.

8. If you followed Forester's Track, pass through a gate and walk along the lower wall of Whiddon Deer Park, enclosed in around AD 1560 to contain a herd of fallow deer.

9. Drogo Weir was built in 1928 to serve the hydroelectric plant downstream. When the river is high, the weir is spectacular.

10. Continuing along Forester's Track, climb the stone stile over the deer park wall and cross the suspension bridge, looking downstream as you cross to see Drogo Weir. At the far side of the bridge you rejoin Fisherman's Path.

11. From the end of the suspension bridge turn left and then right, following signs for Castle Drogo and the Two Moors Way. Follow this route until it joins a tarmac drive near Gibb House and Coombe. Follow the drive uphill.

Herbaceous planting in the Terrace Garden at Castle Drogo.

12. When you reach a wooden gate on the right-hand side of the drive between massive beech trees, turn right and go through the gate, following signs for Hunter's Path. Continue along Hunter's Path, passing below the castle and looking back down the valley. When you reach the bottom of a set of steps (the same ones you came down at point 1), climb the steps and return up the castle drive back to the main car park.

Make the Most of Your Day

Castle Drogo is well worth a visit, as are its beautiful gardens. Further afield, Finch Foundry near Okehampton is the last working water-powered forge in England, where visitors can experience the sights, sounds and smells of three thundering water wheels powering massive hammers, shears and sharpening stones.

Food and Facilities

There is a café at Castle Drogo featuring locally sourced produce, with open-air seating and a play area. Toilets are available at both Drogo and Fingle Bridge.

12. Fowey and Gribbin Head Hike

Fowey
Cornwall PL23 1HW
01726 870146
southeastcornwall@
nationaltrust.org.uk
www.nationaltrust.
org.uk/fowey-estuary-
pencarrow-head

About this walk
Walk of literary interest
Spectacular coastal views
Some steep sections and
narrow paths
Beware of incoming tides
and dangerous currents

Distance 4 miles (6.4km)

Time 1 hour 30 minutes,
plus detours to beaches

The countryside to the west of Fowey offers a variety of landscapes, and includes superb views and many features of historical significance. This coastal walk takes you to beaches, coves, woodlands and grassland rich in wildflowers. Famed for its association with the author Daphne du Maurier, and the setting of many of her books, this area offers breathtaking natural beauty.

Things to see

The Rashleigh Mausoleum
This mausoleum is the final resting place of William and Catherine Rashleigh and their daughter, Edith Stopford Sackville. It was built in 1867, four years before William Rashleigh's death. He chose to live in an Italianate house at Point Neptune instead of his ancestral home at nearby Menabilly.

Polridmouth Cove
This cove is thought to be one of the many places that inspired Daphne du Maurier when writing her novel *Rebecca*. For many years Dame Daphne lived at Menabilly,

a large private house and estate that includes Polridmouth Cove. The series of ponds were built as decoys for Fowey Harbour during the Second World War.

The Gribbin Daymark
The Gribbin Daymark stands 84ft (25.6m) high and was built in 1832 by Trinity House as a navigation aid to prevent mariners from mistaking the shallow waters of St Austell Bay for the deeper waters of Falmouth Harbour. The Daymark is open to the public on Sundays during June, July and August.

Top: Gribbin Head, taken from Coombe Farm.
Above: The Daymark tower navigational aid.

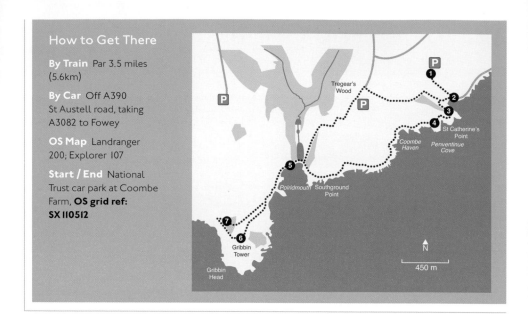

How to Get There

By Train Par 3.5 miles (5.6km)

By Car Off A390 St Austell road, taking A3082 to Fowey

OS Map Landranger 200; Explorer 107

Start / End National Trust car park at Coombe Farm, **OS grid ref: SX 110512**

Stay Safe Please be aware of dangerous cliff edges and unstable cliffs.

1. Leave the National Trust car park and turn right down a wide track. Continue along the track, following the sign to St Catherine's Point. The track bears left and crosses two grass fields. At the second field, keep to the open path on the right of Covington Woods. Go through the wooden gate at the end of the second field and follow the path marked 'Fowey ½ mile'.

2. Bear right and take the path around the edge of Covington Woods. The path then winds towards St Catherine's Castle. You can take a short diversion to the left here, up to the Rashleigh Mausoleum. Return to the main path for the castle.

3. St Catherine's Castle is cared for by English Heritage. It was built between 1538 and 1542 by Henry VIII as a small artillery fort to protect Fowey Harbour from the French. Entry is free. During the summer, you can reach Readymoney Cove by a steep path and steps next to the path for the castle.

4. If you visited the cove, retrace your route past the castle and along the coastal path to Allday's Fields. Continue along the coastal path through Coombe Haven (also know as Coombe Hawne) and on to Polridmouth.

5. Cross the stream at Polridmouth and follow the path around the cove. Turn left and follow the path over the boardwalks and up the hill to Gribbin Head and the Gribbin Daymark.

6. Have a look around and you will notice the remains of a signal station, and various earthworks including a Bronze Age barrow, banks and ditches of long disused cliff gardens and other enclosures. You will also find a brilliant diversity of wildflowers in spring and summer, including early purple orchids. From the Daymark tower, continue along the cliff-top.

7. Follow the path round to the right and trace your steps back down to Polridmouth. Cross the stream and take the left-hand path up to Coombe Farm. Follow the path around the edge of the fields, which leads you onto a lane. This lane will take you back to your starting point at Coombe car park.

Make the Most of Your Day

Once you've blown away the cobwebs with a bracing walk, take a trip to nearby Lanhydrock, a fascinating Victorian country house near Bodmin. You'll get the sense that the Agar-Robartes family, who once owned it, have only just popped out for tea, and appreciate the contrast between their lives 'upstairs' and those of their servants 'downstairs'.

Food and Facilities

Treat yourself to a Cornish cream tea at the café at Coombe Farm, or enjoy the fantastic views as you picnic at Coombe picnic area.

Gribbin Head and the daymark from Polridmouth Cove.

13. Polperro to Chapel Cliff

Explore south-east Cornwall's history and culture as you follow this unspoilt stretch of coastline along Chapel Cliff. Starting out from the bustling, ancient fishing village of Polperro, there are lots of opportunities to sit and admire the views or fly a kite. Look out for caves and the old net loft along the way.

Near Polperro
South East Cornwall
PL 13 2QY
01726 870146
southeastcornwall@
nationaltrust.org.uk
www.nationaltrust.org.uk/
polperro-looe-and-
whitsand-bay

About this walk
An area of historic interest

Stunning coastal views

Some steep, rocky paths on uneven ground

Distance 1 mile (1.6km)

Time 30 minutes to 40 minutes

Things to see

Net loft and lighthouse
The net loft sits nestled within the stony outcrop called Peak Rock and probably dates back to the early 1800s. The ground floor is said to have been used for boat building and the top for storing the pilchard nets and sails. Some believe that this is the true site of St Peter's Chapel, which may possibly have been a chapel and lighthouse combined, as the site would have been ideally located for a beacon.

Polperro allotments
Along the cliff, look out for small, hedged enclosures beside the terraced paths. These plots were once let to local people, often fishermen, to grow flowers and

vegetables because there was so little room for gardens around the houses in the village. Divided by veronica or escallonia hedges to give protection from the wind, they enabled people to grow early crops, even on these seaward-facing slopes.

Preserving pilchards
Chapel (pronounced Chay-pell) Cliff has paths at several levels, but the one nearest the sea is the true coastal path. The sheltered cove has long been a haven for fishing boats. In the nineteenth century, when shoals of pilchards were plentiful, huge quantities were caught here and then packed into barrels and

Top: Polperro Harbour.
Above: Early potatoes at Polperro allotments were once famous.

salted. The preserved fish were then exported to the Catholic countries of southern Europe to be eaten on fast days.

1. Park on the outskirts of Polperro, then either get the shuttle bus or walk to town. From here, follow the signs to the coast path above the harbour. Start the walk by the shelter and head west along the lower path.

2. After 50 yards (45m) branch left; a little further on you'll come across a good viewpoint where you can see east to Rame Head or even further still.

3. Continue keeping left, past a bench and another shelter.

4. Take the steps up the hill. You should see some blocked-off caves on your right. Look out for the rocky outcrop – this is an excellent spot to take in the views.

5. When you come to a junction, head left.

6. Where the path forks, bear left again, walking down the (lower) path and through the privet trees. There used to be fishermen's allotments here – you may just be able to make out the old terraces.

7. Leaving the wooded area, you should get a view west as far as Dodman Point.

8. When you come to a right turn in the path, take this up the steps and across a spring. At the top follow signs for the coast path back towards Polperro.

9. At the fork in the road, take the right path heading down the hill.

10. When you get to the bottom, you should meet the path you were on previously. Turn left.

11. At the next junction, stay left, heading past two benches.

12. At the waymarker, follow the coast path down the hill, making sure to take in the view over the bay, and make your way back to the starting point.

13. If you have time, explore the old National Trust net loft on the rocks at the harbour's edge.

Make the Most of Your Day

While you're here, leave time to visit Polperro, one of Cornwall's most picturesque villages. Head for Hannafore or Port Nadler to explore the rock pools, or Whitsand Bay with its miles of sandy beaches.

Food and Facilities

There is a range of cafés and restaurants in Polperro, as well as public toilets.

14. The Lizard Coastal Walk

The Lizard, near Helston
Cornwall TR 12 7NT
01326 561407
lizard@
nationaltrust.org.uk
www.nationaltrust.org.uk/
lizard-and-kynance-cove

About this walk
A dramatic coastal walk
Good for wildflowers in
spring and summer
Some slopes and steps

Distance 7 miles (11.2km)

Time 2 hours 20 minutes

This walk around the Lizard Peninsula, the southerly tip of mainland Britain, takes in dramatic cliff scenery, rare wildflowers and an interesting coastal history. Kynance Cove is considered to be one of the most beautiful beaches in the world. The bay used to attract visitors in Victorian times and still captivates today.

Above: The sandy beach at Kynance Cove, Cornwall.

Things to see

Kynance Cove
A favourite spot for day-trippers since Victorian times, many of the caves around Kynance have names from that era, such as the Ladies Bathing Pool, the Parlour and the Drawing Room. Today, the café at the Cove is full of eco-friendly features including solar panels, a turf roof, wool insulation and compost toilets.

Wildflowers
One of the richest botanical areas in the United Kingdom, the cliffs are a colourful picture in spring, carpeted in the blue, white and pink of wildflowers such as squill, campion and thrift. Many more quirkily named wildflowers bloom

Thrift along the South West Coast Path.

along the coast through spring and summer, including dropwort, bloody crane's-bill, lady's bedstraw, milkwort and self-heal. The exotic looking pink and yellow flowers of the Hottentot fig can be seen near to the lighthouse.

Seals and basking sharks
Seals and basking sharks are commonly spotted along this route. Basking sharks can reach nearly 30ft (9m) long but cruise these warm waters feeding on nothing more than tiny plankton. In summer 2007, over 40 were spotted in one day.

How to Get There

By Car Lizard village is 11 miles (17.7km) south of Helston, along A3083

OS Map Landranger 203

Start / End Kynance Cove car park, **OS grid ref: SW703125**

1. Set out from the car park at Kynance Cove, heading towards Lizard Point. Look for the Devil's Letterbox on the north side of Asparagus Island – a cave crack with powerful suction caused by the pull of air from the waves below.

2. Steps lead to a headland from the eastern end of Kynance Beach. Walk through the car park and rejoin the cliff path.

3. Continue to follow the cliff path, passing above Pentreath Beach. Along the way, look out for the strikingly beautiful serpentine stone in the cliffs. With veins of red, white and green, the stone was formed millions of years ago by the extreme pressure of rocks being thrust up to the Earth's surface from under the crust.

4. At Lizard Point, look down and you will see the disused Victorian lifeboat station at Polpeor Cove.

5. The Lizard Lighthouse is just round the headland from Lizard Point. An electric foghorn in the lighthouse kicks in when humidity levels rise above a certain level. Make sure you cover your ears! The blast is so thunderous (about 30 times louder than a pneumatic drill), you'll feel the vibrations if passing close by. Tennyson described the twin towers of Lizard Lighthouse as 'the southern eyes of England'. Built in 1752, the lighthouse enbles thousands of ships to pass safely through these rock-filled waters thanks to its 26-mile (41.8km) beam.

6. At this point, look out for the Lion's Den, a 39ft (12m) hole in the cliff created when a cave collapsed one night in the mid-1800s.

7. With its stunning views, Pen Olver provides the perfect spot to stop for a picnic.

8. From Bass Point Old Signal Station, head left inland to Lizard village.

9. After passing the village green, take the path back towards Kynance Cove and your starting point at the car park.

The lighthouse and kissing gate on the Lizard Peninsula.

Make the Most of Your Day

The Lizard Peninsula is renowned as the birthplace of modern communications, where Marconi undertook some of his pioneering radio experiments. Visit the Marconi Centre at Poldhu and the Lizard Wireless Station to find out more about Marconi's work.

Food and Facilities

There are cafés at Kynance Cove and Lizard Point, open from March to October. Toilets are also available in the car parks at both these locations.

The South East

15. Box Hill Natural Play Trail

Visitor Centre
The Old Fort
Box Hill Road
Tadworth, Surrey KT20 7LB
01305 885502
boxhill@
nationaltrust.org.uk
www.nationaltrust.org.uk/
box-hill

About this walk
Spectacular views

Lots of fun for young children

Woodland setting

Distance 2 miles (3.2km)

Time As long as you like

This fun-packed 2-mile (3.2km) walk over level ground gives kids plenty of opportunity to play in the woods. The trail takes anything from an hour to a whole day. There are lots of trees and other structures to climb on, but take care – these might be muddy and slippery in wet weather.

Things to see

Den-making
At Box Hill, children can have lots of fun building a den using branches, twigs, leaves and mud, all of which nature generously provides for free. It helps to start by leaning the sticks against a low branch, like a wigwam.

Balancing skills
Fallen tree trunks and other structures provide lots of fun, and encourage children to develop their balancing skills.

Above: A family explore the Natural Play Trail at Box Hill, Surrey.
Right: The view from Box Hill.

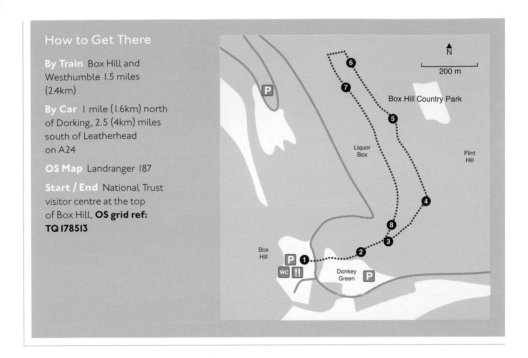

1. Start your adventure at the visitor centre at the top of Box Hill. Carefully cross the road and hop along the stepping stones to the Natural Play Trail archway. Walk under the arch or scramble through the tunnel. Walk, crawl, hop, skip and jump along the path to the next feature.

2. Venture through the tree archway and come back onto the main footpath. Take a left on the path which heads away from the main car park. Follow the path as it goes round the edge of the Donkey Green. The big beech trees have brilliant knobbly roots to climb around.

3. Stay on the path as it curves to the left and heads into the woods. The path forks almost immediately; you need to take the right-hand fork. Continue along this path, keeping a look out to your right. After a while, veer off the path to reach a hidden playful place. You can then loop back towards the path again. At the big yew tree you can rejoin the path by turning right onto it.

4. You'll reach a five-way crossroads. The play trail continues by following the second path on your left. Before doing this, there are lots of loose branches

lying around – perfect for making a den. Lots of the yew trees here are great for climbing on, too. Follow the second path on your left from the crossroads. On your right, you can have a closer look at the roots of a fallen tree or climb all the way along it. Carry on along the path.

5. Where the path forks, take the left-hand fork. Shortly the path splits again: take the right-hand path and carry on along it. Look out for a play feature on your right.

6. Cross the woods using the log bridge shortcut on your left; if you don't want to do that, you can carry on along the path. Take the left turn and then left again at the T-junction. You are close to Broadwood's Tower now, where there are some lovely views. As you walk along the path, keep an eye out for a log bridge on your right. You can be adventurous here and cross this to the more playful pathway. If you've got a buggy with you, you might prefer to stay on the main path.

7. Rejoin the main pathway by crossing the second bridge and turning right. Continue along the track, ignoring any paths turning off it. There are lots of places to stop for a sit down and a rest. Watch out for

Rolling fields at Box Hill.

the magical picnic table on your left. Carry on along this pathway. Look for a secret play place hidden between the trees.

8. Come back to the path, which will bring you back to the Donkey Green, with lots of open space to continue playing.

Make the Most of Your Day

There's lots of wildlife to be seen at Box Hill, such as the beautiful Adonis blue butterfly. It's the perfect spot for flying a kite as well. Add to the fun by visiting Box Hill Fort, built in 1896 as part of the defences of London. Bats have colonised it now, as the dark rooms and cool temperatures suit them well.

Food and Facilities

The Box Hill Café is a great place to indulge in a homemade cream tea or a warming bowl of hot soup. Toilets are available, too.

16. Runnymede: Magna Carta and Memorials

Leave the car behind and take a wander through ancient woodlands, secretive wetlands and open wild-flower meadows. This circular route takes you around Runnymede Nature Reserve. Explore Langham Pond and the ancient woodlands that form a Site of Special Scientific Interest for their many rare and endangered species, and cross the rich wild-flower meadows that are home to the birthplace of Magna Carta.

Egham Station
Station Road
Egham TW20 9LB
01784 432891
runnymede@
nationaltrust.org.uk
www.nationaltrust.org.uk/
runnymede

About this walk

A site of historical and scientific interest

A car-free walk

Dogs welcome under close control

Distance 3.7 miles (5.9km)

Time 2 hours

Things to see

Winter and spring delights

Along Cooper's Hill Lane, small yet mature trees with their crevices and cavities provide a great habitat for small birds. In the late winter and early spring, this path becomes a magical sight as long-tailed tits flutter from tree to tree. During later spring, look out for blue tits and great tits nesting in tree cavities.

Changing seasons

The woodland path through Cooper's Hill Woods proves fascinating throughout the year. Winter is a great time to look at the ancient oaks. Without their leaves, you can see the trees' characteristic

hollows, knots and crooked stems. The woods come to life in the spring as bluebells and wood anemones create a carpet of colour. In summer, search for glimpses of woodland butterflies.

Memorials

If you have time, instead of going through the kissing gate after point 8, turn left and visit the Magna Carta Memorial. Here you can read the history of Magna Carta, considered the foundation of the free world and individual freedom. You can also visit the John F. Kennedy Memorial Stone: a 7-tonne block of Portland stone set in a symbolic acre of American soil.

Top: A view from the bank of Langham Pond at Runnymede, Berkshire.
Above: Wood anemones form a colourful carpet in March.

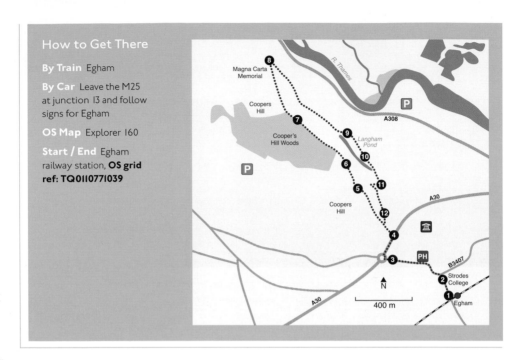

How to Get There

By Train Egham

By Car Leave the M25 at junction 13 and follow signs for Egham

OS Map Explorer 160

Start / End Egham railway station, **OS grid ref: TQ0110771039**

1. If you came by train, exit Egham Station on the London-bound (ticket office) side of the track and turn right onto Station Road. If you came by car, park in any of the pay and display car parks in Egham town centre and make your way to the station.

2. At the traffic lights turn left. Walk down the road towards the roundabout, passing Strodes College on your right.

3. At the roundabout, cross the A30 using the staggered pedestrian crossing to your right and continue in the same direction as the traffic.

4. Turn left into Cooper's Hill Lane, Langham Farm access. Continue up the path, with the Runnymede meadows to your right.

5. When you come to a kissing gate to your right, pass through it onto the meadows. Pass through another kissing gate ahead of you, which takes you into Cooper's Hill Woods.

6. Continue along this woodland path for about 15 minutes.

7. Pass through the kissing gate ahead of you, walking onto the grazed meadows. Walk ahead with the line of oak trees to your left.

8. With the Magna Carta Memorial ahead of you, go through the kissing gate on your right. Turn right again through another kissing gate to enter a grazed meadow. You're now on the return leg of your walk. On your right you'll see an ancient field boundary of willow pollards. These may have originally been pollarded to enable barons and royalty to ride on their horses beneath the trees, without banging their heads. Now, these willows continue to be pollarded, and are home to a wealth of endangered wildlife, including insects, fungi, birds and bats.

9. At the end of the meadow you'll come to Langham Pond, an oxbow lake on your right. Walk over to your left where you'll see a break in the hedge line on your right. Climb over the stile here, and follow the path through the rich wild-flower meadow.

10. Follow the boardwalk through the reed-bed. On leaving the reed-bed, take the diagonal trodden path to your left and go through the metal kissing gate on the opposite side of the meadow.

11. You're now back on the grazed meadows. Turn left and follow the hedge line. When you've passed through the hedge line in front of you, walk diagonally right towards the farm buildings.

12. With the farm buildings on your left, go through the kissing gate in the corner of the meadow. You're now back on Cooper's Hill Lane. Turn left towards the A30 and trace your route back to Egham railway station.

Make the Most of Your Day

Just across the river you can escape from the traffic, noise and crowds at Ankerwycke, where you'll find the ruins of the Benedictine priory and a 2,500-year-old yew tree. It's a bit off the beaten track and there's no car park but, if you're happy to forgo these amenities, you'll discover a hidden gem.

Food and Facilities

Visit the Magna Carta Tea-room for a refreshing break, where you will find a delicious range of food and drink. Toilets are also available here.

A young boy explores inside the hollow trunk of the ancient Ankerwycke Yew, Ankerwycke, Surrey

17. Strolling the Ashridge Estate

This walk takes you through the wonderful Ashridge Estate, linking two of its most prominent features – the monument and the windmill. An ideal day out for the family, it affords some spectacular views across the Chilterns and the Vale of Aylesbury, especially if you climb the Bridgewater Monument.

Ashridge Estate
Moneybury Hill
Ringshall
Berkhamsted HP4 1LT
01442 851227
ashridge@
nationaltrust.org.uk
www.nationaltrust.org.uk/
ashridge

About this walk
Panoramic views

Some steep sections and paths across ploughed fields

Dogs welcome on a lead near livestock

Distance 7.5 miles (12km)

Time 3 hours

Above: The BridgewaterMonument on the Ashridge Estate, Hertfordshire.

Things to see

The Bridgewater Monument
Standing 108ft (33m) tall, the tower was erected in 1832 in memory of the Third Duke of Bridgewater, also known as the 'Canal Duke' because of his role in starting the canal-building boom of the late eighteenth and early nineteenth centuries. A Grade II listed monument, it rewards those who climb its 172 steps with spectacular views over seven counties.

Chalk landscapes
The route takes you across a chalky landscape, formed during the last glaciation as erosion gouged out the chalk, creating a dramatic dry valley at Incombe Hole. More recently Ivinghoe has been sculpted by human occupation and the grassland has been managed to maintain the biodiversity of the landscape. The area is regularly grazed by livestock to prevent the establishment of invasive species, which would push out smaller wild-flowers.

Pitstone Windmill
The Pitstone Windmill is thought to be one of the oldest windmills in Britain – a date engraved into its woodwork suggests it's been here since at least the seventeenth century. The windmill ground flour for the village until a freak storm in the early 1900s left it damaged beyond economic repair. Keen to preserve the mill, its owners donated it to the National Trust in 1937, since when a dedicated team of local volunteers has faithfully restored it.

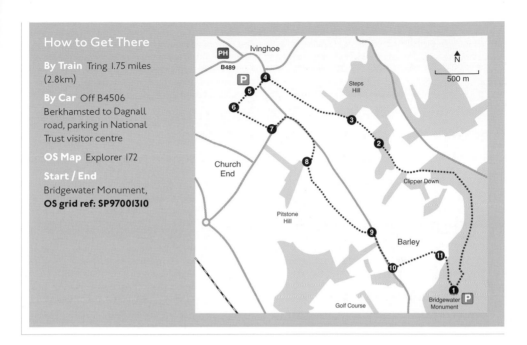

stone Windmill, Ivinghoe, Buckinghamshire.

1. Stand facing the Bridgewater Monument. To the right of the monument there are two paths. One goes straight ahead and down the hill behind the monument. The other, to the right, follows Duncombe Terrace along the contour towards Ivinghoe Beacon. Take the Duncombe Terrace route, following a well-surfaced path and signs for mobility vehicles. Follow this path for approximately 1.5 miles (2.4km) through woodland until fields begin to appear on your left and you pass a house on your right. At the house go through a gate and turn left onto a track. Continue to follow the track as it bears right away from the house.

2. After approximately 200 yards (180m) you will come to a footpath marker. Turn left off the track, following the boundary trail, onto a footpath that descends gently down the hill and through a gate emerging into a more open landscape. You will find fields to your left and chalk grassland to your right. The fields are separated from the grassland by a thin wire fence. Follow the path to the corner of the field in front of you. When you reach the field continue ahead, following the fence line and keeping it to your left.

3. When you come to a point where two paths form a crossroads, marked by a signpost, continue ahead in the direction signed Ivinghoe. Pass through the gate into a more defined field and continue ahead following footpath signs and the line of a hedgerow, keeping the hedge to your right. When you arrive at a gate in the corner of the field go through it and onto a narrow track that seems to be within the hedgerow. Follow this track to the road.

4. When you reach the road, turn left, taking care as this is a very busy road with limited visibility; there is a verge on the left side of the road that you can use but it is uneven. Cross the road where you feel comfortable and continue until you come to the National Trust car park near a very tight bend in the road. Cross the car park and go through a gate at the back. You will now be able to see the Pitstone Windmill very clearly. Follow the path directly towards the windmill.

5. On leaving the windmill continue across the field to the opposite side to which you entered. When you reach the edge of the field turn left and follow the field margin to the road.

6. Cross the road and turn left. This is also a very busy road so take care; there is a verge on the right side but it is uneven in places. Following the road you will eventually come to an opening into a field to your right. Turn in here and then turn immediately left following a narrow track with bushes on both sides. Follow this track as it bends right. Go over a stile and continue ahead on the footpath. The footpath winds uphill through bushes following a road, which you can glimpse to your left, before arriving at the edge of a field. When you arrive at a gate go through into the field. Keep dogs on a lead here as this field is often used for livestock.

7. With your back to the gate go straight ahead, passing in front of the hill to your right. Keep an eye out to your left for the National Trust's Pitstone Hill car park. When you meet the track that comes from the car park and goes up the hill turn, right towards the hill. You don't need to climb the hill itself but can take the left fork and walk around the contour, keeping the hill on your right, if you prefer. This lower route soon bears right and begins to run parallel to a fence. Follow the fence to its corner where you will find a signpost.

8. Follow the sign left through the gate into the field. The path skirts the edge of the field for approximately 100 yards (90m) before bearing left across two fields divided by a rough track. When you reach the tree line beyond these fields turn left and walk around the edge of the field until you come to the road.

9. Turn right and follow the road until you meet a substantial wall to the left and a signpost to your right.

10. Turn left, following the sign for the Bridgewater Monument. Go through a gate into a stableyard. Keeping the stables on your left, cross the yard and continue straight ahead onto a track. Ignoring farm tracks to the right and left you will eventually come to a fork marked by footpath signs.

11. Take the right fork, following the purple arrow. The path climbs uphill into woodland. Follow this path until you come to another fork. This time take the left option past the 'No Horses' sign. Continue straight ahead through a clearing until you come to a well-surfaced track. Turn right onto the track, which will bring you back to the Bridgewater Monument.

Make the Most of Your Day

The National Trust runs a packed events calendar at the Ashridge Estate, with a range of guided walks, talks and family events all year round (see the website for details). The Chilterns Countryside Festival is held in September.

Food and Facilities

If you climbed the monument, treat yourself to a well-earned break at the Brownlow Café (a National Trust concession). Toilets are available at the nearby visitor centre.

Opposite: The Ashridge Estate is awash with colour in the autumn.

18. Hughenden: In Disraeli's Footsteps

Follow in the footsteps of Disraeli in this historic walk through the grounds of his Buckinghamshire home, Hughenden Manor. Begin by walking along the ominously named Coffin Path, before turning to take in the view across Hughenden Valley and finishing with a stroll through open beech woods.

Hughenden
High Wycombe
Buckinghamshire HP 14 4LA
01494 755573
hughenden@
nationaltrust.org.uk
www.nationaltrust.org.uk/
hughenden

About this walk
Woodland walk

Site of historic interest

Dogs welcome under close control

Distance 2 miles (3.2km)

Time 40 minutes

Things to see

Hughenden Manor
Hughenden Manor, once home to Disraeli, is a beautiful manor house surrounded by the Chilterns countryside. Disraeli, the Victorian Prime Minister and founder of the Buckinghamshire police, lived here from 1848 until his death in 1881 and used to regularly walk in the woods of the estate.

Red kites
Red kites can be seen searching for food over open spaces. They are expert gliders and hardly need to flap their wings once at altitude. These magnificent birds were persecuted almost to extinction in England during the nineteenth century but have since been reintroduced to the Chilterns from Spain. They have flourished and are now a common sight gliding on the thermals of these hills. You can recognise them by their large wingspan and deeply forked tail.

The 'Bodgers'
The 'Bodgers' were highly skilled itinerant wood-turners who worked in the beech woods on the chalk hills of the Chilterns. They cut timber and converted it into chair legs. Chair-making was once a major industry in Wycombe, and used much of the woodland in this area (including Woodcock Wood). The beech woods are now maintained as an important habitat for wildlife.

Top: Hughenden Manor, High Wycombe, Buckinghamshire.
Above: Beech leaves in spring.

By Train High Wycombe
2 miles (3.2km)

By Car 1.5 miles (2.4km)
north of High Wycombe,
exit 4 from M40

OS Map Landranger 165;
Explorer 172

Start / End Woodland
car park at Hughenden,
OS grid ref: SU866955

Woodcock
Wood

Hanging
Wood

N

200 m

Hughenden
Manor

A4128

---

1. Start near the notice board in the woodland car park at Hughenden Manor, facing away from the house. Follow the wooden sign for the woodland walks that points up an earth track (the Coffin Path). This ancient road once carried the dead from Naphill to Hughenden Church. From here take the path signposted with the blue arrows. Continue down the Coffin Path (running alongside the woodland car park), heading away from the manor house.

2. After 100 yards (90m) the path divides; take the path that goes straight on and slightly right. Follow the flint track with hedges on both sides.

3. Continue about one-third of a mile (0.5km) until you reach a track crossing the path with metal pedestrian gates on both sides and a large open entrance to the field on the right, where you should turn right.

4. Walk along the field edge, keeping the hedge to your left.

5. Go through the metal gate in the corner of the field and head towards the woods. You can rest here and admire the view of Hughenden Valley.

6. Turn right and through the gate into Woodcock Wood.

7. Follow the track through the wood, continuing down a slope and straight over the crossroads.

8. Pass straight over the second crossroads, and past the bluebells in spring, to enter the woodland car park and the end of the walk.

Make the Most of Your Day
A visit to Hughenden Manor is a must, offering a vivid insight into the charismatic personality of Victorian Prime Minister Benjamin Disraeli. Here, you can browse among an extraordinary collection of personal memorabilia; there are also hands-on activities for children.

Food and Facilities
The tea-room sells a tasty selection of food using delicious home-grown produce from the walled garden. Toilets are also available.

19. An Amble Through Stowe Deer Park

Stowe
Buckingham MK 18 5EQ
01280 817156
stowe@
nationaltrust.org.uk
www.nationaltrust.org.uk/
stowe

About this walk
Peaceful parkland walk

Plenty of architectural interest

Dogs welcome on a lead

Distance 2.5 miles (4km)

Time 1 hour 30 minutes

This delightful walk takes you across the peaceful, open setting of the deer park at Stowe. Green woodpeckers and other wildlife can be seen in the rolling hills, fields and groves of trees. Spot the longhorn cows and sheep that are living lawnmowers, controlling the growth of fast-growing grasses and other plants so that the meadows will be rich with wild flowers in summer.

Above: Visitors at Stowe, Buckinghamshire.

The Corinthian Arch at Stowe.

Things to see

Dead oak tree
This dead oak tree provides invaluable habitats for invertebrates. Standing dead woods are also important for other wildlife such as green woodpeckers, which have a characteristic dip-dip flight and can often been seen pecking on trees and feeding on insects on the mounds of mole hills in the parkland.

Architecture at Stowe
From the parkland there is a wonderful view of the north front of Stowe House with its ornate columns, colonnades and magnificent Neo-classical architecture, which was the height of fashion in the eighteenth century. The surrounding gardens contain 40 historic temples and monuments, each with its own story, incorporating history, nature and beauty in a majestic setting.

Living lawnmowers
The imagery of idealised and peaceful scenes of nature and pastoral landscape were very popular in the eighteenth century. Today the sheep and longhorn cows graze the parkland, maintaining the tranquil atmosphere.

By Train Bicester North
9 miles (14.4km); Milton
Keynes 14 miles (22.5km)

By Car Off A422
Buckingham to Banbury
road

OS Map Explorer 192

Start / End Stowe
Parkland car park, **OS grid
ref: SP670377**

1. Start your walk from the visitor car park beside Home Farm. Walk up the hill on the gravel track towards the main track, where you will see a view of the north front of Stowe House.

2. Turn left and walk up the main tarmac track. At the top of the track, look out for signs of badger latrines and deer prints – these animals are frequent night-time visitors to Stowe.

3. At the bridleway crossroads, go through the gates on the left and walk across a small field towards another small gate. Go through the gate and immediately turn left to follow the track up to General Wolfe's Obelisk, which is a tall and proud monument that commemorates the victorious achievements of General Wolfe, who was killed in action at the battle of Quebec.

4. At the obelisk, enjoy the view of the parkland and trees that are planted in a regimental formation to conjure images of General Wolfe's successful army in battle. Follow the main grass path towards the ridings. Go through a gate and continue following the grass path as it descends down the field towards the stream at point 5.

5. At the stream, follow the waymark and turn left to take the grass path towards the Haymanger Pond. From here you can see a lovely view of the ridings and horses, in the direction of Stowe Corner at Silverstone.

6. At the Haymanger Pond, follow the boundary of the field. Go through the gate and continue to the remains of the walled garden.

7. At the walled garden, follow the grass path back down towards your starting point.

Make the Most of Your Day

There's always lots going on at Stowe, including family fun events and seasonal self-led trails to view the gardens (see website for details) It's well worth a visit to Stowe House, as well, to see the staterooms (not National Trust).

Food and Facilities

The café at Stowe, built in the style of a traditional barn, serves homemade seasonal light lunches, cakes, soups and scones. Toilets are also available.

20. Toys Hill: Octavia Hill Centenary Trail

Celebrate the life of Octavia Hill (1838–1912) on a walk to the picturesque village of Ide Hill and her commemorative seat, passing Emmetts Garden on the way back. One of the founders of the National Trust (established 1895), this remarkable woman was a social reformer, philanthropist, artist and writer whose vision still influences our lives today.

Toys Hill
Chart Lane
Brasted, near Westerham
Kent TN16 1QG
01732 750169
kentcountryside@
nationaltrust.org.uk
www.nationaltrust.org.uk/
toys-hill

About this walk
Site of historic interest

Outstanding views

Some steep slopes and steps

Dogs welcome on a lead in Emmetts Garden

Distance 4 miles (6.4km)

Time 2 hours 30 minutes

Things to see

Toys Hill
Octavia Hill lived in Toys Hill and is buried nearby at Crockham Hill. In 1898 she gave the National Trust one of its first properties, but all that remains of her house in Toys Hill is the terrace with a sunken well. Since then, through the generosity of many different people, the Trust's ownership of Toys Hill has expanded to create an outstanding area of woodland for the enjoyment of all.

Octavia Hill Memorial Bench
The area of woodland at Ide Hill is one of the spaces saved by Octavia Hill for posterity. Octavia once said 'the poor should never

be denied beauty' and certainly her commemorative seat affords a most beautiful view across the weald. The inscription reads 'To the honoured memory of Octavia Hill who loving nature with a great love secured this view for the enjoyment of those who came after her'.

Emmetts Garden
Emmetts Garden was laid out in the nineteenth century as part of an Edwardian estate and the much-loved home of Frederic Lubbock. It contains many exotic varieties of rare trees and shrubs from around the world and has stunning displays of spring flowers and autumn colours.

Top: Octavia Hill, by John Singer Sargent.
Above: The rock garden at Emmetts Garden, Kent.

How to Get There

By Train Sevenoaks and Edenbridge, both 4.5 miles (7.2km)

By Car Off A25 in Brasted village onto Chart Lane

OS Map Landranger 188; Explorer 147

Start / End Toys Hill car park on Chart Lane, **OS grid ref: TQ470517**

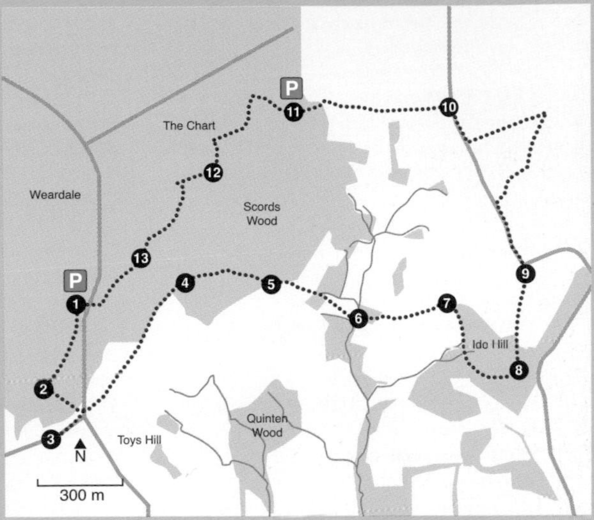

Map labels: The Chart, Weardale, Scords Wood, Quinten Wood, Toys Hill, Ide Hill, N, 300 m, P

1. In the top left-hand corner of the car park by the information panel, go up the steps in the direction of the arrow on the Octavia Hill Centenary Trail waymark disc.

2. At a crossing track and waymark post, turn left and go downhill through a wooden barrier. Then fork left to drop down to Puddledock Lane and a grass triangle with a seat. Turn right through the hamlet and soon reach a low stone wall on the left, with steps leading down to a covered well and a viewpoint with extensive views over the Weald of Kent.

3. Retrace your steps and, keeping to the left of the grass triangle, cross to Scords Lane opposite. Passing the beautiful old Toys Hill farmhouse and Old Cottage farm, maintain your direction at a signpost. The lane finally ends at a private driveway by a metal National Trust sign for Scords Wood.

4. Bear left onto a footpath and immediately right onto a small footpath with a fence on the right. On reaching a wide track turn right and continue downhill. At a waymark post keep straight ahead on the small path marked Greensand Way to emerge via a squeeze stile into a field.

5. Turn left past a seat to follow the boundary of the wood. Ahead can be seen the spire of St Mary's Church at Ide Hill. At the corner of the wood bear slightly right to a gate and maintain your direction down to the corner of the next field and a small footbridge over a stream.

6. Continue straight ahead up the next field and under the telegraph wires to the start of a dirt track. Follow this track through a metal kissing gate and past a solitary oak tree. Very soon on the right is a metal kissing gate in the hedge. Go through, leaving the Greensand Way.

7. Passing between woods on the left and a field on the right, enter woodland. After an uphill section at a fork bear right and continue uphill. The path levels out at a junction of paths. Keep straight ahead to a stone seat commemorating Octavia Hill.

8. Return to the junction of paths and take the second on the right, just to the right of a waymark post. Soon cross an open space with seats and at the end turn left by another waymark post to follow a field fence. On reaching a drive turn left to come out at Ide Hill village green.

9. At the roundabout bear left onto Sundridge Road and, after the last house on the right, turn right onto a signposted footpath. Continue straight ahead to a gap in the hedge and then bear diagonally left across the field to a stile in the hedge by a telegraph pole. Turn left onto a small lane and on reaching a T-junction turn right. Take care on this section.

10. After a short while, on the left next to South Lodge, take the signposted footpath onto a private drive. After some distance the drive passes between the north and south gardens of Emmetts Garden to arrive at the tea-room and shop.

11. To continue, take the footpath next to the tea-room and at a stile go straight ahead to a waymark post. Turn left onto a wide track. In a while, at a crossing track, continue straight over on a sunken path.

12. At the next waymark post turn right uphill, shortly passing through a wooden zig-zag barrier. As the path levels out at a waymark turn left and follow this wide path for some distance.

13. At a junction of five paths continue straight ahead on the level, ignoring two paths on the left and one leading up on the right. Eventually, the path bears right and comes out to a road. Cross to Toys Hill car park.

Make the Most of Your Day

If you want to make a day of it, why not visit Chartwell, Sir Winston Churchill's much-loved family home? The rooms remain much as they were when Churchill lived here, with pictures, books and personal mementoes evoking the career and wide-ranging interests of a great statesman, writer, painter and family man.

Food and Facilities

The nearest refreshments and toilets are available at Emmetts Garden. Pets are not allowed in the tea-room but there is shade and water available outside for your dog.

A view from Toys Hill, Kent.

21. White Cliffs Wildlife Walk

Discover the spectacular coast and countryside of south-east Kent and stroll along the famous White Cliffs of Dover. Walking from Langdon Cliffs to South Foreland Lighthouse, you'll see a host of butterflies and wild flowers along the way. Summer is also a great time to encounter the cliffside antics of kittiwakes, fulmars and peregrine falcons.

Langdon Cliffs
Upper Road
Dover
Kent CT16 1HJ
01304 202756
whitecliffs@
nationaltrust.org.uk
www.nationaltrust.org.uk/
white-cliffs-dover

About this walk
Spectacular cliff-top walk

Some steep slopes

Dogs welcome under close control

Distance 4 miles (6.4km)

Time 1 hour 20 minutes

Above: The White Cliffs of Dover, Kent.

Things to see

Wild flowers
Chalk grassland is a great habitat for wild flowers. It used to cover large parts of Europe but today only fragments remain, mainly in England and France. Look out for the yellow flowers of wild cabbage, from which our garden varieties were bred. Spring and summer bring the colourful blooms of greater knapweed, horseshoe vetch and oxtongue broomrape (a parasitic plant living on the hawkweed oxtongue). In spring, look out for the rare early spider orchid, only found on the South Coast.

Butterflies and moths
This area is well known for its butterflies, especially the small, Adonis and chalkhill blues. As the name suggests, the chalkhill blue is commonly found in chalk grassland habitats where it can find its favourite plant, the horseshoe vetch. Red admiral, painted lady and clouded yellow can be seen in large numbers during migration when some come to the United Kingdom from Europe or Africa. July is the month to spot several rare moths such as the day-flying straw belle.

Birds
Watch out for kittiwakes in summer, breeding on tiny ledges on precipitous cliffs. Also listen out for the song of skylarks and meadow pipits filling the air. As well as kittiwakes, fulmars live here in summer and you may see a peregrine falcon swooping from the cliff walls where it breeds. Some areas of scrub have been left to grow as they provide shelter for warblers including the whitethroat, and for colourful seed-eaters such as the linnet and yellowhammer.

How to Get There

By Train Dover Priory 2.5 miles (4km)

By Car From A2 take A258 towards Dover town centre, turning left into Upper Road after 1 mile (1.6km)

OS Map Landranger 179; Explorer 138

Start / End Gateway to the White Cliffs visitor centre, **OS grid ref: TR336422**

> **Stay Safe** Don't approach the cliff edge as it can crumble at any time, and take special care when the ground is wet, as the grass and exposed chalk can become very slippery.

1. From the Gateway to the White Cliffs visitor centre, head east to the coast path with the sea on your right. The cliffs are being eroded by 2–4in (5–10cm) every year, although in winter storms several tonnes can fall. The battering of the sea means the cliffs stay white, otherwise they would be covered in green vegetation. Here you can also see the remains of the Langdon Convict Prison above the port of Dover.

2. Keep on this path, looking out for where the chalk cliffs meet the English Channel, and take in magnificent views of the French coast from the rim of Langdon Hole. On a clear day you can see 21 miles (33.7km) across the Channel. The chalk downland along the cliff-tops is a Site of Special Scientific Interest (SSSI) and an Area of Outstanding Natural Beauty (AONB) due to the array of flora and insect life that thrives here. Above Fan Bay look out for pyramidal and fragrant orchids in June.

3. South Foreland Lighthouse was built in 1843 on a spot where lighthouses have stood for over 350 years. It helped mariners navigate the infamous Goodwin Sands until it was decommissioned in 1988. It is famed for being the first electrically lit lighthouse and the site of the first ever international radio broadcast. Lighthouses replaced simple beacon fires lit along the cliffs. The remains of a Roman lighthouse (Pharos) can be seen within the grounds of Dover Castle, near the church.

4. Return to the Gateway to the White Cliffs visitor centre, following a surfaced path just inland, this time keeping the sea on your left.

Wild flowers growing in the summer along the coastal path at the White Cliffs of Dover, Kent.

Make the Most of Your Day

The National Trust has got loads of great events happening through the year, from fun nature walks to interesting history talks, so why not take a look and see what you'll discover? Or visit nearby South Foreland Lighthouse, where you can climb to the top and find out what a lighthouse keeper did while on duty.

Food and Facilities

The café at the visitor centre has one of the best views in the county, looking down on the bustling port of Dover and the English Channel. Here you'll find a choice of hot meals and snacks all freshly prepared on site. Toilets are also available at the visitor centre.

22. The Seven Sisters Circuit

Discover stunning views across the Seven Sisters, where the flower-embroidered downs plunge into the sea in a dazzling wall of white. Then turn inland through the peaceful hamlet of Crowlink to reach Friston Church and back across the downs to Birling Gap. With so much wildlife and archaeology to see along the way there really is something for everyone.

Crowlink Lane
Friston, near Eastbourne
East Sussex BN20 0AY
01323 423 197
birlinggap@
nationaltrust.org.uk
www.nationaltrust.org.uk/
birling-gap-and-the-seven-sisters

About this walk
A great wildlife walk

Outstanding views

Some short, steep slopes
and stiles

Dogs welcome on a lead
around grazing cattle

Distance 4.5 miles (7.2km)

Time 3 hours and
30 minutes

Things to see

A field full of flowers
The hay meadow near the beginning of your walk is known as Hobb's Eares. In Sussex dialect 'eares' means 'arable land' and Hobb would have been the name of the owner. In spring, the meadow is a sea of yellow buttercups and white daisies. In summer, a wave of deep purple and gold washes over as knapweeds appear through the drying grass.

Wildlife to spot
Cucumber-scented salad burnet, a nationally rare plant, thrives in the turf around Birling Gap, and on warm days the air is sweet with the coconut aroma of gorse. Listen for skylarks rising from the grass to fill the air with melodious song and, in the combes, watch for the dashing eye stripes and bobbing white rumps of wheatears. During the summer, clouds of butterflies rise from the grass.

Aeroplanes and dragonflies
During the Second World War, the tranquillity of this spot was often shattered by the roar of fighter planes as they flew in from the sea to land at nearby Friston airfield. The unusual stone building on the hillside, seen from point 8, housed the pilots. For airborne drama of a different kind visit the dew pond beside the path, where colourful dragonflies and damselflies stage spectacular summer flying shows.

Top: View across the Seven Sisters, East Sussex.
Above: A marbled white butterfly.

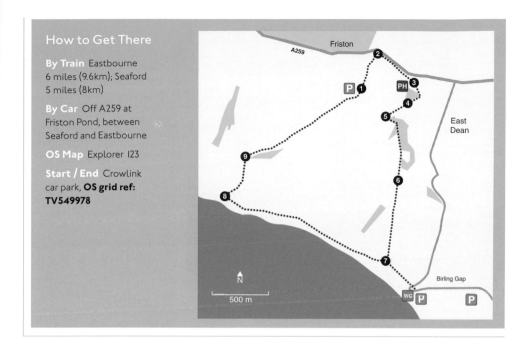

How to Get There

By Train Eastbourne
6 miles (9.6km); Seaford
5 miles (8km)

By Car Off A259 at
Friston Pond, between
Seaford and Eastbourne

OS Map Explorer 123

Start / End Crowlink
car park, **OS grid ref:**
TV549978

1. Go through Crowlink car park and continue along the lane towards the main road, before turning right through the gate into Friston Churchyard.

2. Go through the churchyard, through the far gate, and continue down through the meadow.

3. Near the bottom of the meadow veer right to pick up a path up and through the trees. At the top of the path turn right and climb the hill, keeping close to the wall on your left.

4. In the corner of the field, go over the steps set in the wall and head up the slope to the gate.

5. Go through the gate and skirt around the left of the field. Turn left through the kissing gate, aiming across the field to the red barn.

6. In front of the barn, pick up the sunken track over the brow of the hill and follow it through two gates to join the track down towards Birling Gap.

7. For the Birling Gap Café follow the South Downs Way along the track as it bears left down the hill and behind the toilet block. To continue, without stopping, turn right at the yellow waymark sign, through the pedestrian gate and up onto the downs.

8. Follow the coastline, heading out across a series of hills called the Seven Sisters; count each hill as you go as you're only crossing three 'sisters' plus their 'little brother', Flat Brow. After descending the fourth hill – Flagstaff Brow, with its stone memorial on top – turn right along the combe bottom, away from the sea.

9. Pass the pond and bear right, passing through a bridlegate to your starting point.

Make the Most of Your Day

Chyngton Farm, to the west in the Cuckmere Valley, has some Second World War artefacts such as anti-tank traps, pill boxes and bunkers.

Food and Facilities

The Birling Gap Café, serving locally sourced food, is located beside the car park, where there is also a toilet block.

23. Devil's Dyke and the South Downs Way

This linear walk takes in one of the most stunning sections of the South Downs Way long-distance trail. Spring and summer bring an abundance of wild flowers into bloom; the richness of the plant life is thanks to the chalk soil, which forms a unique grassland habitat. With great bus links from Brighton, why not leave your car at home and make this a green day out?

Ditchling Beacon
West Sussex
01323 423197
ditchlingbeacon@
nationaltrust.org.uk
www.nationaltrust.org.uk/
ditchling-beacon

About this walk
A car-free walk, easily accessible by bus

Site of archaeological interest

Some steep climbs and descents

Dogs welcome on a lead

Distance 5 miles (8km)

Time 1 hour 40 minutes

Above: Sunset over Devil's Dyke, West Sussex.

Things to see

South Downs
The South Downs National Park stretches 90 miles (144km) from Eastbourne to Winchester. The chalk landscape was formed over 100 million years ago from the remains of animals and plants. Today these grasslands are rich in wild flowers and herbs – over 50 species can live in one square yard. Lady's bedstraw, devil's-bit scabious, squinancywort, ribwort plantain and burnet saxifrage are just a few of the quirkily named wild-flowers found here. Many species of orchid also thrive.

Devil's Dyke
Devil's Dyke is the largest dry valley in the United Kingdom. It has thrilled day-trippers since Victorian times, when there was a fairground here, a cable car that crossed the hillside and a small train line that brought visitors up from Brighton. It's also the site of a prehistoric hill fort and settlement. Today, you'll see hang-gliders catching thermals and updrafts from the valley slopes.

Butterflies and birds
The best places for spotting butterflies and wild-flowers on the downs are the steep slopes that don't have a history of ploughing and farming; this makes Devil's Dyke ideal. Look out for chalkhill blue and Adonis blue butterflies, distinguished from the common blue by their chequered wing tips. If you're lucky, you might catch a sight of warblers, linnet, yellowhammer, grey partridge and corn bunting along the route. Also listen out for skylarks as they soar overhead.

How to Get There

By Bus Brighton and Hove Buses, 79 Brighton to Ditchling Beacon, 77 Devil's Dyke to Brighton (check online for details)

By Train Brighton 5 miles (8km)

By Car Ditchling Road, off A27 north of Brighton

OS Map Landranger 198; Explorer 122

Start / End Ditchling Beacon, **OS grid ref: TQ332113**

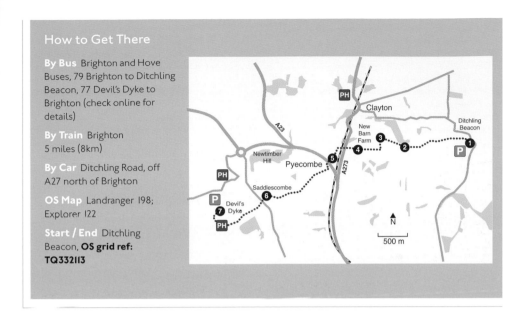

1. Ditchling Beacon lies on the South Downs Way (SDW) long-distance trail. Follow the blue acorn markers west along the chalk ridge, keeping the sea on your left. At around 820ft (250m), this is one of the highest points in the South Downs and gives great views in all directions. For this reason, it was a defensive stronghold in the early Iron Age. You can still see some of the fort banks and ditches today.

2. Just before you reach the windmills is Clayton Holt. This is an ancient woodland estimated to be 10,000 years old and is worth a diversion off the main path. The majority of the trees are ash and beech, some a few hundred years old. There's a Saxon church in Clayton village with an eleventh-century fresco depicting the Last Judgement.

3. Return to the SDW path and continue to Clayton windmills. The landscape is undulating and many of the mounds are not natural features, but tumuli or ancient burial mounds. The windmills are affectionately called Jack and Jill. Jack is not open to the public, but Jill is open daily. From here you can see the northern edge of Brighton.

4. Continue on the SDW path, which runs due south of the windmills, passing New Barn Farm; then west to Pyecombe. There's a gastro pub in the village called the Plough Inn.

5. Cross the A273 then the A23 by way of a footbridge. From here on it's National Trust land and the landscape quickly becomes stunning again. The path twists back into the downs and to the historic hamlet of Saddlescombe, with its sixteenth-century manor farm.

Devil's Dyke.

6. Take a quick signposted detour to the farm's donkey wheel and well, which is thought to be 400 years old. Cross a road then follow the path to Devil's Dyke.

7. Marvel at this landscape that was carved out during the last Ice Age. Constable called the view up here 'the best in all the land'. From here you can walk or take the bus back to Brighton.

Make the Most of Your Day

Saddlescombe Farm is a hidden gem, documented in the Domesday Book and well worth a visit. It's a unique example of a downland farm that shows what life was really like throughout the last 1,000 years. A working farm, it can be visited on special open days.

Food and Facilities

Along the way, visit the Plough Inn at Pyecombe, or the pub next to the car park at the top of Devil's Dyke. Toilets are available in Ditchling village and at Devil's Dyke car park.

A chalk path ascending Devil's Dyke.

24. Harting Down Wildlife Wander

Harting Down
West Sussex GU31 5PN
01730 816638
woolbedingcountryside@
nationaltrust.org.uk
www.nationaltrust.org.uk/
harting-down

About this walk
Wonderful views
Some steep ascents and
descents
Dogs welcome on a lead

Distance 4 miles (6.4km)

Time 2 hours

This wonderful wildlife walk takes you through Harting Down Nature Reserve, a tapestry of pristine Sussex downland blended with scattered scrub and woodland. Reaching the summit affords panoramic views over the weald to the North Downs and south to the Isle of Wight, while your descent takes you into secluded valleys of natural and historic interest.

Above: Crosswort, buttercups and daisies beside the South Down Way, on Harting Down.

Things to see

Abundant insects
The hillsides are strewn with countless ant hills of the yellow meadow ant. The ants help care for the caterpillars of the common blue butterfly in return for a sugary secretion produced by the caterpillars. Lots of other insects enjoy the downland, including the Duke of Burgundy fritillary and grizzled skipper butterflies, and the blue carpenter bee. On dark summer nights, take a look on Round Down for glow-worms.

Plant life
The grassland on Harting Down supports 30 to 40 plant species, such as cowslips and the pyramidal and fragrant orchids. Bird's-foot trefoil, with its yellow flowers, is food for the caterpillars of the common blue butterfly. The site is also one of Britain's best places for juniper – the fragrant black berries are used in gin-making.

Wrestling wildlife
If you're really lucky, you may see the rare sight of male adders 'dancing' (wrestling) for territory at Granny's Bottom. There's more chance of seeing fallow deer bucks putting on a show in the October rut when they call loudly and lock antlers in an attempt to secure the doe's attention. Make sure to stop here and listen for the nightingale on summer afternoons and evenings.

Fallow deer grazing.

How to Get There

By Train Petersfield
5 miles (8km)

By Car 5.5 miles (8.8km)
south-east of Petersfield,
off B2141

OS Map Landranger 197

Start / End Down car park,
OS grid ref: SU791180

1. Start in Harting Down National Trust car park, where you'll get a fantastic view across the flat plain of the weald towards the Hog's Back ridge and North Downs. Walk through a gate and cross Harting Hill.

2. Go over the undulating Cross Ridge Dykes. These parallel mounds date back to the Iron Age and may have been boundary markers or a 'checkpoint' across the ridgeway.

3. Follow the right-hand track up Round Down, keeping the hedge on your left. You'll see a huge variety of plants here all year round. Just over the top of the hill, turn left and go through a gate before walking down into the next valley. After passing through another gate at the bottom, walk across to the base of Beacon Hill. Stop a moment and smell the berries that grow on the female juniper bush, and in springtime enjoy the buttery-yellow carpet of cowslips – a plant often used to make potent local wine.

4. Here is the ridge of an Iron Age hill fort, probably created as an animal enclosure and symbol of status rather than a defensive stronghold. Either climb up to the summit of Beacon Hill or turn right and skirt across the hill's lower slopes.

5. If you do walk over the top, turn right at a crossroads of paths on the other side and skirt back round the lower slopes of Beacon Hill until you meet the shortcut route.

6. At a signpost turn away from Beacon Hill and follow the path downhill towards a dew pond and a little hill called Granny's Bottom on your right. The dew pond in the valley bottom was re-created in the 1990s on the site of a seventeenth-century pond. There are several dew ponds across Harting Down; they were originally used to supply water for grazing animals but now they serve a different purpose, being inhabited by frogs and dragonflies.

7. Pass the pond and cross into a yew wood known as 'the darkest place on the downs'. Yew trees are home to birds such as wren, thrush and finch so keep an eye out.

8. Climb up through the shade back onto Harting Hill. Follow the path until you emerge through an opening (rather than a gate) on the right. Stay on the grassy path to take you back to the car park.

Uppark, South Harting, West Sussex, a late seventeenth-century house set high on the South Downs.

Make the Most of Your Day

While you are in the area, why not visit Uppark, a tranquil and intimate late-seventeenth century house rescued after a major fire in 1989. A Georgian dolls' house, with its original contents, is one of the highlights, as are the servants' quarters in the basement, shown much as they were in Victorian days when H.G. Wells' mother was housekeeper.

Food and Facilities

Refreshments and toilets can be found at nearby Uppark or in South Harting village.

25. Cissbury Ring Butterfly Walk

Cissbury Ring
Near Findon
West Sussex BN14 0HT
01903 740233
cissburyring@
nationaltrust.org.uk
www.nationaltrust.org.uk/
cissbury-ring

About this walk
Site of archaeological interest

Some short, gentle slopes,
usually with steps

Dogs welcome under close
control

Distance 3 miles (4.8km)

Time 2 to 3 hours

This lovely walk across an ancient hill fort takes you through one of
the best butterfly sites in Sussex, where you'll find numerous Adonis
and chalkhill blues, dark-green fritillaries and marbled whites, with
some grizzled skippers and small blue, and the occasional brown
hairstreak. It's also rich in flora, with bee orchids, field fleawort and
round-headed rampion.

Above: A chalky path winds along
the top of a bank at Cissbury Ring,
West Sussex.

Things to see

Rich in wildlife
The area following point 2 on the
map is an excellent stretch for chalk
downland butterflies, including
numerous chalkhill blues in July
and August, dark-green fritillaries
in July, and dingy and grizzled
skippers in May. Also look out for
chalk downland flowers, including
various orchids. The rare and legally
protected fairy shrimp appears in
the dew pond during periods of
heavy rain – the rest of the time it
remains as eggs in the ground.

Butterflies and birds
The open grassland after point
3 is an extremely rich area for
butterflies, with a few brown
hairstreaks during August and
September, a host of browns
including some wall brown (May
and August), some dark-green
fritillaries, plus wandering species
such as red admiral and painted
lady. This is not an important area
for blues, though, which are far
more abundant around the short
turf at the head of Rifle Range
Valley and around the flint mines.

Butterflies, flowers and lichen
The area around the flint mines is
very rich in butterflies, with dingy
and grizzled skippers in spring and
also brown argus, Adonis, chalkhill
and common blues, dark-green
fritillaries and marbled white. It is
also good for downland flowers,
including bee orchids and the
round-headed rampion – the pride
of the Sussex Downs. The short
turf around the flint mines also
supports 'lichen lawns', including
several rare species.

How to Get There

By Train Worthing 3 miles (4.8km)

By Car Take A24 north of Worthing and follow signs for Cissbury Ring parking

OS Map Explorer 121

Start / End Storrington Rise car park (not National Trust), **OS grid ref: TQ 129076**

Canada Bottom

Cissbury Ring

Rifle Range Valley

Hill Barn Covert

Shiptons Holt

Vineyard Hill

300 m

Bee orchids can be found around the flint mines.

1. Take the path out of the Storrington Rise car park, heading across a neglected field towards the corner of a copse. Go through the kissing gate and follow the path along the copse edge, under old sycamore trees. Cross the stile and follow the path across a grass field, through a kissing gate and onto Cissbury Ring, by the Trust omega sign and a bench.

2. Cissbury Ring is the largest hill fort in Sussex, with a history dating back over 5,000 years. Turn left onto the outer ramparts. The fence on your left gradually drops away. Go down the steps to the small car park in the northern corner (before the car park is an old sunken dew pond).

3. Turn right in the minor car park, before the gate into the field, and follow the vehicle track that leads through scrub and open flowery glades, with a steep slope on your left. It soon becomes more open, with a big grassy area appearing on your left. Go straight over the minor crossroads, staying on the upper of the two paths. Go through a bridlegate (not National Trust, but Open Access land) into a large area of open grassland with developing scrub. Explore this area for a while, then retrace your steps back to the bridlegate.

4. After the bridlegate, turn left at the crossroads. Go through another bridlegate, and aim for the main (eastern) entrance to the hill fort. (Before the entrance, you can do a detour to explore the steep south-facing slope at the head of Rifle Range Valley.)

5. After the kissing gate leading into the hill fort, turn right to follow the path along the outer ramparts initially, before bearing left at the top of the steps to follow the inner rampart ditch. This leads past an area of flint mines.

6. Follow the inner rampart ditch, past where you entered, round to the south-west entrance. Near the old beech plantation, turn right out of the hill-fort entrance, go through the kissing gate and meander around the flint mines before heading towards the bridlegate by the corner of the wood.

7. From the wood-edge bridlegate, follow the straight diagonal path back towards the old sycamore trees, and return to the Storrington Rise car park.

Make the Most of Your Day
Visit nearby Slindon Estate, with its countless historic landscape features, such as a Roman road, and unspoilt Sussex village, where autumn boasts Slindon's famous pumpkin display and a fantastic leafy show of colours in Park Wood. The flaming torch walk, Halloween walk of doom and mini-beast safari are equally unmissable.

Food and Facilities
Tea shops are available in Findon village, or source local produce for a picnic in the delicatessen. Toilets are available for patrons of pubs in Findon.

English longhorn cattle on Cissbury Ring, West Sussex.

26. Petworth Park Through Turner's Eyes

Enjoy stunning scenery as you walk in the footsteps of England's greatest landscape painter. The trail takes you through the undulating parkland of Petworth Park, stopping along the way to take in views that inspired J.M.W. Turner. Turner was a regular visitor to Petworth House as a guest of the 3rd Earl of Egremont, who collected and commissioned a wealth of art.

Petworth House and Park
Petworth
West Sussex GU28 0AE
01798 342207
petworth@
nationaltrust.org.uk
www.nationaltrust.org.uk/
petworth-house

About this walk
Site of historic interest

Parkland walk

Dogs welcome under close control

Distance 2.5 miles (4km)

Time 2 hours

Things to see

A moment of inspiration
The Upper Pond, as seen from Petworth House, inspired Turner (1775–1851) time and time again in paintings such as *Sunset, Fighting Bucks*. Petworth House is home to 20 of Turner's oil paintings, constituting the largest collection outside of the Tate Gallery.

Turner at work
The view you see today of Upper Pond (seen from point 4 on the map) may differ slightly from that immortalised in Turner's paintings, because Turner often drew from memory. After a quick pencil sketch he would complete the painting indoors, normally at his studio in London. He also painted an idealised view of the landscape, which accounts for some of the differences. The park has also grown in size since the early nineteenth century when Turner visited Petworth.

Top: Deer in the park at Petworth, West Sussex.
Above: The Upper Pond in Petworth Park, which inspired Turner.

Wildlife
Petworth Park is home to a herd of fallow deer, along with geese and numerous birds of prey. The deer can be seen depicted in Turner's work. Look out for them on your walk.

How to Get There

By Train Pulborough
5.25 miles (8.4km)

By Car Follow signs from centre of Petworth (A272/A283)

OS Map Explorer 121

Start / End House car park on A283, **OS grid ref: SU974224**

1. To start the trail turn right as you enter the pleasure grounds and follow the path through the gate to the park, past the kennels (on your right) and towards Lower Pond.

2. After an early morning sketch Turner would go fishing at Lower Pond. While the 3rd Earl of Egremont was used to this daily routine, it landed Turner in trouble at Tabley House in Cheshire. When commissioned by Sir John Leicester in 1809 for an oil painting of the lake, he would often be found by mid-morning fishing rather than painting, and when pressed would respond that the sketch had already been completed. The finished painting was bought by the 3rd Earl of Egremont on the death of Sir John, and can be found in the North Gallery in Petworth House. You will still often find fishermen at Lower Pond where there are healthy pike, tench and carp populations.

3. From the top end of Lower Pond any of the three paths towards Arbour Hill will lead you to Upper Pond. Follow the path to the right of Upper Pond, and stop shortly after the gate. You should have the two spring-fed stew ponds ahead of you and a lumpy grass

hill on your right. Look across Upper Pond towards the house to see the scene from Turner's oil painting entitled *Dewy Morning*, one of a set of four exhibited in the White Library at Petworth. The paintings took over four years to complete due to Turner trying out different subjects and compositions.

4. Walk across Mansion Lawn until you are roughly halfway between Upper Pond and the house, and then turn around to look back across the lake – this was the inspiration for *Sunset, Fighting Bucks*, which is currently located in the Carved Room. If you visit Petworth in late September or October the deer are often seen rutting very close to the house.

5. Petworth House is home to many more Turner oil paintings – 13 in the North Gallery, four in the Carved Room and two in the Red Room. From Mansion Lawn take the gate to the left of the house through to the pleasure grounds. From here, take a right turn to visit the house or a left turn to return to the visitor centre and car park.

Don't miss the magnificent *batterie de cuisine* in the kitchen at Petworth House.

Make the Most of Your Day

A visit to Petworth House is a must, with its internationally important art collection, including works by Turner, Van Dyck, Reynolds and Blake, along with ancient and Neo-classical sculpture, fine furniture and carvings by Grinling Gibbons. The servants' quarters contain fascinating kitchens – including a copper *batterie de cuisine* of more than 1,000 pieces – and other service rooms.

Food and Facilities

There's plenty of choice at Petworth House, where you'll find a restaurant serving local, seasonal homemade food, along with a coffee shop in the servants' hall and a vintage van selling ice creams, cake and coffee. Toilets are also available.

27. The Vyne: Morgaston Woods Bluebell Walk

The Vyne
Morgaston Road
Basingstoke
Hampshire RG24
01256 883858
thevyne@
nationaltrust.org.uk
www.nationaltrust.org.uk/
vyne

About this walk
A gentle stroll through
ancient woodland

Good for bird watching

Dogs welcome under close
control

Distance 2.3 miles (3.7km)

This gentle walk takes you through Morgaston Woods, part of the Vyne Estate in Hampshire. These ancient woodlands are a great place in every season, carpeted in bluebells in the spring and awash with the colour of autumn leaves later on in the year. Along the way, sneak into the wetland bird hide and enjoy watching the wildfowl and wading birds.

Things to see

Bluebells and native flowers
In spring, large areas of the woodland floor are carpeted by richly scented native bluebells. Look out for other woodland wild flowers too, such as wood anemone, wood sorrel, violets, primroses, foxgloves and common spotted orchids.

Woodland trees
There are a variety of trees in the woodland that you can look out for on this walk, including ancient oak with hazel coppice, beech, sweet chestnut, ash and more recently plantations of larch, Douglas fir and Scots pine.

Bird hide
The wetlands are frequented by numerous species of wildfowl and wading birds, and the bird hide offers

a great place to spot them. Look out for lapwing, redshank, heron and snipe. Wey Brook is also a haven for water voles; sightings are rare, but the voles can often be heard along the brook making a distinctive plop as they jump into the water.

Top: A carpet of spring bluebells.
Above: The wooden bird hide in the park at The Vyne, Hampshire.

How to Get There

By Train Bramley 2.5 miles (4km); Basingstoke 4 miles (6.4km)

By Car 4 miles (6.4km) north of Basingstoke between Bramley and Sherborne St John, off A339

OS Map Landranger 175 and 186; Explorer 144

Start / End Middle Gate car park, **OS grid ref: SU625572**

1. From Middle Gate pass through the kissing gate and bear to your left, following the concrete path.

2. At the woodsheds, bear left. Leave the concrete track, keeping the large woodsheds to your left, and the smaller wooden shed on your right. Follow the brown arrows on the waymark posts from now on.

3. At the edge of the woods, with the parkland in front of you, turn right and walk along the disused historic main driveway to The Vyne house.

4. At the bottom of the path, turn right onto Beech Ride, named after the beech trees planted either side of the path.

5. Continue along the path until you reach the bird hide. Here you can view the inland waders.

6. As you walk along Beech Ride, note Wey Brook to your left. This feeds the wetlands and main lakes of The Vyne. As you continue along Beech Ride, you will pass the medieval fish-ponds, formed by the dam on your right. Trees were planted in the disused ponds in the 1950s to provide wood for making matchsticks.

7. At the woodland corner turn right. This corner is known as Loaders Gate, as it was where timber products from the woods were loaded for transportation.

8. The path passes over a small culvert. The culvert supplied water to the medieval fish-ponds, now on your right. The main path rises in front of you, but don't follow it. Instead, turn left, following the brown waymarks.

9. Continue straight on, passing a small glade on your right, where numerous species of butterflies can be seen in the summer months.

10. When you reach the concrete track, turn left onto it to return to Middle Gate.

Make the Most of Your Day
The Vyne is well worth a visit. A grand yet intimate family home, its history spans centuries, from its royal beginnings in Tudor times.

Food and Facilities
The tea-room at The Vyne was originally a sixteenth-century brew-house. Toilets are also available.

28. Isle of Wight Butterfly Paradise

Butterflying doesn't get any better than this; walking along the chalk ridge that runs through the middle of the Isle of Wight you'll find an abundance of insect life, pure escapism into the real world! This is a great site for Adonis and chalkhill blue butterflies, and in late summer you can often catch a glimpse of the clouded yellow.

Compton Bay and
Downs
Shippards Chine
Military Road
Brook
Isle of Wight PO30 4HB
01983 741020
comptonbay@
nationaltrust.org.uk
www.nationaltrust.org.uk/
compton-bay-and-downs

About this walk
Wonderful coastal views

A total ascent of 900ft (274m)

The chalk is slippery in
wet conditions

Dogs welcome kept on
a lead around cattle

Distance 5 miles (8km)

Time 2 hours 30 minutes

Above: A view along the cliffs at
Compton Bay, Isle of Wight.

Things to see

The downs

'For words, like Nature, half reveal And half conceal the Soul within', wrote the poet Alfred, Lord Tennyson, who lived for many years just west of Freshwater and loved these downs. His neighbour, the celebrated Victorian photographer Julia Margaret Cameron, lived at Dimbola Lodge, which can be found along the B3322 in Freshwater. The Lodge Museum garden also contains a life-size statue of Jimi Hendrix, who famously headlined the Isle of Wight Festival in 1970.

Downland management

Since the 1940s, Brook and Compton downs have been grazed by a free-ranging herd of Galloway cattle, run by the National Trust's tenant farmers at Compton Farm. The cattle are well adapted to the challenging environment and graze the slopes to create perfect conditions for wild flowers and insects. The gorse is controlled by cutting and burning.

Brook Down

The quarry slopes at Brook Down are good for spotting butterflies. Look out for the Glanville fritillary, which often breeds among the gorse above the quarry. The main track up to the crest of the downs is also a great viewing point.

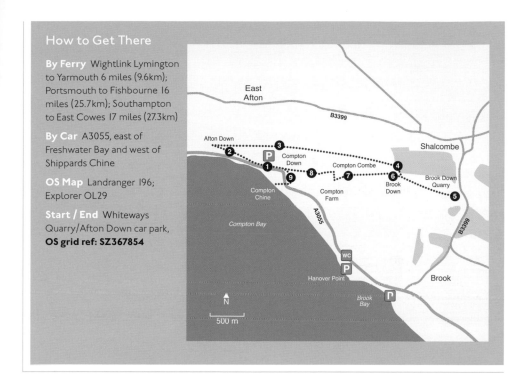

How to Get There

By Ferry Wightlink Lymington to Yarmouth 6 miles (9.6km); Portsmouth to Fishbourne 16 miles (25.7km); Southampton to East Cowes 17 miles (27.3km)

By Car A3055, east of Freshwater Bay and west of Shippards Chine

OS Map Landranger 196; Explorer OL29

Start / End Whiteways Quarry/Afton Down car park, **OS grid ref: SZ367854**

---

1. Start your walk in Whiteways Quarry car park (the National Trust sign reads 'Afton Down car park') by the main road. This area is usually great for spotting blue butterflies.

A Glanville fritillary.

2. Turn right out of the car park and go onto the downs, heading up the Freshwater Way footpath on Afton Down until you reach the summit. This area is a golf course

3. Head eastwards on the bridleway along the summit of the downs. Dark-green fritillaries abound among the burnt and cut gorse that flourishes here.

4. Continue along this path until you reach another path; drop down to join the path and follow it in an easterly direction to the car park at Brook Down.

5. From Brook Down Quarry, explore the quarry slopes and gorse glades for butterflies such as the Glanville fritillary, before heading west back towards the main track and dropping down to the cattle tracks along the lower south-facing slope. Look out for the Adonis blue here.

6. Head west along the lower slopes towards Compton Combe. Clouded yellows are often seen here and on the upper slopes of the campsite field.

The chalky cliffs of Compton Down on the Isle of Wight.

7. Compton Combe is the best-known site for the Glanville fritillary, although the timing of the flight season varies from mid- to late May in good springs and early to mid-June in late springs. The butterflies can be found along the lower cliff slopes, on either side of the wooden steps, but move their headquarters periodically. Colonies of Glanville fritillary also occur along the south slope of Compton Down and in the mown or burnt gorse on Brook Down. Blue butterflies are similarly best found in and around Compton Combe, above Compton Farm.

8. Carry on westwards along the lower slopes, crossing the fence into the ungrazed section. This area is best for spotting graylings, green hairstreaks and small blues.

9. During the Glanville fritillary season (June to early August), make a detour here via the road verge to the small coastal gully known as Compton Chine. Go south along the cliff-top and then down the wooden

steps to the beach – this is a great place for bathing. From here, carry on heading west until you reach your starting point at Whiteways Quarry car park.

Make the Most of Your Day
Compton Bay is one of the best spots on the Isle of Wight for swimming, surfing, fossil hunting or just sitting around and enjoying the sun, the sea and the sand. Further afield, visit the iconic Needles chalk stacks or, on the other side of the island, Bembridge Windmill, another of the island's most iconic images, built around 1700. Here you can climb to the top and follow the milling process as you work your way down its four floors.

Food and Facilities
There is a licensed van selling hot and cold snacks, drinks and ice cream at Compton Bay. A tea-room and toilets can be found at the Needles Old Battery (National Trust).

East England

29. Wicken Fen Ghost Walk

Wicken Fen
Lode Lane
Wicken, Ely
Cambridgeshire CB7 5XP
01353 720274
wickenfen@
nationaltrust.org.uk
www.nationaltrust.org.uk/
wicken-fen

About this walk
An Adventurer's Trail
Dogs welcome on a lead

Distance 2.75 miles (4.4km)

Time 1 hour

Explore a fragment of the wilderness that once covered East Anglia on this eerie ghost walk across the fenland. As one of Europe's most important wetlands, Wicken Fen is also a National Nature Reserve, so there's lots of wildlife to look out for, too, including birds such as wigeon, teal, lapwing, bearded tit, heron and marsh harrier.

Above: Wicken Fen National Nature Reserve, Cambridgeshire.

Things to see

Monk's Lode
Monk's Lode starts as a chalk spring at Landwade Hall, Newmarket. Many of the lodes (water courses) in the area were thought to be constructed by the Romans and used for transport. It's believed Monk's Lode is so-called because it was used by the monks of Spinney Abbey, west of Wicken, for fishing and transport.

Phantom black dog
As with other wild and remote places, such as Dartmoor, it's widely believed that a huge black dog stalks through the fens. Some even say that if you look into its big eyes they turn an orangey red.

Roman legions
The area is said to be the haunt of a long-dead Roman legion that briefly appeared to passers-by before vanishing into thin air.

The legion's presence here could be related to a canal route from Lincolnshire through the fens, established centuries ago by the Romans.

The windpump at Wicken Fen.

How to Get There

By Train Ely
9 miles (14.4km)

By Car 17 miles (27.3km)
north-east of Cambridge
via A10, 3 miles (4.8km)
west of Soham and south
of Wicken, just off A1123

OS Map Landranger 154;
Explorer 226

Start / End Wicken Fen
National Trust visitor centre,
OS grid ref: TL563705

1. First, take a look in the visitor centre to find out more about the area. As you exit, Wicken Lode is on your right. Follow the path, keeping the water to your right. You'll pass Wicken Poor's Fen on your left. This is common land where, traditionally, local villagers had the right to collect sedge and peat.

2. Cross Monk's Lode at Norman's Bridge, looking out for plants such as arrowhead and water lilies. Turn left after the bridge.

3. Walk along Monk's Lode, then turn right through the lower set of gates.

4. Note the two hides on your right. Look out for birds such as wigeon, teal and shoveler in winter and lapwing and redshank in summer on the flooded fields. Bearded tit, heron and marsh harrier live here year round.

5. Turn right along the next path and on your right is the site of Norman's Mill, originally used to drain the turf (peat) pits. The windpump is now restored on Sedge Fen. On your left, roe deer can often be spotted.

6. Note the reed-beds on your left and the many birds and insects that live there. Turn right again to walk alongside Wicken Lode. There is a squeeze gap and path on the right leading to West Mere Hide, which overlooks the mere's west end and the island.

7. Continue on to a hide, from where you'll get views across the whole mere.

8. Cross back over Norman's Bridge and return towards the visitor centre.

Make the Most of Your Day
Family events and children's activities are held throughout the year at Wicken Fen – check online for details. Or visit nearby Anglesey Abbey, renovated by Lord Fairhaven in the 1930s into a sumptuous country home.

Food and Facilities
A café can be found at the visitor centre, along with toilets.

30. North Norfolk Coastal Ramble

**Blakeney National
Nature Reserve**
North Norfolk Coast
Norfolk NR25 7BH
01263 740241
blakeneypoint@
nationaltrust.org.uk
www.nationaltrust.org.uk/
blakeney

About this walk
Uninterrupted views of the
coastline
Good for bird spotting
Dogs welcome under close
control

Distance 4.75 miles (7.6km)

Time 2 hours

This circular walk takes you across Blakeney National Nature Reserve,
passing through a variety of habitats. Stroll along a soft shingle beach
for about a mile (1.6km), then head up to the heathland on top of the
coastal ridge before journeying back down again, looking out for wildlife
such as wading birds and wildflowers along the way.

Above: Blakeney Point, Norfolk.

Things to see

Shingle ridge
The shingle ridge runs for 8 miles
(12.8km) from Weybourne Cliffs
to the end of Blakeney Point. It's
constantly being reshaped by the
sea, and is growing westwards
and moving inland over time. The
beautiful horned sea poppy grows
among the shingle – look for its
distinctive yellow flowers in the
summertime.

Walsey Hills
This area offers a tremendous
vantage point to look out across
the marshes and out to sea. The
Norfolk Ornithological Association
(NOA) looks after Walsey Hills,

A snow bunting.

carrying out research into bird
populations and migration.

Salthouse Heath
This is an important area of coastal
lowland heath, dominated by
heather and gorse – a prickly
yellow-flowered shrub with a
subtle coconut-like scent. In the
spring, a variety of birds can be
heard singing here; listen out for
the beautiful song of the
nightingale. The reed-beds near
Salthouse host a variety of birdlife,
and the reeds are cut for thatching.
Look out for marsh harriers and
bearded reedlings.

How to Get There

By Train Sheringham
6 miles (9.6km)

By Car A149 King's Lynn to
Cromer coast road

OS Map Landranger 133;
Explorer 251

Start / End Salthouse
Beach car park, **OS grid
ref: TG083442**

1. From the car park, walk on to the shingle bank towards the sea and turn left. Carry along the coast, keeping the sea on the right. You can walk on either side of the shingle bank, but don't miss the turning if you walk on the beach.

2. After about a mile (1.6km), there's a concrete slope across the path on the landward side of the shingle bank. Turn your back on the sea here and go left along the raised bank that leads inland. The path takes you through Arnold's Marsh, owned by the National Trust but managed by the Norfolk Wildlife Trust as part of Cley Marshes Nature Reserve. The pools here host a variety of wading birds and in the spring avocets are often to be seen feeding in the shallow water.

3. Arriving at the A149, turn left and follow the path for 100 yards (90m). At the NOA watchpoint sign, cross the road and follow the footpath by the blue Walsey Hills signpost, marked 'To Salthouse'. The steps along on the left lead up to a viewing platform.

4. Continue on this path, going straight on at the next signpost to Salthouse Heath, with the sea still behind you, until you come to a road.

5. Go left until you reach a signposted public footpath (just before a crossroads); turn left here and continue along this path.

6. When you get to the road, turn left. Cross the road and turn right at the next public footpath sign onto Salthouse Heath.

7. At the marker post with the blue Sculpture Trail sign, keep straight ahead, avoiding paths on the left-hand side. The sea is now down on the left and the wide grassy path winds round until the last left-hand bend takes you onto a road again. In the winter months look out for flocks of snow bunting around Gramborough Hill; the birds return north to Scandinavia for the spring and summer to breed.

8. Go left, seeing the sea ahead as you come out into the open. Stay on the road as it bends to the left, then go through the hedge at the next public footpath sign on the right.

9. Cross the field, aiming for the public footpath sign opposite, to the left of the church. If the field is in cultivation, walk in single file, keeping to the narrow trodden footpath.

10. Go down the steps and turn right to walk through the village.

11. Arriving again at the A149 coast road, go right by the bus stop and continue on past the ponds to the turning signposted 'Beach'.

12. Go left here and follow the straight road back to the car park.

Make the Most of Your Day

Visit Blakeney Point, an impressive 4-mile-long (6.4km) stretch of coastline encompassing a sand and shingle spit, salt-marshes, sand dunes and a range of plant life. The Point is home to a colony of common and grey seals that are here most of the year round and can be seen from any of the seal boat trips that leave from Morston Quay.

Food and Facilities

Refreshments and a seafood stall can be found at Morston Quay (not National Trust), and there are several pubs in the nearby villages of Stiffkey, Morston, Blakeney, Wiveton and Cley. Toilets are available at Blakeney Quay and Morston Quay.

The lapwing is just one of the many birds to look out for on this lovely walk.

31. Sheringham Park
Late Spring Walk

Sheringham Park Visitor Centre
Upper Sheringham
Norfolk NR26 8TL
sheringhampark@
nationaltrust.org.uk
www.nationaltrust.org.uk/
sheringham-park

About this walk
Glorious displays of
rhododendrons in late spring

Famous for its views, planned
by Repton

Keep dogs on a lead near livestock

Distance 2 miles (3.2km)

Time 1 hour to 1 hour
30 minutes

Take a gentle stroll through the glorious landscaped parkland at
Sheringham, designed by the visionary Georgian landscape designer
Humphry Repton. Enjoy stunning sea views as well as countryside vistas
along the way, and relish the glorious spectacle of rhododendrons and
azaleas in full bloom from mid-May to early June.

Things to see

The Ling House

Set among the rhododendrons, and
affording wonderful views across
the valley, the wooden hut known
as the Ling House has been used as
a shelter since the 1900s. This point
was intended by Repton to provide
a glimpse over the coastline for
visitors arriving by horse and
carriage. Skelding Hill viewpoint
can be seen from here over by
Sheringham Golf Course.

Rhododendrons

More than 80 species of
rhododendron and azalea can be
found in Sheringham Park. Between
1900 and the 1930s, owner Henry
Morris Upcher sponsored botanical

trips to collect wild species. From
1946, Thomas Upcher carried on
the wild rhododendron planting,
holding rhododendron champagne
parties to show them off, during
which ladies in fine gowns, some
wearing Wellington boots, would
walk down the main carriageway,
sipping champagne and admiring
the colours.

The temple

Designed by Humphry Repton, the
temple was not built until over 160
years later. It was finally opened in
1975 to celebrate the 70th birthday
of Thomas Upcher, who was the last
of the family line to live at the hall.

Top: A quiet walk in Sheringham
Park, Norfolk.
Above: Rhododendrons
in full bloom.

How to Get There

By Train Sheringham
2 miles (3.2km)

By Car Entrance at
junction of A148/B1157,
2 miles (3.2km) south-west
of Sheringham, 5 miles
(8km) west of Cromer

OS Map OS Landranger
133; Explorer 252

Start / End Sheringham
Park visitor centre,
OS grid ref: TG 135420

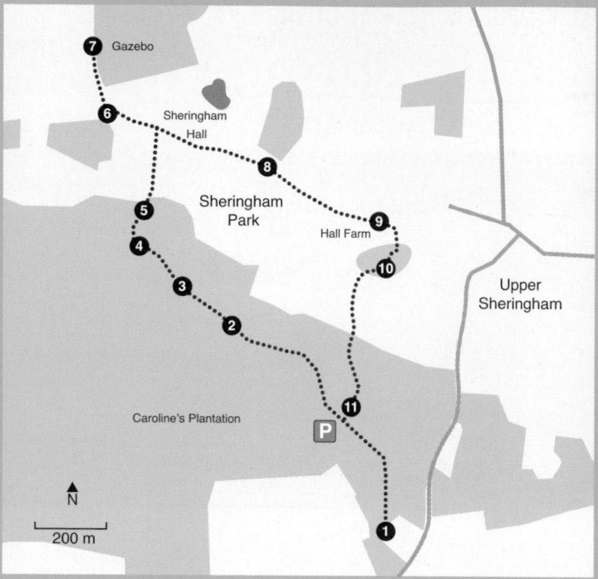

Map labels: Gazebo, Sheringham Hall, Sheringham Park, Hall Farm, Upper Sheringham, Caroline's Plantation, N, 200 m

---

1. Starting from the visitor centre, head straight past the turning for the 'Bower', staying on the main pathway. This takes you through the stunning collection of rhododendrons and azaleas, which are shaded by the woodland canopy.

2. As you continue down the drive take time to look at the moosewood tree on your left, with its bright green bark. In front of you you'll see a wooden hut called the Ling House. Stop for a moment to take in one of the best views in the park, looking down a valley framed by rhododendrons, over parkland and out to sea.

3. Continue along the path, taking in the different varieties of rhododendron, which first appeared in the park around the mid-1800s.

4. Approaching the black railings you now come to one of Humphry Repton's famous scenes, called 'The Turn', as featured in the Sheringham Red Book (a copy of which can be seen in the exhibition centre). This is the point from which Repton wished the hall to be viewed, creating a strong first impression. As you descend down the drive Sheringham Hall appears sitting in front of Oak Wood, with sea views on either side.

5. Continue along the path and over the cattle grid that leads you out into the open parkland. As you approach Sheringham Hall (not open to the public), take the path to the left. If you wish to bypass the gazebo go right and pick up the route at point 8.

6. Head through the gate and turn right. Follow the path to the gazebo viewing tower, climbing to the top to see the amazing views over the oak-wood canopy. Looking out to sea, when visibility is good, you can see Blakeney Point from here.

7. Retrace your steps back through the gate until you are back outside Sheringham Hall. Continue straight along the path.

8. Park Lodge will be on your left as you approach another cattle grid. Take a moment to view the

View from the temple towards Sheringham Hall, with the sea beyond.

parkland with the woods running along to your right. Centre stage is the temple, designed by Repton but not built until 1975. Note how the parkland dips and rises to create a spectacular hide-and-seek game as you move along the path.

9. Continue along the path, passing by Hall Farm on your left, and take the right-hand pathway leading to the temple.

10. Once at the temple take a good look at Sheringham Hall. Does the temple seem to be at the same height as the hall? Follow the red, blue and orange arrows to the right, keeping to the right as you cross the field to the five bar gate. Pass through the gate and make your way up the track.

11. At the waymark turn left and head back along the main path to the visitor centre.

Make the Most of Your Day

It's well worth a visit to the Repton exhibition centre to learn more about Humphry Repton, and how the turbulent events of the time influenced his designs for Sheringham Park. Here you will find copies of his Red Book, and information on the Upcher family. Or head down the coast to the Elizabeth House Museum, an amazing 'hands-on' museum that's a treasury of sixteenth-century domestic history.

Food and Facilities

The Courtyard Café at Sheringham Park serves a selection of hot and cold snacks and ice cream. Toilets are available near the visitor centre.

32. Blickling Estate: In Anne Boleyn's Footsteps

Blickling Estate
Norwich
Norfolk NR II 6NF
01263 738030
blickling@
nationaltrust.org.uk
www.nationaltrust.org.uk/
blickling-estate

About this walk
Good for bluebells in spring

Some stiles

Keep dogs on a lead near
livestock

Distance 4.5 miles (7.2km)

Time 2 hours

This refreshing walk takes you across the beautiful Blickling Estate, once the home of Anne Boleyn. With its narrow hedges and tree-lined lanes, woodlands and red-brick buildings, this quintessentially Norfolk landscape has changed little over the centuries. Along the way you'll find plenty of points of interest, including a tower and mausoleum and an old ice house.

Things to see

The Tower and mausoleum
Now let as a holiday cottage, the Tower was built in the eighteenth century as a grandstand for the steeplechase racecourse that ran across the area now known as Tower Park. This area has been returned to grass, with extensive grazing designed to encourage biodiversity. The mausoleum was built in 1794 in the shape of a large pyramid to house the remains of the 2nd Earl of Buckinghamshire and his two wives.

Buckinghamshire Arms
An alehouse has stood on this site since the 1600s, although the current inn, which was used occasionally for 'the horses of

Gentlemen', dates from the 1700s. Owned by the National Trust, it's a great place to stay on an overnight visit to Blickling, with good food, log fires and four-poster beds.

Great Wood
The medieval Great Wood has changed little since the late eighteenth century, with its mix of English oaks, groves of beech and ancient sweet chestnuts, as well as small-leaved limes on the banks to the south-west of the wood. Bluebells are a sight here from late April to early May.

Top: Blickling Hall, Norfolk.
Above: Bluebells carpet the medieval Great Wood.

How to Get There

By Train Aylsham 1.75 miles (2.8km); North Walsham 8 miles (12.8km)

By Car North-west of Aylsham on B1354, off A140 Norwich to Cromer road

OS Map Landranger 133

Start / End Blickling main car park, **OS grid ref: TG 178286**

1. From Blickling main car park, facing the visitor centre, skirt the left-hand side of the building and follow the path down to the lane.

2. Cross the lane and turn right past the Buckinghamshire Arms, then turn left and walk past the front of the main house driveway.

3. Continue on ahead, stopping to visit St Andrew's Church if you choose.

4. Now cross the road with care and follow the minor road opposite (signposted 'Weaver's Way'), towards Silvergate. At the end of the fence (100 yards/90m or so) on the right-hand side, you can enter the wood and have a look at the old eighteenth-century ice house, hidden in Icehouse Plantation; used until the 1930s, it is now Grade II listed. Returning to the road, turn right and continue until, on the right-hand side, you reach a stile and a waymark with a blue arrow.

5. Cross the stile and walk through the small woodland where there is a second stile to be crossed. Continue across the meadow (known as Pond Meadow) where there is another stile. The brick building in front of you once housed a pump that fed water to the house during the Second World War. Cross the carr (just past the pump house) and turn left into the field. The name 'carr' is derived from the old Norse word 'kjarr', which means 'wet (sometimes swampy) woodland'.

6. Follow the path along the field margin until you exit onto the lane, opposite Hall Farm. Turn right along the lane for about 100 yards (90m) or so and look for a waymark on the left. Turn left up the track, go past a cottage and, just before reaching the main road, turn left and follow the path that runs alongside the road and wood.

7. At the end of this path, turn right and, crossing the busy road with care, head towards a kissing gate. Just before reaching the gate, turn left into Long Plantation and follow the path.

8. After a short walk you will arrive at the Tower, built as a grandstand.

Woodland on the Blickling Estate.

9. After leaving the Tower, continue along the waymarked path until almost reaching the road. Ignoring the path directly ahead, turn sharp right and continue along the edge of Buck's Common woodland until you reach a gate at its end. Go through the gate and continue across Hyde Park (cattle freely graze this area) until you reach another section of woodland and another gate. Go through the gate and turn immediately right. The path now continues downhill alongside Bunker's Hill Plantation towards Great Wood.

10. When you reach the bottom of the hill, turn right and follow the edge of Great Wood uphill until reaching the second seat on the left. Now turn left and follow the path until you get to an open area with the mausoleum to your left.

11. After visiting the mausoleum head back along the edge of the woodland and take the second path on the left. Follow the path, bearing right further on, and head towards, then follow, the edge of the arable field in front of you, enjoying extensive views down to the River Bure and beyond. Eventually you reach a small area of woodland known as the Beeches.

12. After entering the woodland, turn immediately right; leaving the Beeches behind you head downhill, watching out for grazing animals, and continue until you reach the park gates at the bottom. Exit through the small gate and after about 25 yards (23m) turn left and head towards the entrance to the main car park and the visitor centre.

Make the Most of Your Day
There's so much to see and do at Blickling that one day is never enough. Explore the imposing turreted red-brick mansion, with its nationally important book collection, and hear the real voices of the servants who once worked 'downstairs'. Then discover the top-secret work carried out by the RAF during the Second World War.

Food and Facilities
The Muddy Boots Café is a relaxed, informal eating-place serving fresh, seasonal food – ideal for a post-walk snack. Alternatively, try the Buckinghamshire Arms (when open). Toilets can be found in the main car park and restaurant.

33. Horsey Windpump: Windmills and Wildlife

Horsey Windpump
Horsey
Great Yarmouth
Norfolk NR29 4EF
01263 740241
horseywindpump@
nationaltrust.org.uk
www.nationaltrust.org.uk/
horsey-windpump

About this walk
An internationally important
site for wildlife

Some stiles and steps

Dogs welcome under close
control

Distance 4.5 miles (7.2km)

Time 2 hours

Experience the Broadland landscape and a wealth of wildlife as you
stroll through the Horsey Estate, with its mere, reed-beds, marshes and
drainage mills. Along the way visit the imposing Horsey Windpump, a
five-storey drainage mill that provides stunning views across the flat
scenery of the Norfolk Broads and coastline.

Things to see

Brograve Mill
Brograve Mill is a windpump that
lies approximately 1 mile (1.6km)
north of Horsey Mere. It was built in
1771 by Sir Berney Brograve and is
thought to have last worked around
1930. The mill is Grade II listed and
is the earliest surviving tower mill
in the Broads.

Horsey Mere
Horsey Mere and the surrounding
reed-beds are a haven for wildlife.
The mere offers superb sailing and
fishing, while in winter a wildfowl
refuge operates. The mere hosts
over 5,000 wildfowl, and boat-
users are asked to avoid it from
November to March each year.

Horsey Windpump
Standing sentinel over Horsey
Mere, this is the last tower mill built
in the Broads, dating from 1912. It
was designed to control the water
levels of the surrounding marshes
whenever there was wind to turn
its sails. This area has flooded
many times throughout history and
remains at the mercy of the sea.

Top: Sunset over the Horsey Estate
in the Norfolk Broads.
Right: Brograve Mill is over
240 years old.

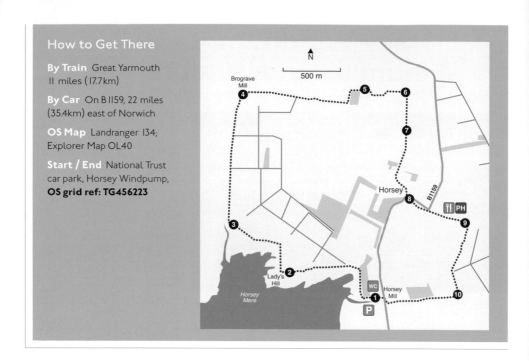

How to Get There

By Train Great Yarmouth 11 miles (17.7km)

By Car On B1159, 22 miles (35.4km) east of Norwich

OS Map Landranger 134; Explorer Map OL40

Start / End National Trust car park, Horsey Windpump, **OS grid ref: TG456223**

1. From the car park head back towards the entrance and the Horsey Staithe Stores (where you can get further information on the area). From the stores, head to the Staithe and follow the path along the flood-bank, adjacent to the car park and around the edge of Horsey Mere.

2. At Lady's Hill turn right, heading north to follow this new flood-bank; then turn left towards Waxham Cut.

3. Where the path rejoins the flood-bank turn right and continue along a large dyke, the Waxham Cut. You will see the derelict Brograve Drainage Mill ahead of you.

4. Turn right opposite the mill and leave the flood-bank. Enter a field. Walk along the edge of the field until you reach the stile and a bridge over a dyke. Cross both and continue to the houses at Horsey Corner.

5. When you reach the metalled road turn right, then left between the houses and continue on a narrow path into a field.

6. Continue along the field edge and turn right where the path meets a hedge. As you continue, the path widens and has a hedge either side.

7. The grassy track joins a metalled road (Binsley Close). Continue on past the houses and All Saints' Church at Horsey. Follow the road round to the left and continue before turning right and reaching the main road (B1159).

8. Taking care, cross the road and turn left and over a small footbridge. Go left and walk along the field edge to the field entrance. Turn right and walk down the narrow lane to your right (The Street), looking out for traffic. Continue down The Street past houses, National Trust holiday cottages and the Nelson Head pub and restaurant.

9. Approximately 100 yards (90m) past the pub, look for a wide grassy path on your right. Follow this path, keeping the ditch on your left-hand side. Continue and you'll see a stile ahead of you. From now on, the remainder of the walk is via a permissive path provided by the Horsey Estate Trust.

10. Cross the stile and turn right, and you will see Horsey Windpump ahead of you. Continue to the main road and cross with care, returning to your starting point.

Make the Most of Your Day

Make the effort to climb Horsey Windpump, from where you'll get fabulous views across the Broads.

Then head for the Elizabeth House Museum, an amazing 'hands-on' museum that's a treasury of sixteenth-century domestic history.

Food and Facilities

You can get a well-deserved cup of tea and some cake in Horsey Staithe Stores, or try the Nelson Head pub and restaurant, which serves snacks all day. Toilets are available in the car park.

Horsey Windpump stands sentinel over Horsey Mere in the Norfolk Broads.

34. Oxburgh Hall Heritage Hike

Oxburgh Hall
Oxborough
Norfolk PE33 9PS
01366 328258
oxburghhall
@nationaltrust.org.uk
www.nationaltrust.org.uk/
oxburgh-hall

About this walk

A heritage walk

Several stiles

Dogs welcome under close control

Distance 3.5 miles (5.6km)

Time I hour 30 minutes

This delightful rural walk along farm tracks and bridleways takes you from Oxburgh Hall to Gooderstone, passing through nationally protected farmland along the way. In the course of your walk, take time to explore the area's rich heritage, including two medieval churches, an old drovers' road and the remains of a tower mill.

Above: Oxburgh Hall, Norfolk, completed in 1482 for Sir Edmund Bedingfield.

Things to see

Gooderstone Water Gardens

In 1970, Billy Knights, a retired farmer in his 70th year, began designing and creating these water gardens (not National Trust). After his death in 1994 at the age of 93, the gardens became somewhat forgotten and overgrown. In 2002 in memory of her father, his daughter Coral commenced restoration work and the gardens re-opened the following year.

Rich wildlife

As you walk down past Elm Place (point 5 on the map), the farmland to your left is designated a Special Protection Area and a Site of Special Scientific Interest (SSSI), due to its rich variety of birds, such as stone curlew, nightjar and woodlark, and other wildlife including brown hare and bats. The nightjar is a nocturnal bird that can be seen hawking for food at dusk and dawn. It arrives in the United Kingdom between April and May, and leaves around August to September.

Chalkrow Lane Tower Mill

The tower mill in Chalkrow Lane was built around 1829 for a Mr George Seppings. It was quite a small mill, standing around 33ft (10m) high and comprising only three storeys. The mill used four double-shuttered sails, each with eight bays of three shutters. Unusually, the sails turned clockwise and were struck via a lever with a swing hook. The boat-shaped cap held a gallery and a six-bladed fan. A bakehouse was attached to the mill house.

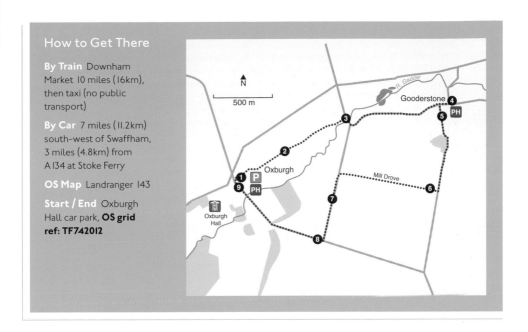

How to Get There

By Train Downham Market 10 miles (16km), then taxi (no public transport)

By Car 7 miles (11.2km) south-west of Swaffham, 3 miles (4.8km) from A134 at Stoke Ferry

OS Map Landranger 143

Start / End Oxburgh Hall car park, **OS grid ref: TF742012**

---

1. Starting at Oxburgh Hall, turn left out of the car park and then turn right along the lane next to the Bedingfield Arms. Pass Chantry House on your right and after 100 yards (90m) or so look out for a-not-very-well signposted public footpath on your right with a fence on one side. The footpath enters

a field via a stile, adjacent to Church Farm. Turning immediately left over the stile, follow the footpath along the right-hand side of the hedge line, changing from right- to left-hand side of the hedge further down. After about 500 yards (460m) you will reach another stile (with barbed wire, so be careful).

2. Cross this stile and enter another field currently full of rabbit holes. At some times of the year you might see piglets in the field on your left. Carefully make your way across the field from the left- to the right-hand corner, past the sewage works, to another stile.

3. Climb the stile and turn right along the road. Follow the road for approximately half a mile (0.8km) into the village of Gooderstone, passing Gooderstone Water Gardens (not National Trust) along the way.

4. Continue down until you reach St George's Church (not National Trust). A medieval church dating from the thirteenth century, it's well worth taking 10 minutes or so to explore it.

5. After exploring the church, retrace your steps back out of Gooderstone until you reach Elm Place on the left, where the surrounding farmland is nationally protected.

Look out for rabbits along the way.

6. Continue walking for around half a mile (0.8km) until you reach a public bridleway on the right, called Mill Drove. This is an old drovers' road, which in years gone by hosted a post-mill (hence the name). The mill appears on maps from the late 1700s to the early 1800s but little is now known about it. Follow this bridleway until the end and turn left onto Chalkrow Lane.

7. Follow the lane and on the way look out for the remains of Chalkrow Lane Tower Mill on the right. The gate to the yard has an interesting plate, seemingly of LNER railway vintage.

8. When your reach the T-junction turn right and follow the road back towards your starting point at Oxburgh Hall.

9. At the end of your walk visit the church of St John the Evangelist, dating from the fourteenth century. At the east end of the south aisle lies the Bedingfield Chapel, which was founded in 1496 and contains very rare terracotta screens from about 1530.

Make the most of Your Day
Take time to visit Oxburgh Hall, which was built in the fifteenth century for the Bedingfield family, who have lived here ever since. Inside, the family's Catholic history is revealed, complete with a secret priest's hole and stunning needlework by Mary, Queen of Scots and Bess of Hardwick.

Food and Facilities
The tea-room at Gooderstone Water Gardens is open most days; the Swan in Gooderstone or the Bedingfield Arms in Oxborough also make good refreshment and toilet stops.

The needlework panels at Oxburgh Hall were made by Mary, Queen of Scots and Bess of Hardwick.

35. Ickworth Monument Walk

This long circular walk takes you through the tranquil parkland of Ickworth, in Suffolk, past a range of attractive features, from the walled garden and Fairy Lake to the Old Deer Park, via the Round House and monument. There are some stunning views across the parkland along the way, and lots of things to do once you've finished your walk.

Ickworth
Horringer
Bury St Edmunds
Suffolk IP29 5QE
01284 735270
ickworth@
nationaltrust.org.uk
www.nationaltrust.org.uk/
ickworth

About this walk
A tranquil parkland setting
Some stiles
Dogs welcome under close control

Distance 5.8 miles (9.2km)

Time 3 hours

Things to see

Bees at the walled garden
The walled garden is now home to several beehives, which have been installed on the far side of the right-hand wall as part of a nationwide 'conserve bees' initiative. It is also part of a project to restore the walled garden to how it would have looked 100 years ago.

The Round House and monument
Built around 1850 the Round House was originally used as a shooting lodge and gamekeeper's cottage. It's recently been completely restored and is now a holiday cottage. The monument was erected in 1817 by the people of Derry as a memorial to Frederick Hervey, the 4th Earl of Bristol, who was also the Bishop of Derry and creator of Ickworth House. His remains are buried in St Mary's, the Ickworth family church.

The Old Deer Park
The Old Deer Park was the first part of the estate to be converted to parkland, the deer being introduced in 1706. Evidence of the original medieval strip cultivation of the land (comprising long narrow fields called 'strip lynchets') can still be seen in the way the oaks are positioned in lines, having been retained from the ancient lynchet boundaries.

Top: View across the lake and summer-house towards the Rotunda at Ickworth, in Suffolk. Above: The Round House dates from the mid-nineteenth century.

How to Get There

By Train Bury St Edmunds 3 miles (4.8km)

By Car From A14, take J42 towards Westley

OS Map Landranger 155

Start / End Ickworth main car park, **OS grid ref: TL810610**

Twist Wood

Ickworth Park

Ickworth

Adkins Wood

Downter's Wood

Lownde Wood

N

500 m

A143

1. Heading towards the main house, take the right-hand fork towards the former vineyard and walled garden. Go through the gate (shutting it behind you) and follow the road down the hill towards the old St Mary's family church (now open for visitors), passing Parson's Pond on your right. On the horizon you may well be able to see the top of the monument.

2. When you reach the church, leave the road and head towards the wall (behind which is the walled garden). Go through the five bar gate and follow the wall to the end. Turn right through the black metal gate into the walled garden, beside what is known as the Canal Lake. Look out for bees in summer.

3. After exploring the walled garden, return the way you came: exit through the black metal gate and back track up the path beside the wall to the five bar gate. Just before the gate, turn hard right, and after a few yards stop at the bird hide.

4. A few yards further down, follow the path straight along the valley, enjoying views of the Rotunda to your left. Cross the wooden bridge and walk through a sometimes-muddy section, then climb the small set of steps. You're now at the Fairy Lake, dug between 1842 and 1866 as a boating lake, but now more a haven for wildlife.

5. Turn left and follow the dam. Following the red and blue waymark posts, turn right at the other side of the dam. After a few yards keep straight on, following the path at the edge of the woods close to the field. Continue to the top.

6. At the crossroads, turn right by the sign for Lady Hervey's Wood and then by the next red waymark keep straight on.

7. Pause and take a look at the Round House to your right. When you get to the end of the path, turn left and then right, following the red waymark for a fairly long way.

View across the Fairy Lake at Ickworth.

8. At the end of the field (with spectacular views of the Rotunda), keep right, still following the red waymarks. Now look out for the monument in the field to your left. When you get to the stile, cross into the field and walk across to it.

9. From the monument, return to the stile and turn left back onto the red waymarked path and follow it for quite a long way, until you meet a gate where the path meets the road. Turn right and follow the path past Stoneyhill Wood on your left and Downter's Wood on your right.

10. Continue until reaching a cattle grid. Cross the grid and turn left; this is known as the Old Deer Park. Follow the path along the valley to the wooden footbridge, over the stream to your right.

11. Cross the wooden bridge and follow the edge of the field to the top, then enter the woods by the orange waymark post. Turn right and follow the path past views to the right over the valley; the monument can be seen in the distance from here.

12. You're now entering part of the Albana Walk. Follow the path, without turning off, and shortly, after passing a 500-year-old oak tree, turn right. Upon reaching the gate, turn left and then right into the car park.

Make the Most of Your Day
Take time to visit Ickworth's impressive Rotunda, an architectural marvel built by the 4th Earl of Bristol to house his priceless Grand Tour treasures. Then experience 1930s domestic service in the restored servants' basement, sharing the real stories and memories of former staff who kept this country estate running.

Food and Facilities
Refreshments can be found at the West Wing Restaurant, or the Porter's Lodge outdoor café. Toilets are also available.

36. Dunwich Heath Ramble

This walk around the perimeter of Dunwich Heath offers you peace and quiet and a true sense of being at one with nature. A rare and precious habitat, the heath is an Area of Outstanding Natural Beauty, home to species such as the Dartford warbler and nightjar. Go from July to September and you'll find it alive with the colour of gorse and heather.

Dunwich Heath
Suffolk IP17 3DJ
01728 648501
dunwichheath@
nationaltrust.org.uk
www.nationaltrust.org.uk/
dunwich-heath

About this walk
An Area of Outstanding Natural Beauty

Rich in wildlife

Dogs welcome on a lead

Distance 2.5 miles (4km)

Time 1 hour 30 minutes

Above: A footpath leading through the heather on Dunwich Heath, in Suffolk.

Things to see

Sea Watch hut
Located just after the start of this walk, stay a while at the Sea Watch lookout hut and you may be lucky enough to spot porpoises, seals and birds. Telescopes and wildlife identification charts are available for keen naturalists.

The Bund
The bank or 'Bund' (just after point 14 on the map) was constructed in 1999 and is now covered in reeds. Its purpose is to protect the freshwater habitats of the RSPB Minsmere Reserve (adjoining the heath) in the event of an inundation by the sea. The purpose-built sand quarry acts as an important habitat for a variety of solitary wasps and bees. These insects, some of them nationally scarce, dig individual nests for their young in the soft, hot sandy banks and ground.

Centenary Pond
This pond, which has a good stock of smooth newts, was created in 1995 for the study of water creatures, to mark the centenary of the founding of the National Trust. Pond-dipping has since become a popular part of Dunwich Heath's educational programme. The pond needs regular work to control an invasive weed called *Crassula helmsii*; affected areas around the edge are covered with butyl tarpaulin for a large part of the year.

Pond-dipping is a popular pastime at Dunwich Heath Coastal Centre.

How to Get There

By Train Darsham
6 miles (9.6km)

By Car 1 mile (1.6km)
south of Dunwich,
signposted from A12

OS Map Landranger 156

Start / End National
Trust car park at Dunwich
Heath information hut,
OS grid ref: TM476685

500 m

N

Dunwich
Heath

---

1. From the information hut, facing the front of the Coastguard Cottages and tea-room, walk round the right-hand side of the building and locate the waymark post with yellow banding.

2. Walk on past the Sea Watch hut on the right.

3. After 100 yards (90m) or so there's a natural branch in the path; bear right at this point.

4. Continue along the path until you reach the National Trust access road. Cross the road, go straight ahead for a few yards and then bear left, and shortly afterwards bear right.

5. Take the next turn to the right and continue until you reach a waymark for the sheepfold. This area, bounded by banks and ditches, was once thought to have been a medieval sheepfold, but a recent survey has concluded it's a later feature and is therefore not a sheep enclosure. Look out for Dartford warblers here as they fly low across the heath.

6. At the next junction, keep to the left and head around the enclosure. This fine piece of open acid grassland is a great place for spotting birds and insects.

7. Bear left around the enclosure.

8. At the next junction keep to the left.

9. After a few yards you'll reach a public footpath/bridleway with several possible directions. Ignore the public footpath sign to your left and turn right, following the yellow and purple waymark post.

10. Now keep to the left for about 300 yards (275m), along what is known as the North Boundary Walk.

11. At the end of the North Boundary Walk (with a five bar gate and stile ahead of you onto public land), turn left and follow the path for 600 yards (550m).

12. With Bunker Hill on your left, turn right at the waymark with yellow and green bands, then immediately left. After 200 yards (180m) the path turns left, and in 150 yards (140m) you'll reach Nightjar Corner.

A wintery morning on Dunwich Heath, Suffolk.

13. Nightjar Corner is a lovely secluded spot to look out for dragonflies, damselflies and lizards, as well as the elusive adder and grass snake. Continue to follow the path.

14. Here, you reach the start of Docwra's Ditch, dug in 1970 and named after the first National Trust warden for Dunwich Heath. The ditch follows the lines of the original freshwater channel and encourages a rich diversity of wildlife. Listen out for Cetti's warbler and water rails wherever a viewing point is located. A little further on, on the right-hand side, you reach what is known as the Bund.

15. Docwra's Ditch extends for approximately 200 yards (180m) between points 14 and 15.

16. After another 150 yards (140m) or so you reach Centenary Pond. Take a sharp left turn and continue straight up the hill towards the Coastguard Cottages and tea-room, and your starting point.

Make the Most of Your Day

At Dunwich Heath there's a wide range of family activities, including beach scavenger hunts and the new Smugglers' Trail. There's lots of fun to be found on the beach, as well, so bring a bucket and spade for the kids.

Food and Facilities

The old Coastguard Cottages are home to a small but enjoyable tea-room, with a viewing room at the top of the building. Toilets are available in the building next door.

37. Sutton Hoo Circuit

This hauntingly beautiful estate, with far-reaching views over the River Deben, is home to one of the greatest archaeological discoveries of all time – an Anglo-Saxon royal burial site. The walk links the visitor centre with the river and the wider surrounding landscape. In spring, look out for a show of daffodils on the path that leads down the valley.

Sutton Hoo
Woodbridge
Suffolk IPT2 3DJ
01394 389700
suttonhoo@
nationaltrust.org.uk
www.nationaltrust.org.uk/
sutton-hoo

About this walk
Site of enormous archaeological interest

Lovely views

Some steep gradients

Dogs welcome on a lead in park

Distance 3 miles (4.8km)

Time 2 hours

Things to see

Deben Valley
You can get fine views over the Deben between points 4 and 5 on the map. Look out for the tide mill complex on the opposite side of the river. It was the last working tide mill in the United Kingdom. The wheel last turned in 1957, when its $22in^2$ ($140cm^2$) oak main shaft broke. It was descending into a perilous state of decay, but with the help of a lottery grant was fully refurbished in 2004, and now welcomes visitors.

Gar Seat
Look out for the Gar Seat before the end of the walk. Cleverly crafted to link in with the royal ship burial, it was commissioned by Dick

and Lisa Robinson in memory of Elizabeth Robinson, Dick's beloved mother known affectionately as Gar. Elizabeth was a volunteer at Sutton Hoo until her death in 1997. The carvings on the seat echo the beautiful Anglo-Saxon designs found in Mound 1 of the ancient ship burial site.

Tranmer House
Built in 1910, this is the Edwardian home of Edith Pretty, where it is said she saw a vision that led to the excavations of Sutton Hoo. Enter the dark, wood-panelled hallway and relax in the lounge. See if you can spot a burial mound from the drawing room.

Top: Burial mounds at Sutton Hoo, in Suffolk.
Above: Tranmer House, home of Edith Pretty.

How to Get There

By Train Melton
1.25 miles (2km); Woodbridge
Station 3 miles (4.8km)

By Car On B1083, Melton
to Bawdsey, following
signs from A12 north of
Woodbridge

OS Map Landranger 169

Start / End Sutton Hoo
reception and car park,
OS grid ref: TM288487

1. Turn right out of the reception and head towards the rear of the restaurant and terrace. From the rear of the restaurant, head down the valley, following the path.

2. When you reach a T-junction at the bottom of the valley, turn left and follow the path past Dairy Farm on the right-hand side.

3. Immediately after Dairy Farm take the signed footpath on the right.

4. Follow the path between the gardens; cross the meadow and ascend the path to the river wall. Now turn left and carefully follow the path along the river wall to Ferry Cliff Woods.

5. At the end of Ferry Cliff climb some steps, turn left and follow the steps to the top of the cliff. Turn left and follow the bridlepath to the right around the edge of the woods, keeping to the tree line.

6. Ignoring all the other paths, at the end of a field where the track goes through the trees, turn right (do not go through the trees) and follow the path along the field, keeping the wood on your left.

7. When you reach the end of the wood, follow the path across the field to a gap in the hedge and turn left onto a tarmac bridleway; follow this until you reach an estate road. Walk along the estate road for at least a mile(1.6km), until you reach the main road.

8. Upon reaching the main road (with a wooded area to the left), turn left and, taking care, follow the road for about 250 yards (230m).

9. When you reach the end of the woods, turn left and follow the track to the top of the field.

10. At the top of the field look out for the National Trust sign signifying the entrance onto National Trust land. Walk past the sign and then turn sharp right through the pedestrian gate.

11. Now follow the path back towards Tranmer House, looking out for the Gar Seat on the way.

12. Have a peep into Tranmer House and relax here for a while, soaking up the 1930s atmosphere. Then make your way back to the reception and exhibition centre, where you started your walk.

Make the Most of Your Day

While you're here, a visit to the Anglo-Saxon burial mounds is a must. Mound 1 was excavated in the early summer of 1939 by Basil Brown from Ipswich Museum, who uncovered the remains of a 90ft (27m) long clinker-built wooden ship dating from the seventh century, outlined by its iron rivets in the sand. Further excavations in the following years led the excavators to believe this was the burial site of Raedwald, leader of the Wuffing dynasty of the East Angles, dating from about AD625. To find out more, explore the award-winning exhibition where there is a full-size reconstruction of the burial chamber, stunning replica treasures and original finds, including a prince's sword.

Food and Facilities

There is a licensed restaurant in the visitor centre, and toilets both here and outside for walkers.

The burial mounds at Sutton Hoo.

38. Flatford: In Search of Constable Country

Explore the picturesque Stour Valley and Dedham Vale, made famous by the paintings of one of Britain's foremost landscape artists. John Constable painted many idyllic views of the area, depicting scenes that remain recognisable to this day. This walk is easily accessible by train, so why not leave the car at home?

Flatford Bridge Cottage
Flatford
Suffolk CO7 6UL
01206 298260
flatfordbridgecottage@
nationaltrust.org.uk
www.nationaltrust.org.uk/
flatford-bridge-cottage

About this walk
Site of historic interest

A car-free walk

Dogs welcome on a lead

Distance 4 miles (6.4km) or
7 miles (11.2km) on optional loop

Time 2 hours 30 minutes or
3 hours 45 minutes (with loop)

Things to see

Cattawade Marshes
The Cattawade Marshes, where the fresh water of the Stour meets the tidal estuary, is a great place to spot waterfowl and waders. The little egret can also be seen fishing in streams and ditches downstream of Flatford.

Flatford
The little riverside hamlet of Flatford is the setting for some of Constable's most famous paintings, such as the well-known *The Hay Wain* and *Boatbuilding near Flatford Mill*. Wandering beside the River Stour or looking at Flatford Mill and Willy Lott's House, you can feel as if you are actually walking through one of his paintings.

Dedham
From his home in East Bergholt, a mile or so (c1.6km) to the north, Constable used to walk across the riverside meadows to Dedham every day on his way to school. Dedham is a pretty village, where the church of St Mary the Virgin is home to an original Constable painting, entitled *The Ascension*. Painted in 1821, this is considered to be the best of Constable's three religious works.

Top: Willy Lott's House at Flatford, in Suffolk.
Above: View over the Stour Valley.

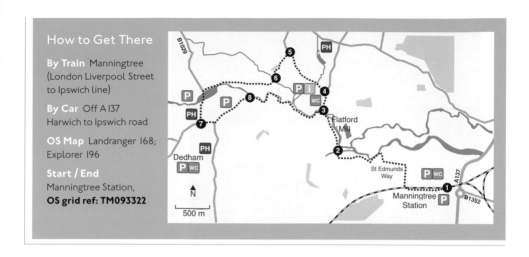

How to Get There

By Train Manningtree
(London Liverpool Street
to Ipswich line)

By Car Off A137
Harwich to Ipswich road

OS Map Landranger 168;
Explorer 196

Start / End
Manningtree Station,
OS grid ref: TM093322

1. Leave Manningtree Station, descending the ramp to the right into the car park. After leaving the car park, turn right along a track, then right again under a railway bridge. Follow the path until you reach the river and turn left along a streamside path that takes you through the Cattawade Marshes.

2. Walk behind the Fifty-Six Gates, the original flood defence designed to stop salt water inundating the low-lying Dedham Vale. Follow the path along the bank to Flatford.

3. From here, take a short detour to see Flatford Mill (not open), Willy Lott's House and the site of *The Hay Wain*. Now you can either return to Manningtree by the same route or continue on to Dedham.

4. To extend your walk, leave Flatford by walking from Bridge Cottage towards the RSPB Wildlife Garden. Go up the steps on your left and follow the path to the car park. Turn left at the top of the car park and after about 100 yards (90m) take the footpath running parallel to the road.

5. Turn left into Fen Lane, looking out for the views that inspired Constable to paint *The Cornfield*.

6. Shortly after crossing a bridge, turn right along a tree lined footpath. Cross the riverside meadows until you reach a bridge at Dedham.

7. Leave the village on a footpath after the drive to Dedham Hall. Follow this back to Flatford, bearing left at a National Trust sign to Dedham Hall Farm

8. The river leads back to Bridge Cottage across water meadows. A kissing gate marks the site of an old stile featured in another Constable painting, *The Leaping Horse*. Retrace your path back to Manningtree Station.

Make the Most of Your Day
Find time to visit Bridge Cottage in Flatford, owned by the National Trust and home to a small exhibition on Constable.

Food and Facilities
A National Trust tea-room can be found at Bridge Cottage. Toilets are available at Manningtree Station, and Flatford and Dedham villages.

39. Nature's Autumn Harvest at Pin Mill

Discover a peaceful woodland and heathland landscape alive with the colours and fruits of autumn. Take in the tranquillity of the wooded foreshore and savour the spectacular views of the River Orwell on this seasonal ramble at Pin Mill, near Ipswich. Along the way look out for the products of nature from which to make decorations, teas or tasty snacks.

Pin Mill
Suffolk IP9 1JW
01206 298260
flatfordbridgecottage@
nationaltrust.org.uk
www.nationaltrust.org.uk/
flatford-bridge-cottage

About this walk
Good for autumn walking
Steps and one steep slope
Be aware of high tides along the foreshore

Distance 2 miles (3.2km)

Time 1 hour 30 minutes

Above: High tide at Pin Mill on the River Orwell in Suffolk.

Things to see

Fruits of the forest
The beautiful woodland is full of autumn seeds and fruits, many scattered on the woodland floor. This is a great spot for collecting fallen pine cones to make natural Christmas decorations. Look out for the prickly cases of sweet chestnuts – the nuts make a tasty snack.

Heathland colours
Twenty-five years ago the heathland was the site of a conifer plantation, but during the storms of 1987 many of the trees were uprooted. The fallen trees and stumps were removed and the land was re-sown with wildflower seeds from Dunwich Heath, further up the Suffolk coast. The result is the fantastic wildlife-rich heathland you see today.

River Orwell
The wooded cliff-top path offers breathtaking views of the River Orwell. As well as a range of smaller boats commonly seen at Pin Mill, you might also see large ferries on the river on their way from Ipswich to the Continent or even a Thames barge in full sail.

A collection of twigs and pine cones is great for making Christmas decorations.

Map: River Orwell, The Cliff, Pin Mill, Cliff Plantation, Clamp House, Dawns Covert, Chelmondiston, B1456, N, 200 m

1. From the car park turn right along the lane for about 40 yards (35m), then left up a set of concrete steps. Follow the footpath up the slope and along the back of the gardens to enter Pin Mill Woods via a kissing gate.

2. Continue past a pine plantation – a good spot to hunt for pine cones. Turn left at a junction, keeping the plantation on your right. The track turns to the left and after 380 yards (350m) opens out into the first heathland area.

3. Take the first left-hand path by the tall gorse bushes blooming with yellow flowers – these are great for making tea and wine. The path then leads to another area of heath. Follow the path into the woodland and see what autumn fruits and seeds you can forage from the woodland floor. At the T-junction, turn left.

4. This cliff-top path offers wonderful views through the trees down to the River Orwell. Follow the path and descend a steep slope.

5. At the bottom of the slope, turn right at a path junction to follow the route along the shore. Keep an eye out for shipwrecks and houseboats along the foreshore. Some boats are lived in, but others have been abandoned as dramatic wrecks.

6. The path leaves Pin Mill Woods and descends a few steps to the foreshore in front of the Butt and Oyster pub. Follow the foreshore to pass in front of the pub, then turn left on the lane to return to the car park. Be warned, if there's a high tide, it's not safe to walk along the foreshore in front of the pub. You'll need to retrace your steps about 150 yards (140m) to the steps and follow them back up to the top path. Turn right and return to the car park.

Make the Most of Your Day
After you've refreshed yourself at the Butt and Oyster, visit nearby Flatford where Constable painted many of his famous landscapes. There's a small exhibition on the painter at Bridge Cottage.

Food and Facilities
Refreshments and public toilets are available at the Butt and Oyster pub in Pin Mill.

40. Hatfield Forest Family Walk

No other place evokes the atmosphere of a medieval royal hunting forest so completely as Hatfield Forest. The ancient trees are like magnificent living sculptures, peaceful giants worn from centuries of seasons and use. This family walk takes you through wood pastures, along an abandoned railway line and past the remains of a 1,000-year-old oak and an Iron Age settlement.

Hatfield Forest
Near Bishop's Stortford
Essex CM22 6NE
01279 870678
hatfieldforest@nationaltrust.org.uk
www.nationaltrust.org.uk/hatfield-forest

About this walk
Dogs welcome on a lead near livestock

Distance 3.5 miles (5.6km)

Time 2 hours 30 minutes

Above: There's fun for all the family at Hatfield Forest in Essex.

Things to see

Flitch Way
The Flitch Way is open to walkers and cyclists, and is now classed as a country park. It follows 15 miles (24.1 km) of the route of the former Bishop's Stortford to Braintree railway.

Site of the Doodle Oak
It's believed that the Doodle Oak began growing about AD950. It is mentioned in the Domesday Book of 1086, and by 1630 was a significant landmark, thought to be one of the largest trees (by circumference) in England. The tree died in 1858 and all that's left are its fenced-off remains, but the oak to the right is believed to be growing from one of the roots of the original tree.

Shell House and lake
The Shell House was a summer-house used for picnics by the Houblon family, who owned the forest between 1729 and 1923. The lake was created in 1746 and, along with the marsh area, now provides a home to a wealth of different species of birds and other animals.

Greylag geese gather beside the lake IN Hatfield Forest.

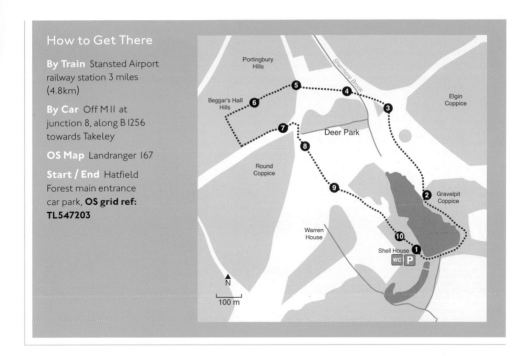

How to Get There

By Train Stansted Airport railway station 3 miles (4.8km)

By Car Off M11 at junction 8, along B1256 towards Takeley

OS Map Landranger 167

Start / End Hatfield Forest main entrance car park, **OS grid ref: TL547203**

1. From the car park, head along the entrance road until you reach a boardwalk path to your left. Turn right opposite the boardwalk and head across the plain.

2. Continue straight ahead, keeping the line of trees close to you on your left. This area, and the next plain, is covered with buttercups in May and used as grazing land for cattle. The wood pasture, commonly known as the plain, is a very rare habitat in Britain and even Europe. Eventually you will reach the exit road from the forest. Cross this road with care (checking for any traffic) and continue across the plain, heading slightly to the right.

3. Head across the plain towards a red-roofed building in the distance, going up the slope to the top of Takeley Hill and continuing straight on, keeping the building (Hatfield Forest Estate Office) on your right. Keep ahead then exit Hatfield Forest through the metal gate and turn left onto the Flitch Way.

4. Now it's a pleasant level walk along the Flitch Way for about 1 mile (1.6km), with the boundary of Hatfield Forest on the left. Pass through three gates across the Way until you reach Elman's Green. Then stop at the third gate.

5. Turn left into Hatfield Forest, at Elman's Green, and onto the Forest Way path. There's an information map on the left as you enter. Keep left of the open pasture, alongside the trees, then, when you reach the first left opening, fork left off the Forest Way path and go diagonally left across the pasture to the far corner to the trees.

6. To your right, amidst the trees, you'll find the site of the Doodle Oak. Take time to look and read about the oak. Go back out the same way and turn left along the edge of the pasture to meet the Forest Way path again. Turn left and immediately right (in effect crossing over the Forest Way path) and follow along until the third opening/path on your left at a site known as Six Wantz Ways, where six paths meet.

Rowing on the lake is a popular pastime at Hatfield Forest.

7. Take this path and at the first crossroads stop and explore the Portingbury Hills Iron Age settlement on your left, at Beggar's Hall Coppice. Rejoin the path and go straight over the crossroads to a T-junction at a wide ride (there's a yellow waymark sign with the number 13 on a post at this junction).

8. Turn right then almost immediately left (crossing over the ride) onto a smaller path, and continue to Round Coppice, bearing left at a sort-of crossroads. Then, when you arrive at the open plain, walk straight across to the gravel track at the far side. Cattle and deer often graze in this area.

9. At the gravel track, turn left and follow it round to the right past Warren Cottage, then round to the left and up to a road junction. Cross over the road and straight over the grass to a yellow waymark post. Turn right and over a small bridge, through a hawthorn coppice and bear left to the boundary gate of the lake area. Go through the gate and walk alongside the lake on your left, passing a large old oak tree on your right, to reach the Shell House and Discovery Room, where you can stop for a break.

10. From the Shell House, turn right onto the path and follow it left over the dam, taking in the views of the lake on your left. Join a boardwalked path and stay on this through the woods, going through one gate then across a plain until the path comes to a road. At the end of the boardwalked path, turn right and follow the road back to the car park. Many of the pollarded hornbeam trees in this area are in excess of 400 years old.

Make the Most of Your Day

There's plenty to do at Hatfield Forest. You can hire a boat or get a fishing permit at the lake (seasonal), go bird watching or join one of the numerous family events, such as learning medieval archery or joining in the muddy play week. Download the Hatfield Forest smartphone app before you go, or visit the Discovery Room at Shell House to find out more about the area.

Food and Facilities

There is a licensed outdoor café at the lakeside beside Shell House, selling fresh, locally sourced, homemade food. Toilets are also available in the lakeside area.

The Midlands

41. Clent Hills Ramble

Romsley
Worcestershire B62 0NL
01562 712822
clenthills@
nationaltrust.org.uk
www.nationaltrust.org.uk/
clent-hills

About this walk
Good for autumn colour

Breathtaking views

Some steep climbs and
uneven paths

Distance 2 miles (3.2km)

Time 40 minutes

Join the many day-trippers who have travelled to the Clent Hills from nearby towns and cities for over 200 years. Sitting only 8 miles (12.8km) outside Birmingham, these hills offer a haven of peace and tranquillity, with beautiful woodland and plenty of wildlife on offer. The hills are awash with colour in autumn, when nature's fruits are plentiful.

Above: View across the surrounding countryside from the Clent Hills, Worcestershire.

Things to see

Ancient woodland
As you wander through the ancient woodland, look out for berries to pick. You will also notice deadwood lying around the woodland floor; this plays an important role in creating a rich environment by adding nutrients back into the soil and providing a habitat for many invertebrate species, which in turn attract birds and mammals.

Beautiful autumn colours
As you walk through the woodland in the Clent Hills you'll be greeted with a spectacular display of autumn colours and bustling wildlife. You may notice lots of old beech pollards; these are 250-year-old trees that were cut just above head height so that they sprouted a mass of branches low down, providing food for livestock. Today, these pollards are home to insects, beetles and nesting birds.

Grassland and woodland
The open grassland and woodland provides plenty of opportunities for wildlife spotting, in particular wintering birds. Redwing, wintering thrush and fieldfare can all be spotted from October onwards. Redwing, with its distinctive creamy stripe above the eye and orangey-red flank, is Britain's smallest thrush and a threatened species, due to a decline in its breeding activity over the last 50 years. Look out for migrating birds, such as wheatear and ring ouzels, too.

Woodland on the north-west face of the Clent Hills.

How to Get There

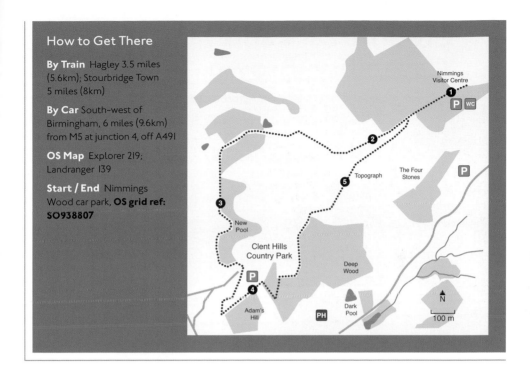

By Train Hagley 3.5 miles (5.6km); Stourbridge Town 5 miles (8km)

By Car South-west of Birmingham, 6 miles (9.6km) from M5 at junction 4, off A491

OS Map Explorer 219; Landranger 139

Start / End Nimmings Wood car park, **OS grid ref: SO938807**

1. From Nimmings Café, climb up a gentle zig-zag slope into the woodland. Turn right and follow the lower path leading down into woodland. At the next crossroads, again stick to the lower path taking you around the boundary fence of Hagley Hall Estate.

2. Continue to follow the same path round the boundary fence, which becomes a red-brick wall.

3. The path will take you to New Pool, a natural pond awash with autumn colour from the surrounding mixed deciduous woodland. Leave the path that you have been following and take the smaller path to your left. Follow this path up to the open grassland, where you will be able to see the Hill Tavern pub down to your right.

4. Walk towards the pub and at the wooden gate, before the road, take the lower path that runs alongside the fence. This takes you up to a bench from where you can admire views of Clent village. Follow this path round and look out for a wealth of

blackberry bushes to your right. Take the path back to the top of the hill. Walk along the top, past the Scots pine and towards the topograph.

5. At the topograph, there are amazing views of the Cotswolds, Shropshire Hills and Welsh borders. Follow the lower path below the topograph, and to your right you will see areas with bilberry bushes full of fruit. This path takes you back towards the car park and your starting point.

Make the Most of Your Day

Make a day of it by visiting Hanbury Hall and Gardens after your walk. The beautiful red-brick house was built in 1701 by Thomas Vernon, a lawyer and Whig MP for Worcester.

Food and Facilities

The café at Nimmings car park serves hot food and drinks. Toilets are also available here.

42. Croome Park and 'Capability' Brown

Croome Park
Near High Green
Worcestershire WR8 9DW
01905 371006
croomepark
@nationaltrust.org.uk
www.nationaltrust.org.uk/
croome

About this walk
Influential landscape design
by 'Capability' Brown

Beautiful architectural
features

A relatively steep decline and
incline and some stiles

Distance 3.5 miles (5.6 km)

Time 1 hour 30 minutes

This relatively easy stroll takes you through Croome Park, the first parkland designed by the ground-breaking eighteenth-century landscape designer Lancelot 'Capability' Brown, and often described as 'Europe's most influential landscape'. Along the way marvel at the beautiful structures and follies dotted around the park, positioned to draw attention to the impressive views.

Things to see

Transforming Croome
Between 1751 and 1809, the 6th Earl of Coventry had Croome Park and Court extensively remodelled and redesigned, employing the as yet unproven talents of one Lancelot Brown, who in 1751 was still establishing his reputation as a landscape designer. During the course of his work Brown transformed the morass of Seggy Mere into the glorious landscape you see before you.

Croome Court
As you follow the meanders of Brown's artificial river, you draw closer to the centrepiece of his design – Croome Court. In

the course of his work, Brown extensively remodelled the house in the Palladian style, saving just the chimney stacks from the original building.

Mary Magdelene Church
As you reach the end of your walk, you approach Mary Magdelene Church, designed by 'Capability' Brown with an interior by Robert Adam.

Top: Mist rising from the lake at Croome Park, Worcestershire.
Above: The south front of the house seen across the lake.

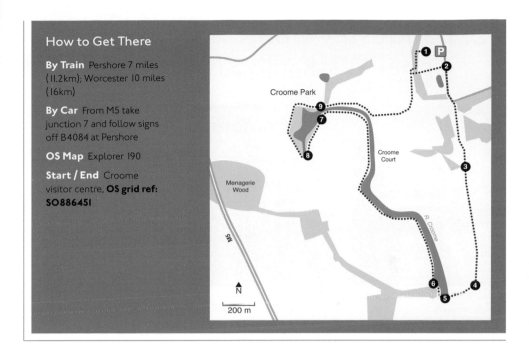

How to Get There

By Train Pershore 7 miles (11.2km); Worcester 10 miles (16km)

By Car From M5 take junction 7 and follow signs off B4084 at Pershore

OS Map Explorer 190

Start / End Croome visitor centre, **OS grid ref: SO886451**

---

1. Starting at the visitor centre, follow the path through the Wild Walk shrubbery and on through the gate. Just before Mary Magdelene Church, turn left through the churchyard. Exit through the gate on the other side and continue straight on until you reach the road.

2. Turn right and follow the road to the London Arch, designed by Robert Adam as a grand entrance. On the bend you will see a gate and stile; cross the stile and follow the concrete path until it ends.

3. Keep walking, past a line of oak trees on your left.

4. Walk along the ridge and just before you reach a wooden gate, turn right and follow the fence line downhill. On your left you will see the Park Seat, designed by Adam in 1770 as a viewing station. Continue downhill until you reach the river, then turn left.

5. Follow the path around the weir at the end of the river and across the bridge.

6. Climb over a stile and follow the footpath, with the river on your right.

7. Continue along the river, round the bend and along the line of the sunken fence.

8. At the third gate, leave the field and turn right onto the lane. Follow the lane until you reach the Pier Gates. Pass through them and follow the carriage drive as it rises ahead.

9. Passing over the Dry Arch Bridge, head through the gate and follow the river towards the court. Continue round the edge of the field and back to the church and your starting point.

Make the Most of Your Day
Take time to visit Croome Court. On Sundays, Croome's characters are re-created by local actors. You can also see Croome's secret Second World War airbase, now restored as a visitor centre.

Food and Facilities
The visitor centre has a 1940s-style restaurant.

43. Baddesley Clinton Canal Walk

This gentle walk takes you through country lanes, across fields and along the towpath of the Grand Union Canal. On the way you'll discover Baddesley Clinton, a secluded moated manor house, two historic churches and the Heart of England Way. There's a choice of routes, allowing you to choose between a 5-mile (8km) walk or a shorter 3-mile (4.8km) one.

Baddesley Clinton
Rising Lane
Warwickshire B93 0DQ
01564 783294
baddesleyclinton@
nationaltrust.org.uk
www.nationaltrust.org.uk/
baddesley-clinton

About this walk
A gentle canal-side walk

Some steps and stiles

Beware of water hazards

Distance 5 miles (8 km) or shorter option of 3 miles (4.8 km)

Time 2 hours 30 minutes for the longer walk, 1 hour 30 minutes for the shorter option

Things to see

Baddesley Clinton
Baddesley Clinton is a picturesque medieval moated manor house dating from the fifteenth century. It has been home to the Ferrers family for 500 years. The house and interiors reflect its heyday in the Elizabethan period, when it was a haven for persecuted Catholics – three priest's holes can be found inside the house.

The Grand Union Canal
The Grand Union is Britain's longest canal, stretching from London to Birmingham and passing through rolling hills, quiet villages and industrial cities. It was not built as a single entity but is the result of

an amalgamation of several canal systems which took place between 1894 and 1929.

St Michael's and St Lawrence's
Built of Arden sandstone from the same quarry as the house at Baddesley Clinton, St Michael's Church dates from 1305. Many owners of Baddesley are buried here, including Nicholas Brome (d.1517) who is buried standing up just inside the door, as penance for murdering the local priest. St Lawrence's in Rowington dates from the early twelfth century; the top course of red sandstone on the tower came from Kenilworth Priory as a gift from Mary I.

Top: View across the moat to Baddesley Clinton, Warwickshire.
Above: The gardens at Baddesley Clinton.

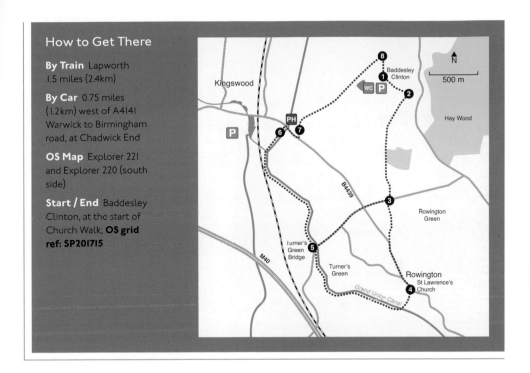

How to Get There

By Train Lapworth
1.5 miles (2.4km)

By Car 0.75 miles
(1.2km) west of A4141
Warwick to Birmingham
road, at Chadwick End

OS Map Explorer 221
and Explorer 220 (south
side)

Start / End Baddesley
Clinton, at the start of
Church Walk, **OS grid
ref: SP201715**

1. The walk starts along Church Walk, opposite the entrance to the visitor reception at Baddesley Clinton. Follow the path through the churchyard, go through the kissing gate and then through the metal horse gate on the right into a field.

2. Walk along the edge of the field with the hedge on your left, through a gate into the next field and over a small wooden bridge. At a choice of two gates, take the left-hand one to walk up the field with the hedge on your right. Continue along this footpath until you reach the road. For the shorter walk turn right and follow this road past the cricket club and over a crossroads, until you reach a canal bridge. Join the canal towpath and turn right along it. Then pick up the directions from point 5.

3. For the longer walk, turn briefly right along the road, and then take the lane on the left, signed 'Queen's Drive'. At a T-junction turn left and follow the road into Rowington village.

4. At St Lawrence's Church, take the lane on the right, signposted as a public footpath and bridleway. Go over the canal bridge and join the towpath on the other side. With the canal on your right, walk back under the bridge and follow the towpath along the Grand Union Canal.

5. Pass under Turner's Green Bridge (number 63) and continue along the towpath, with the canal on your right, until you reach Kingswood junction, where the Grand Union and Stratford canals meet. Continue straight on over the bridge, in the direction of Birmingham, until you reach bridge 65.

6. Take the steps up to the road and turn right along the road, past the Navigation Inn. Then take the footpath on the left to join the Heart of England Way – a 104-mile (167km) Long Distance Walking Route from Cannock Chase in Staffordshire to Bourton-on-the Water in the Cotswolds.

Visitors look across the moat to Baddesley Clinton.

7. Follow the Heart of England Way along a drive, through a stableyard, to the right of the building and across the fields to meet the drive at Baddesley Clinton.

8. Turn right here and make your way back to the car park and entrance to the property.

Make the Most of Your Day

Explore the cosy rooms of Baddesley Clinton and discover how generations of the Ferrers family lived in isolated splendour within its moat. Outside, enjoy the intimate garden, play in the woodland, walk around the lake or simply find a quiet seat and relax. There are also lots of family events throughout the year, from Easter egg trails to pond-dipping and much more.

Food and Facilities

The Barn Restaurant at Baddesley Clinton has a varied menu, with vegetables sourced from its own garden and home-baked bread. Toilet facilities are also available.

44. Coughton Court and Kinwarton Dovecote

Coughton Court
Near Alcester
Warwickshire B49 5JA
01789 400777
coughtoncourt@
nationaltrust.org.uk
www.nationaltrust.org.uk/
coughton-court

About this walk

Across gently rolling farmland

Some kissing gates and stiles

Dogs welcome on a lead

Distance 8 miles (12.8km)

Time 3 hours 30 minutes

Extend a visit to Coughton Court with this gentle stroll through the Warwickshire countryside to Kinwarton Dovecote, a rare survivor from the fourteenth century. The route takes you across gently rolling fields, along country lanes, through kissing gates and over stiles, giving you the opportunity to explore three churches along the way.

Things to see

Coughton Court
Home to the Throckmorton family for 600 years, this imposing Tudor mansion stands testament to a family's courage in maintaining their Catholic faith. They fell from a position of high favour to one of fear and oppression following the Reformation, but their fortunes changed in the nineteenth century when they helped to bring about Catholic emancipation.

A tale of two churches
The church of St Peter was built by Sir Robert Throckmorton between 1486 and 1518. This is still the parish church for the villages of Coughton and Sambourne. The Roman Catholic Church of Saints Peter, Paul and Elizabeth was built

in 1853, following the Catholic Emancipation Act of 1979, after which the Throckmorton family were free to worship as they wished.

Kinwarton Dovecote
This rare survival of a fourteenth-century circular dovecote has 3ft (0.9km) thick walls, hundreds of nesting holes and its original rotating ladder. It is the only relic of a moated grange once belonging to the Abbey of Evesham. Only the Lord of the Manor was allowed to own a dovecote, and enjoy eating pigeon at a time of year when fresh meat was scarce. But the pigeons would often eat the crops of the lord and tenants alike, causing much resentment

Top: St Peter's Church, Coughton, Warwickshire.
Above: Kinwarton Dovecote.

How to Get There

By Train Redditch
6 miles (9.6km)

By Car 2 miles (3.2km)
north of Alcester on
A435h

OS Map OS Explorer
220 (south sheet) and
205

Start / End Coughton
Court visitor centre,
OS grid ref: SP083606

1. With the visitor reception behind you, walk along the drive in front of the house, passing the sixteenth-century gatehouse and St Peter's Church of England church, next to Coughton Court.

2. At the end of the drive you will see the Roman Catholic Church of Saints Peter, Paul and Elizabeth on your left. Cross the road into the field and walk diagonally left across two fields to a footbridge and rejoin the lane.

3. Follow the lane for about 300 yards (275m) and turn right into Church Farm.

4. Pass through the farm and carry straight on until you reach a fork. Take the right-hand fork leading to a farm building.

5. At the farm building turn left along the edge of the field. Then turn right, walking along the field edge leading to a left turn into the industrial estate.

6. When you reach Estate Road, cross straight over and walk to the end of the road and into the field.

7. Walk up the hill to join Arden Way at the top. Go through the hedge and turn right.

8. Follow the path, keeping to the left, and come out onto the Alcester to Great Alne road.

9. Turn left and follow the road to Great Alne until you come to a right turn, signposted 'Kinwarton' and the Dovecote. Take this road down to the farm, bearing left towards the church. The Dovecote is straight ahead.

10. A small door gives access into the dovecote, which was given to the National Trust in 1958.

11. Retrace your steps to the main road, turn right along the road and back up Coughton Fields Lane on the left.

12. After passing a farm on the right, you should climb a stile on the right and follow the Monarch's Way, climbing gently across the fields until you meet a road.

13. Turn left along the road and, after some houses, left again along a track now following the Arden Way.

14. Follow this track for 2 miles (3.2km), passing newly planted woodland – a private venture to replant the Forest of Arden – and Windmill Hill. The track then joins Coughton Fields Lane. Turn right along the lane, and right again along the drive back to Coughton Court.

Make the Most of Your Day

Extend your day with a visit to Coughton Court, where you can explore the fascinating stories of the personalities who once lived here through the 'family album' of portraits and Catholic treasures dotted around the house. Coughton is still very much a family home with an intimate feel: the Throckmorton family still lives here, managing the stunning gardens they've created.

Food and Facilities

Visit the Stables Coffee Barn in the Stableyard, where you can indulge in a delicious local ice cream or warm up with a nice cup of tea. Toilet facilities are also available.

Looking from the roof across the lawn at the rear of Coughton Court.

45. Attingham Park Wildlife Ramble

This delightful walk starts in the Stables Courtyard at Attingham Park and follows the Deer Park Walk through the beautiful parkland of this great estate. Attingham is home to a wide range of wildlife, from buzzards and bats to dragonflies and other insects – you may even be lucky enough to spot an otter. There's also an observation hive where you can watch bees hard at work.

Attingham Park
Atcham
Near Shrewsbury
Shropshire SY4 4TP
01743 708123
attingham@
nationaltrust.org.uk
www.nationaltrust.org.uk/
attingham-park

About this walk
A gentle stroll through beautiful parkland

A few short inclines

Paths not suitable for buggies in muddy conditions

Dogs welcome on a lead in the deer park

Distance 2.5 miles (4km)

Time 45 minutes to 1 hour

Things to see

Walled garden and orchard
Attingham's walled garden and orchard were probably built in the 1780s, at the same time as the mansion. This productive area would have provided the Berwicks, who owned the estate, with a constant supply of fruit, flowers, vegetables and honey. The walled garden is still home to the Attingham bees, which can safely be watched hard at work in the new observation hive.

Otter spotting
The River Tern is only 30 miles (48km) long and flows into the River Severn about a mile (1.6km) downstream. Its source is considered to be a lake in the grounds of Maer Hall in Staffordshire. Otters have been spotted from the bridge, so look out for them as you pass by on your walk.

The Repton Oak
This venerable oak may have started life in the reign of King Edward III (1327–1377) – the best guess is that it's about 650 years old. Originally marking the boundary between the parishes of Wroxeter and Atcham, this old oak is now one of the wonders of Attingham Park.

Top: Cattle graze in front of the house at Attingham Park, in Shropshire.
Above: Dahlias thrive in the walled garden.

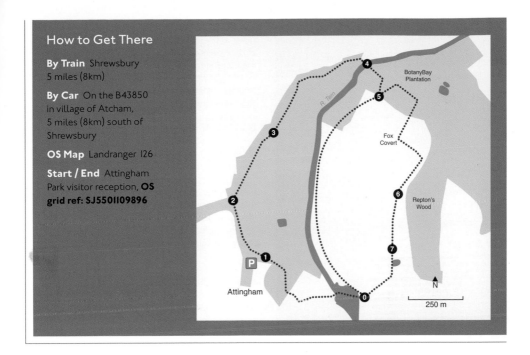

How to Get There

By Train Shrewsbury
5 miles (8km)

By Car On the B43850
in village of Atcham,
5 miles (8km) south of
Shrewsbury

OS Map Landranger 126

Start / End Attingham
Park visitor reception, **OS
grid ref: SJ550II09896**

BotanyBay
Plantation

R. Tern

Fox
Covert

Repton's
Wood

Attingham

N

250 m

1. From the car park make your way to the visitor reception and through the Stables Courtyard, bearing left towards the walled garden. You are now on part of the Mile Walk – a 'hoggin path' designed by Thomas Leggett in 1770 for Noel Hill, 1st Lord Berwick of Attingham Park. Hoggin is a mix of gravel, sand and clay ideal for building paths. In 2009, when the National Trust restored the pond in the adjacent paddock, they dug out hundreds of tonnes of hoggin to rebuild the Mile Walk.

2. Pass the walled garden on your left as you continue along this section of the Mile Walk, stopping off on your way to see the historic bee house and new observation beehive. The observation hive is made of clear acrylic and allows visitors to see the busy bees at work.

3. At this point the path diverges – bear left, following signs for the Deer Park Walk.

4. Cross the cable stay bridge (constructed in 2009) over the River Tern. Attingham is host to around 5 miles (8km) of river, featuring beautiful stretches of the Severn and Tern. The many ponds are a haven for

wildlife of all sorts, from ducks and swans to otters and dragonflies.

5. At the fork in the path carry straight on up a gentle incline to continue with the walk. At further forks in the path follow the signs for the Deer Park Walk. (For buggies in muddy conditions and mobility scooters follow the right fork – labelled 'Shortcut' – through the gate, which takes you along the bank of the Tern to rejoin the walk at point 8.) Along the way, you'll pass an area where families have been building dens, so why not stop and let the children have a go?

6. After walking through the woodland the path opens out along the top of the deer park, with the woodland on your left and the deer park to your right. If you look closely in the bracken and ferns here you might be lucky to spot some of the deer herd. (Please note that during parts of the year sections of the deer park may be closed, so please follow any signed diversions on your route.)

7. Keep walking along the grass path, keeping the woodland on your left, until you get to the Repton Oak. Lots of different animals live in the deer park

If you're very lucky, you may spot an otter.

and woodland areas at Attingham, especially in old trees, which are havens for wildlife, including bats, birds, insects, mosses and lichens. Five species of bat can be found at Attingham Park, including over 1,000 pipistrelle bats. The barn owl, raven and buzzard are the top predators here – see if you can spot any of them flying overhead.

8. A short while after passing the Repton Oak the path begins to lead you down the hill towards the mansion. Go through the gate, across the bridge and turn right to take a look at the ice house. There's no artificial light in here and it's lit by natural light from its entrance, so be careful walking down the narrow uneven steps. After you've visited the ice house follow the path, passing the mansion on your right, and continue to bear right, past the tea-room and toilets before turning left to return to the Stables Courtyard.

Make the Most of Your Day

Complete your day with a visit to Attingham Hall. Built for the 1st Lord Berwick in 1785, it was owned by one family for more than 160 years. As their fortunes rose and fell, the family proved themselves to be variously spenders, savers and saviours – providing a fascinating story of love and neglect which still marks Attingham's rooms today. The saviours are the current owners, the 8th Lord and Lady Berwick, whose restoration programme aims to bring the mansion back to life.

Food and Facilities

The Carriage House Café in the Stables Courtyard is a great place to stop and have a cake and a cuppa, or visit the Mansion tea-room and relax with a light lunch, made using home-grown ingredients from the walled garden. Toilets are available at the visitor centre.

46. Across the Shropshire Hills

Carding Mill Valley
Church Stretton
Shropshire SY6 6JG
01694 725000
cardingmill@
nationaltrust.org.uk
www.nationaltrust.org.uk/
cardingmill

About this walk
Fabulous views

A site of archaeological interest

A steep incline, with steep drops to the side

Distance 5 miles (8km)

Time 2 hours 30 minutes to 3 hours

This dog-friendly walk takes you through an Area of Outstanding Natural Beauty and an important site for wildlife, geology and archaeology. Starting at the head of Carding Mill Valley, you climb up a rugged route to the highest point of the Long Mynd ('long mountain'), from where you can take in fantastic views across the Shropshire Hills and beyond.

Above: Long Mynd at the head of Carding Mill Valley

Things to see

Mott's Road and the Portway
Mott's Road is named after a local doctor who improved it in the 1850s in order to visit patients in remote areas. The Portway is a 5,000-year-old ridgeway that once carried Neolithic traders high and dry above the wet wooded valleys.

The Long Mynd
The Long Mynd is situated in the Shropshire Hills Area of Outstanding Natural Beauty, and is a Site of Special Scientific Interest. It is also one of the oldest and most important geological sites in the country.

Shooting box
Past point 5, beside the road to Ratlinghope, lies a rare bell barrow, an ancient monument that has survived since Neolithic times. The Victorians converted the site into a shooting box, with its steep gabled roof, during the nineteenth century.

Sheep grazing the steep hillside of the Long Mynd in autumn.

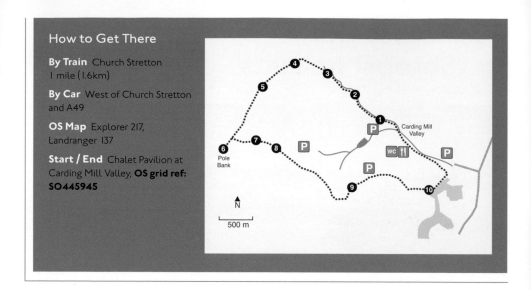

How to Get There

By Train Church Stretton
1 mile (1.6km)

By Car West of Church Stretton
and A49

OS Map Explorer 217,
Landranger 137

Start / End Chalet Pavilion at
Carding Mill Valley, **OS grid ref:
SO445945**

500 m

1. From the Chalet Pavilion, follow the stream uphill to the top car park. Continue straight ahead, on the stony track alongside the stream to the head of Carding Mill Valley.

2. Where the valley forks, go right and follow Mott's Road uphill.

3. As you make your way along the path, Calf Ridge is high up on your left. Soon you'll emerge on the top of the hill.

4. Continue to follow the path as it runs on across the moor to join a broader stony track. Go left and, almost immediately, left again, onto the ancient Portway.

5. After about 400 yards (365m), where the main track bends left, turn off to the right and go straight ahead on a narrower continuation of the Portway.

6. Cross the road and take the path straight ahead, uphill and through the rolling heather. About two-

thirds of a mile (1km) further on, beyond paths to Priory Cottage and Medlicott, is Pole Bank. Rising 1,696ft (517m) above sea level, this is the Long Mynd's highest point, from where on a clear day you can see as far as the Brecon Beacons and the Malverns.

7. From Pole Bank, retrace the path for about 250 yards (230m) to its junction with the Medlicott Track. Turn right here to join the tarmacked Burway Road below, beside the spring at Boiling Well.

8. Go straight on along the road. Within 100 yards (90m), on the right is a waymarked path to Townbrook. Turn right here onto a grassy path, running roughly parallel with the Burway.

9. Continue downhill around a low ridge to the lip of the dramatic Townbrook Hollow.

10. Follow the narrow path down the valley. Beyond the Victorian reservoir at the foot of the valley, bear left along the top of Old Rectory Wood to emerge on the Burway. Cross the road and descend the Burway Track back to your starting point in Carding Mill Valley.

Wilderhope Manor, built c1586.

Make the Most of Your Day

Pick up an Adventure Trail leaflet and get exploring. The leaflet gives you lots of ideas for family activities, including paddling in the stream, bird watching in the hide, pulling yourself up the rope pull and den-building. Or head for Wilderhope Manor near Much Wenlock, a beautiful Elizabethan manor house restored by John Cadbury in 1936 (check opening times at www.nationaltrust.org.uk).

Food and Facilities

The tea-room at the Chalet Pavilion in Carding Mill Valley provides everything from hot and cold meals to homemade cakes and ice creams, made where possible using local and seasonal produce. From here, head to the roof terrace to relax in the sun after your strenuous walk. Toilets are also available.

47. Dovedale Stepping Stones Trail

Ilam Park
Peak District
Derbyshire
01335 350503
peakdistrict@
nationaltrust.org.uk
www.nationaltrust.org.uk/
white-peak

About this walk
A site of geological interest
Wonderful views
Stiles and a slight gradient

Distance 2.5 miles (4km)

Time 1 hour

Discover the limestone countryside of the southern Peak District, famed for its wildlife and geology. Starting at the tranquil Victorian wooded landscape of Ilam Park, this easy walk takes you into Dovedale, an iconic and spectacular gorge carved out by the River Dove. You'll find plenty to explore at both ends of this glorious walk.

Above: View looking north-west across Ilam Park, situated in the Peak District, Derbyshire.

Things to see

Ilam Park
Designed in the nineteenth century as an idyllic setting for Ilam Hall, the Manifold and Hamps rivers re-emerge here after several miles flowing underground. The places where they rise are known as boil holes, as the water appears to bubble and boil at the surface. A Tudor mansion once stood at Ilam, but in the 1820s local industrialist Jesse Watts-Russell built the current hall. The hall fell into ruin in the 1930s and two-thirds of it was demolished.

Thorpe Cloud and Bunster Hill
Rising up on either side of the River Dove, these hills are both 'reef knoll' – immense piles of calcareous material, or underwater life forms, which accumulated on an ancient sea floor over 350 million years ago. Thorpe Cloud is an especially distinctive, conical hill – it's a short but challenging walk to the top. Despite hosting over a million visitors a year, the 3-mile (4.8km) Dovedale gorge supports a vast range of rare habitats and wildlife.

The stepping stones and beyond
The stepping stones at Dovedale were first set down for Victorian tourists to enable them to cross the river. If you're still feeling energetic when you reach them, you can extend your walk. The footpath continues for 2.5 miles (4km) to Milldale at the north end of the gorge where a set of steps climbs to a limestone promontory called Lover's Leap. The original steps were built by Italian prisoners of war captured in the Second World War.

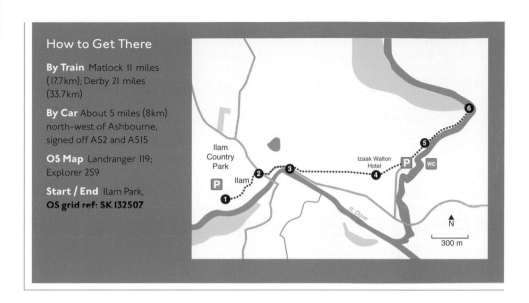

How to Get There

By Train Matlock 11 miles (17.7km); Derby 21 miles (33.7km)

By Car About 5 miles (8km) north-west of Ashbourne, signed off A52 and A515

OS Map Landranger 119; Explorer 259

Start / End Ilam Park, **OS grid ref: SK 132507**

1. Start your walk at Ilam Park and take the footpath towards Ilam Church. Look out for the shafts of two 1,000-year-old Saxon crosses in the churchyard.

2. Follow the path past the church into Ilam village. Here you'll find a group of alpine-style houses and a school, built in the nineteenth century for the local residents by Ilam's owner, Jesse Watts-Russell. Continue through the village until you reach the Mary Watts-Russell Memorial Cross, built in 1840 in memory of Jesse Watts-Russell's wife. Carry on along the road until you leave the village.

Unusual alpine-style cottages in Ilam village.

3. On leaving Ilam village at a lay-by, cross the road, go through a wooden gate and up a short steep slope to the footpath. Turn right onto the track and go through a squeeze stile into the fields, from where there are wonderful views of the Manifold Valley.

4. Follow the paths across the fields behind the Izaak Walton Hotel, named after the author of the book, *The Compleat Angler*, who fished the River Dove in the mid-seventeenth century. The hills of Thorpe Cloud and Bunster can be seen from this point.

5. Cross a stile and follow the footpath downhill to join a road. Turn left and walk along this path, with the River Dove on your right, to enter Dovedale. The name is derived from the old Norse word 'dubo', meaning 'dark'. An information panel here tells you more about the National Trust's work in this area.

6. Continue along the path until you reach the stepping stones, taking time to absorb the fantastic scenery along the way. Put in place in the mid-nineteenth century, the stones have long been a magnet for visitors to the area. Cross the stones to continue your walk through the gorge towards Lover's Leap or retrace your steps back to Ilam Park.

Make the Most of Your Day
Take time out to explore the crags, caves, spires and deep limestone ravine of the iconic landscape at Dovedale; or discover Hinkley Hollow at Ilam Park, where there are natural play places by the river. Other events include an Easter egg trail and visits to a local mine.

Food and Facilities
The Manifold tea-room at Ilam Park serves a wonderful array of tasty food and drinks, or look out for the barn at the entrance to Dovedale, where you can buy delicious ice creams. It may look like a normal barn, but it's actually on wheels so it can be removed at night! Toilets are available in the stableyard at Ilam Park.

View from the summit of Thorpe Cloud, looking across the gorge to Bunster Hill.

48. Derwent Valley Ramble

Derwent Valley
Near Derwent Dam
Peak District
Derbyshire
01433 670368
peakdistrict@
nationaltrust.org.uk
www.nationaltrust.org.uk/
dark-peak

About this walk
Many beautiful views

Rough walking through open moorland

Some stiles and steep inclines

Dogs welcome under close control

Distance 4 miles (6.4km)

Time 1 hour 30 minutes

The Derwent Valley is a wonderful place for taking in the many habitats of the Peak District. This walk takes you alongside the Ladybower Reservoir, through farmland and steep wooded cloughs, before emerging high up on the moors, from where you'll get fantastic panoramic views of the Derwent Valley and much of the High Peak Estate.

Above: Golden plovers can be spotted in the Derwent Valley.

Things to see

Derwent Valley and Dam

This area is good for certain types of bats, including the noctule, pipistrelle and Daubenton's bat. The brown long-eared bat is also to be found here, although sightings are rare. Derwent Dam and its twin, Howden Dam, were built at the beginning of the century and became famous for being used in 1943 for RAF flying practice for the Barnes Wallis bouncing bomb; they were subsequently used in the Second World War film, *The Dam Busters*.

Pike Low

This Bronze Age barrow, or burial mound, can be found at the highest point on the moor. The varying heights of the heather in this spot produces a 'patchwork' effect that is the result of conservation management by burning, which allows for sheep and grouse. The practice also benefits other wildlife in the area. You may be lucky enough to spot some of England's only mountain hare population, introduced to the moors many years ago as an alternative to grouse. In winter the hare's fur turns white, providing the animal with camouflage in the snow.

Golden plover

You are most likely to spot golden plovers in summer, when they inhabit upland moorlands. In winter they move to lowland fields in large flocks, where they are often found in the company of lapwings, and their black plumage is replaced with buff and white.

How to Get There

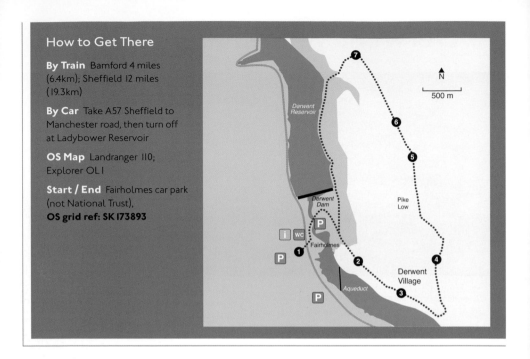

By Train Bamford 4 miles (6.4km); Sheffield 12 miles (19.3km)

By Car Take A57 Sheffield to Manchester road, then turn off at Ladybower Reservoir

OS Map Landranger 110; Explorer OL1

Start / End Fairholmes car park (not National Trust), **OS grid ref: SK 173893**

1. Start your walk at Fairholmes car park, turning right out of the car park and following the road towards Derwent Dam.

2. Walk past the dam and follow the road uphill, walking alongside Ladybower Reservoir on the right and Old House Farm on the left, towards the site of Derwent village.

3. The village was flooded when the dam was built in the Second World War. Only two buildings remain: the Lodge and the schoolroom, which you pass as you walk along the lane. To view the site of the village and an information panel, continue down the slope and across a bridge. Retrace your route back up the short slope and, at the top, turn sharp right at the end of a high wall onto a track, over a stile and past the ruins of a farm.

4. Continue uphill until just after a cottage where the path divides. Keep left and climb uphill through open fields and then over a stile onto moorland. After about half a mile (0.8km) and a right turn by a wall corner, as the track levels, you will pass a burial mound called Pike Low 100 yards (90m) on your left.

5. Continue along this track above Mill Brook, which runs below on your right. At one point this whole area was wooded, but due to clearances that have taken place since Roman times very little now remains. The National Trust is working to preserve and increase the woodland here, using natural regeneration and some planting of native trees such as oak, rowan and Scots pine. You are free to enter the enclosures to see the result of the Trust's work, but please avoid crossing large areas of heather between April and June, during the bird-nesting season. Follow the track to the Scots-pine shelter belt ahead, the site of a substantial shooting cabin, with two lines of grouse butts running towards Green Sitches (a sitch being a ditch or wet area). Keep left at a fork just before the pines.

6. Follow the track until it turns right at a fence. Cross the fence by the stile and continue to Bamford House (a derelict farmstead) along the edge of the moor, with Derwent Reservoir below on your left.

7. On reaching Bamford House, turn left and take the steep path downhill towards the reservoir. Turn left again once you reach Derwent Reservoir and follow this track alongside the reservoir and back towards Derwent Dam and Fairholmes car park.

Make the Most of Your Day

Geocaching in the Peak District is a fun way for people to explore and engage with this beautiful area. It's an exciting high-tech treasure hunting game in which GPS devices are used to locate hidden containers, called geocaches. Check www.nationaltrust.org.uk to find out more.

Food and Facilities

Head for the Penny Pot Café in nearby Edale, where you will find hot and hearty food and drink – the perfect place for a bite to eat. You'll find toilets here as well.

Derwent Reservoir in winter with a backcloth of conifers and snow-dusted hills.

49. Along the Edges at Big Moor

Curbar Gap
Peak District
Derbyshire
01433 631757
peakdistrict@
nationaltrust.org.uk
www.nationaltrust.org.uk/
longshaw

About this walk
Dramatic views from the
Edges

Several steep sections

Dogs welcome, but kept on a
lead from March to July

Distance 6 miles (9.6km)

Time 2 hours 30 minutes to
3 hours

Explore the Eastern Edges on Big Moor, which forms part of the iconic Dark Peak landscape in the Peak District. Jointly managed by the National Trust and RSPB as the Eastern Moors Partnership, this area is a truly special place for walking, with its diverse wildlife, ancient woods and tumbling streams.

Things to see

Top: View towards Froggatt Edge in the Peak District, Derbyshire.
Above: An adder basks in the sun.

Adders
Big Moor is known for being a place where you might be lucky enough to spot an adder. Britain's only venomous snake, the adder is rarely dangerous, although you should treat it with respect if you find one! These cold-blooded creatures can be seen basking on spring and summer days, warming themselves in the sun. Identified by the zig-zag pattern down the middle of their back, adders usually move away when they hear someone coming.

Red deer
The United Kingdom's largest land mammal, the red deer is a favourite sight on Big Moor. Sometimes, all you see of the stags are their antlers sticking up above the heather. Along with the hinds, their russet-coloured coats help them to blend into the moorland. If you watch for a while, you'll find there are always more than first glanced. They are most visible during the rut (mating season), when stags battle to mate with the hinds.

Heather moorland
Heather moorland is common in the uplands of Britain and provides an internationally important habitat for the wildlife that thrives here. Heather is seen at its best after the 'Glorious Twelfth' (the 12th of August, start of the grouse-shooting season) when the flowers turn the drab moor into vibrant shades of purple.

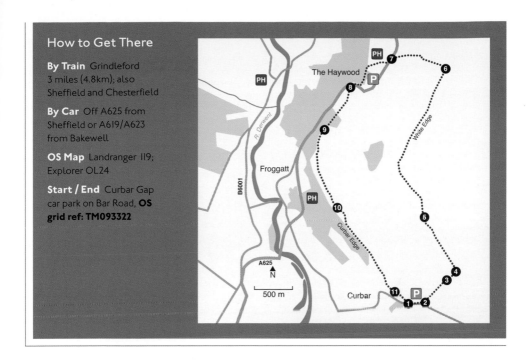

How to Get There

By Train Grindleford 3 miles (4.8km); also Sheffield and Chesterfield

By Car Off A625 from Sheffield or A619/A623 from Bakewell

OS Map Landranger 119; Explorer OL24

Start / End Curbar Gap car park on Bar Road, **OS grid ref: TM093322**

1. From Curbar Gap car park, head east through a gate on a vehicle track.

2. Where the track forks, take the right fork towards Sandyford Brook and cross the brook over a bridge, with the dry stone-walled fields on your left.

3. Climb the steep bank, following the wall on your left to the top of the bank and the corner of the wall.

4. At the corner of the wall, follow the well-trodden path that leads you north along White Edge. The edges are sandstone, or 'gritstone', escarpments that bound parts of the Peak District. These gritstone edges were once extensively quarried for their rough, coarse stone. Remnants of discarded round millstones can be found around the edges, giving the stone its common name, millstone grit. In past centuries, many corn and textile mills were sited on this landscape.

5. A deviation to the trig point on the right provides a great place to spot red deer across the expanse of Big Moor, with the redundant Barbrook Reservoir in the background.

6. Continue for some distance along White Edge to the hole in the wall. Turning left, a redundant dry stone wall leads from here through fields down to the Grouse Inn.

7. Take a break at the Grouse, but don't dally too long, as you're only halfway round. The next section leads you across the fields, behind the National Trust car park at Haywood.

8. From Haywood car park, head south across a small brook and carefully cross the main road to a gate opposite that leads to Froggatt Edge.

9. A wooded track leads to another gate, preceded by another brook. As the woodland opens out, with views across to the limestone of the White Peak, a small stone circle can be found on the left.

Dry stone walls made of gritstone boulders at Curbar Gap.

10. Follow the track along the full length of Froggatt and Curbar Edges. Once famous for millstones, these scarps are now known as great places to rock climb.

11. At the end of Curbar Edge, a small gate leads back to the car park at Curbar Gap.

Make the Most of Your Day
There's always plenty to do in the Peak District, with a host of activities and events such as talks, woodworking, dry stone walling and Easter egg and ant trails (see website for details). Or explore 'Play Longshaw!' – lots of fun for young children as they search for hidden places, explore tunnels among the rhododendrons and delve into the natural habitat of the Boggarts. There's also a visitor centre at nearby Longshaw, where you can find out more about the estate.

Food and Facilities
The nearest National Trust café can be found at Longshaw, which is famous for its tasty scones, freshly baked on the premises and arguably the best for miles around. You'll find toilets here, too.

50. Mam Tor Circuit

Mam Tor
Near Castleton
Peak District S33 8WA
01433 670368
peakdistrict@
nationaltrust.org.uk
www.nationaltrust.org.uk/
dark-peak

About this walk
Panoramic views

Some stiles, steep steps and climbs

Dogs welcome on a lead

Distance 3 miles (4.8km)

Time About 2 hours

Standing at 1,695ft (517m) high, Mam Tor provides some of the most dramatic views in the Peak District, stretching north over the Edale Valley to Kinder Scout and the Derwent Moors. This circular route takes you round Mam Tor, from where you can appreciate the stunning views and watch out for classic Peak District wildlife.

> **Stay Safe** Take care around the cliffs as the edges can be unstable – please keep to the paths.

Things to see

Meadow pipit
Often mistaken for a song thrush, the pipit can be identified by its olive-brown upper parts with dark streaks and dull pink legs. It can be seen all year round in the Peak District, mostly on the ground rummaging for insects or in its nest of dry grass. Listen out for its distinctive short and repetitive song.

Red grouse
'Go-back, go-back' is the distinctive call of this reddish-brown game bird, which can be heard on the heather moorlands all year round. It inhabits the moorlands because of

the lack of trees on the landscape and the wealth of heather shoots, seeds and flowers that it feeds on.

Mountain hare
The mountain hare is shorter than the brown hare, with shorter ears and legs, and inhabits the moorlands to graze on the many plants. It uses depressions in the ground for shelter under heather and rock outcrops. To prepare for winter, it sheds its black/grey summer coat, replacing it with a distinctive partially white coat, keeping its black-tipped ears.

Top: View from Mam Tor in the Peak District National Park, Derbyshire.
Above: A meadow pipit in the snow.

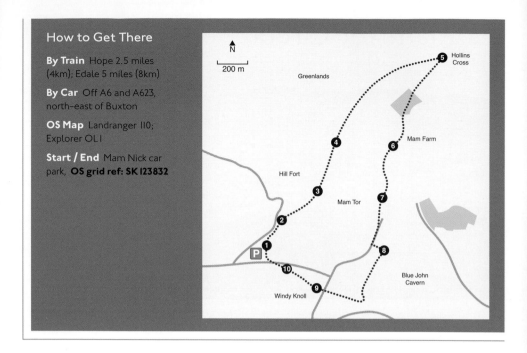

How to Get There

By Train Hope 2.5 miles (4km); Edale 5 miles (8km)

By Car Off A6 and A623, north-east of Buxton

OS Map Landranger 110; Explorer OL1

Start / End Mam Nick car park, **OS grid ref: SK 123832**

200 m

N

Greenlands

Hollins Cross

Mam Farm

Hill Fort

Mam Tor

Blue John Cavern

Windy Knoll

---

1. Climb the steps at the top of the car park and follow the path alongside the road to a small gate and National Trust sign. Go through the gate, bearing left.

2. Climb the stone steps until the ground begins to level out not far below the summit of Mam Tor.

3. Continue to follow the path up to the summit of Mam Tor. This path, which is stepped and stone pitched, has been rebuilt by the National Trust's Estate Team to replace the original track.

4. Follow the flagstone path north along the ridge until it gets noticeably steeper.

5. Continue to follow the path down to a small monument in a dip in the ridge.

6. Turn right, downhill, back towards Mam Tor. Take the right fork in the path, just before the trees, skirting around the woods. Continue on the path to the road.

7. Walk up the road, through a gate, to a broken road (caused by a landslide).

8. Continue up the broken road and pass through a gate and parking area. Turn left down the track to Blue John Cavern. Take a look in this show cave (not National Trust) to see the rare mineral after which the cave is named.

9. Pass the building that gives access to the mine entrance and go through a small gate and up a grassy path. Bear right at the top of the hill and go through a gate. Cross the field and road and take the left fork uphill, to the entrance of another cave, Windy Knoll. Take care! Don't enter the cave as there have been recent rock-falls.

10. From the cave, cross the field to a small gate by the road. Cross this road and walk along the grass verge back to the car park.

The stepped path leading to the summit of Mam Tor.

Make the Most of Your Day

There's always something to do in the Peak District, with events for all ages running throughout the year, from storytelling in Edale to sowing heather seeds on Mam Tor. Or visit the Blue John Cavern (not National Trust), a series of limestone caverns considered to be the finest range in Britain.

Food and Facilities

Visit the Penny Pot Café in nearby Edale and sample the wide range of delicious homemade food, drinks and cakes. Toilets are also available here.

51. Hardwick Hall: Walking in Bess's Footsteps

Hardwick Hall
Doe Lea
Chesterfield
Derbyshire S44 5QJ
01246 850430
hardwickhall@nationaltrust.org.uk
www.nationaltrust.org.uk/hardwick

About this walk
Site of historic interest
A lovely walk in all seasons
Dogs welcome on a lead

Distance 3.5 miles (5.6km)

Time 1 hour 30 minutes

Once home to Bess of Hardwick, Hardwick Hall's Elizabethan splendour dominates the landscape. Much of Hardwick looks the way it does today because of the way Bess and her Devonshire descendants shaped the countryside to meet their needs. As you walk through the estate you'll see features from Bess's time, as well as those developed in the 400 years since her death.

Above: The west front of New Hall at Hardwick, Derbyshire.

Things to see

Bess of Hardwick
'Hardwick Hall more glass than wall', goes the popular saying, and you'll soon see why. Bess was born in the Old Hall in 1527, but she completed the far grander New Hall in 1597. It has her initials, 'ES' for Elizabeth Shrewsbury, emblazoned along the top. Hardwick symbolises Bess's achievement in moving up through Elizabethan society, from the daughter of an obscure gentry family to a countess and the second richest woman in the country – second only to the Queen.

Hardwick ponds
The ponds at Hardwick were created to provide the estate with fresh fish and duck for the table, and fishing still continues today. As you'll see from the sculpture at the edge of the pond, dragonflies are a regular sight here in summer. Listen for the characteristic plop of the elusive water vole or look out for the blue flash of a kingfisher.

Stableyard
The stableyard has played a key role in running the estate for well over 400 years. Housing a smithy, wash-house, brew-house, dairy, crops, livestock, horses, coaches and even a fire engine at one time, these buildings have had a variety of uses to meet the changing needs of the estate. Look out for the new interpretation panels and listening posts to discover more, or rest your feet a while on the wonderfully carved sculpture benches.

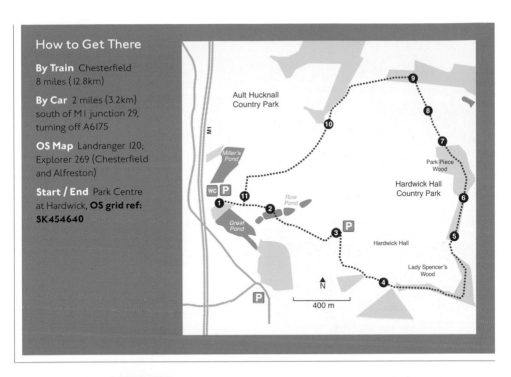

How to Get There

By Train Chesterfield
8 miles (12.8km)

By Car 2 miles (3.2km)
south of M1 junction 29,
turning off A6175

OS Map Landranger 120;
Explorer 269 (Chesterfield
and Alfreston)

Start / End Park Centre
at Hardwick, **OS grid ref:
SK454640**

Ault Hucknall
Country Park

Miller's
Pond

Row
Pond

Great
Pond

Park Piece
Wood

Hardwick Hall
Country Park

Hardwick Hall

Lady Spencer's
Wood

N

400 m

View across one of the ponds in the park at Hardwick Hall.

A walk through the garden leading to the south front at Hardwick Hall.

1. From the Park Centre follow the track over the footbridge, walking away from the motorway.

2. When you reach the pond with the dragonfly sculpture turn right and go through the gate into the field. Walk straight up the field towards the halls. The ponds date from before Bess's time. These ponds are fished by the Bess of Hardwick Angling Club, which helps to maintain a good habitat for the resident water voles.

3. At the hall turn right along the road until you get to the stableyard's arch on your left. Turn left through the stableyard and continue through the second arch. Look out for a glimpse of the herb garden and orchard through the gate.

4. Follow Lady Spencer's Walk, turning left at the bottom of the steps. Lady Spencer was the mother of Georgiana Cavendish (wife of the 5th Duke of Devonshire). She created this walk with her granddaughter while staying with her at Hardwick in the late 1700s.

5. Cross over the farm track and go through the gate into the field in front of you. Follow the fence line into the wood.

6. Follow the track through Park Piece Wood – this path can be very muddy in wet weather.

7. When you come out of the wood, walk straight down the hill through the field to the road, heading for the gate.

8. Cross over the drive and continue through the field to the gate into the next wood.

9. Follow the path through the woodland. When you reach the track, turn left and follow the track until you reach a big blue gate.

10. Go through the blue gate and walk straight ahead, following the grass path downhill, over the drive. Continue until you reach a gate in the fence near the ponds.

11. Once through the gate, turn right past the quarry to return to the Park Centre.

Make the Most of Your Day
A visit to the 'new' Hardwick Hall is a must. Designed by the Elizabethan architect Robert Symthson to symbolise Bess's wealth and status, it pushed the boundaries of architectural design with its vast areas of glass windows. Inside you'll discover sumptuous Elizabethan furnishings and tapestries, reflecting Bess's passion for embroidery, while outside visitors young and old can enjoy the Fairy Tree, a recent addition to the gardens.

Food and Facilities
The Great Barn Restaurant is a perfect place to refuel after your walk, serving delicious home-cooked meals and tasty sweet treats. Toilets are available in the stableyard.

52. Exploring Clumber Park

Clumber Park
Worksop
Nottinghamshire S80 3AZ
01909 544917
clumberpark@
nationaltrust.org.uk
www.nationaltrust.org.uk/
clumber-park

About this walk
Through beautiful parkland

A car-free walk

A wide variety of tree species

Distance 6 miles (9.6km)

Time 3 hours

Leave the car at home and travel by bus to explore Clumber Park's glorious landscape. Here you'll discover a range of different habitats, a rich variety of wildlife and over 200 species of tree. The walk starts at the bus stop, and passes through some of the quieter parts of the park, taking in Clumber's famous Lime Tree Avenue along the way.

Above: Clumber Bridge in Clumber Park, Nottinghamshire, designed in the Palladian style and built of local limestone.

Things to see

Ornamental features
Clumber Bridge was designed by Stephen Wright and built in the Palladian style in 1770. In 1774 the River Poulter was damned to create an 87-acre (35ha) lake, which is now home to many water birds and dragonflies. In the 1900s the cascade and grotto were created as ornamental features. Later a more practical role was fulfilled when a turbine was installed to provide water for the house.

Pleasure grounds
The pleasure grounds were designed for walking, picnicking, boating and reading. The 2nd Duke of Newcastle laid out the gardens in the late 1700s and planted exotic trees collected from North America. Ornamental statues and classical temples added to the grandeur. Apart from the boating, all of these activities can still be enjoyed here today.

Lime Tree Avenue
Between 1840 and 1860 the Lime Tree Avenue was planted and is now the longest double lime tree avenue in Europe. In the spring and early summer the blossom has a glorious scent and in the autumn the leaves turn a lovely pale gold.

View of the Greek Temple across the lake at Clumber Park.

How to Get There

By Bus Sherwood Arrow service from Worksop and Nottingham, alighting at Piper Lodge

By Train Worksop 4.5 miles (7.2km); Retford 6.5 miles (10.4km)

By Car 11 miles (17.7km) from M1 junction 30, and 1 mile (1.6km) from A1/A57

OS Map Explorer 270

Start Piper Lodge bus stop on B6034, **OS grid ref: SK60540 73444**

End Clumber Road bus stop, **OS grid ref: SK59540 76177**

1. If you came by bus, follow the public bridleway sign on the opposite side of the road from Piper Lodge, taking care if you need to cross the busy road. (If you came by car, pick up the walk at point 4 at the visitor centre.) Follow the bridleway for approximately a third of a mile (0.5km), passing Manor Farm and Carburton Church.

2. At the road junction cross the road with care and turn left to walk along the grass verge. After about 360 yards (330m) you'll reach Carburton Lodge and the entrance to Clumber Park. Walk over Carburton Bridge and take the first road on your right (Clumber cycle route marker 22). After the wooden barrier the road is usually car free.

3. At the crossroads turn right and walk to Clumber Bridge, from where you can take in the lovely view of the lake and a glimpse of Clumber's Victorian Gothic chapel. Go back to the end of the bridge and immediately look for a path on your right that takes you down into woodland. Pass Clumber Grotto and soon you'll see the lake on your right. The path bears

right through the trees and after a short walk uphill you reach a road where you turn right.

4. Walk along this usually car-free road and after about a quarter of a mile (0.4km) follow it round to the left. At the signpost turn right into the Turning Yard to find the visitor information point, café and Discovery Centre.

5. From the Turning Yard, follow the sign for the lake, mansion site and the pleasure grounds. Walk across the grass towards the lake and just before you reach the water turn left to walk along the lakeside path.

6. At the end of the path you reach metal railings and the derelict site of the boathouse. Turn left along a path that goes through the trees. Where you meet another path turn right. Go through the stone archway and metal gate and continue straight ahead. In a short distance you walk between two stone pillars and go up into Ash Tree Hill Wood. You are now on one of the many cycle tracks in the park, which have blue numbered markers; this one is number 8.

7. At a crossroad of tracks carry straight on downhill. Just after a wooden barrier you reach a road. Cross the road with care and continue in the same direction along another track. You're now following cycle route marker 16.

8. At the next wooden barrier take care crossing the road and carry straight on, still following cycle route marker 16. In approximately a quarter of a mile (0.4km) you pass three wooden stumps and arrive at Lime Tree Avenue. Beware of traffic as you cross the road to another track and continue with cycle route marker 16.

9. At a junction of tracks with an information board carry straight ahead following cycle route marker 17. After approximately 20 yards (18m) the track divides. Take the left fork and continue to follow cycle route marker 17. In about a quarter of a mile (0.4km) you reach a T-junction of paths where you turn right. You have now picked up cycle route marker 18.

10. After about a mile (1.6km) you reach a dark green National Cycle Network millennium milepost. Here you turn left to follow cycle route marker 19 and National Cycle Network route 6.

11. Continue on this track until you reach a road where you turn right and walk along the grass verge to Truman's Lodge. Beware of traffic as you walk under the archway. Walk along the right side of the road for about 300 yards (275m) until you see a public bridleway sign. Cross the road with care to follow the bridleway. (Truman's Lodge gates are open 8am to 7pm. If you arrive at the gates and they are closed retrace your steps and look out for a narrow path on the left, mid-way between Truman's Lodge and the pay point. Follow this path through the trees and after approximately 150 yards (140m) you'll come to a road. Turn left and it will bring you to the road on the other side of Truman's Lodge. Please note the path through the trees is not maintained.)

12. After about half a mile (0.8km) you'll reach the B6034. Turn right and follow the footpath to the Clumber Road bus stop where you can get the bus to Nottingham via Ollerton; alternatively, cross the busy road with care for the bus to Worksop. Hopefully you've timed it just right! (If you came by car, follow points 1 to 4 to take you back to your starting point.)

The spire of the Gothic chapel viewed across the lake at Clumber Park.

A view of Lincoln Terrace which runs the length of the pleasure grounds at Clumber Park.

Make the Most of Your Day

Make a visit to the Discovery Centre to find out more about Clumber's wildlife. With hands-on activities, talks and ever changing displays, you can get up close to some of the park's more reclusive residents, whether they are furry, feathery, creepy or slimy. Then complete your day by exploring the pleasure grounds, dating from the late eighteenth century, and the beautiful walled kitchen garden, which grows hundreds of varieties of fruit, vegetables and herbs and has beautiful herbaceous borders and an impressive glasshouse.

Food and Facilities

There are plenty of options for refreshments: choose from the Clumber Park Café for a wide selection of hot meals and snacks, the Reading Room Bookshop and Café or The Burrow for drinks and snacks to eat in or take away. Toilets are available at the visitor centre.

Opposite: The Lime Tree Avenue at Clumber Park.

53. Belton Deer Park Walk

This gentle stroll focuses on Belton Deer Park, which accounts for nearly half of Belton Estate's 1,350 acres (550ha). The walk passes ancient woodland and a deserted medieval village, looking at key architectural features, such as Bellmount Tower and the Alford Monument, and points of geographical interest along the way.

Belton House
Belton
Grantham
Lincolnshire NG32 2LS
01476 566116
belton@nationaltrust.org.uk
www.nationaltrust.org.uk/
belton-house

About this walk
Through beautiful parkland

Architectural and geographical interest

Dogs welcome on a lead

Distance 3 miles (4.8km)

Time 1 hour 30 minutes

Above: The South Front at Belton House.

Things to see

Fallow deer
Look out for direct descendants of the wild herd that was enclosed here in 1690. These deer have large flat antlers and can be a variety of colours.

A white-clawed crayfish.

The young are born in June and are then hidden in the grass by their mothers to protect them from predators; if you find a fawn please don't be tempted to touch it as human scent will make it more vulnerable to attack.

Alford Monument and Lion Gates
The Alford Monument was built in memory of Viscount Alford, who died aged 21. The Latin inscription reads: 'Farewell my dearest son. Among these trees, once fortunate in aspect, I, your weeping father, place this here, offered in your name with a prayer.' The Lion Gates once marked the main route into the Belton Estate and originally stood by what was the main road to Lincoln.

Towthorpe village and Hollow Ponds
Towthorpe is mentioned in the Domesday Book of 1086 but is thought to date from much earlier, as prehistoric and Saxon artefacts have been found in the area. Today there is little trace of the village, although earthworks can be seen on the western side of the river. Towthorpe Hollow Ponds were created around 1820 and are now a haven for white-clawed crayfish, after special reefs were built in 2009.

How to Get There

By Train Grantham
3 miles (4.8km)

By Car On A607 Grantham
to Lincoln road, signposted
from A1 and A52

OS Map Landranger 130

Start / End Belton House
main car park, **OS grid ref:**
SK928391

Map labels: Belton Nurseries, Belton, WC, Tar Lane Pond, Boathouse Pond, N, 400 m, A607, R. Witham, Belton Park, P, Towthorpe Hollow Ponds, Villa Pond, Manthorpe Mill, Manthorpe, Londonthorpe Woods

---

1. Make your way from the car park towards the front of the main house. As you look at the front of the house you'll see a gate on the right that leads into the gardens and another gate that leads into the parkland; go through the gate into the parkland.

2. Follow the tree line all the way to a gate in a wooden fence, and go through the gate. Make your way across the parkland towards the brow of the hill. You may notice Bellmount Tower in the distance. Completed in 1751, it was designed as both a focal point and a viewing tower. It contains a room reached by a spiral staircase and is open for exploration on selected Sundays each year (see website for details).

3. Turn right and head towards Old Wood (even marked 'Old' on estate maps of 1690) and pick up the woodland path. Belton's herd of around 300 fallow deer often seek sanctuary in Old Wood, so take care not to disturb them, especially during June when they are fawning.

4. Along the path you will eventually see the fence line that denotes the edge of the golf course. Head right and follow the fence line around the edge of the golf course. You will see the Alford Monument

(c.1852) within the golf course to your left, created in memory of Viscount Alford who died aged 21 (son of the 1st Earl Brownlow).

5. Continue to follow the fence line and make your way towards the Lion Gates.

6. With your back to the Lion Gates, head left and towards the River Witham. You are now walking around the site of the deserted medieval village of Towthorpe. Look out for signs of earthworks and evidence of the ridges and furrows associated with medieval farming methods.

7. Walk beside the river bank, passing Towthorpe Hollow Ponds and looking out for the excellent examples of river features such as an oxbow, riffle, meander, pool and flood plains along the way. Head towards a small wood, at the edge of which turn right and follow the path to a kissing gate.

8. Make your way towards the old driveway and head through the gate and back onto the oval in front of the house, from where you can make your way back to the car park.

A fallow deer stag.

Make the Most of Your Day

While you're here, take time to visit Belton House. Home to the Brownlow family for over 300 years, it is a superb example of a seventeenth-century English country mansion with stunning interiors and many layers of history to explore. Or take the family to the outdoor adventure playground, a perfect place to let off steam.

Food and Facilities

Enjoy hearty homemade soup, freshly prepared seasonal dishes and tempting treats in the Stables Restaurant, or visit the Ride Play Café for a variety of lighter snacks, cakes and coffee. Toilets are located in the parkland, stableyard, Ride Play Café and gardens.

The North West

54. Alderley Edge Woodland Walk

This car-free walk begins at Alderley Edge railway station, just 12 miles (19.2km) south of Manchester. Set around a dramatic sandstone escarpment in rolling Cheshire farmland and mature Scots pines and beech woodlands, Alderley Edge has spectacular views, intriguing legends and an ancient mining history.

Alderley Edge
Wilmslow Road
Cheshire SK9 7QA
01625 584412
alderleyedge@
nationaltrust.org.uk
www.nationaltrust.org.uk/
alderley-edge

About this walk
A car-free walk

Site of archaeological and geological interest

Some steps and stiles

Dogs welcome on a lead near livestock

Distance 4.5 miles (7.2km)

Time 2 hours 30 minutes

Things to see

The landscape
The rocky escarpment of Alderley Edge is made up of layers of Triassic sandstone, which developed in semi-arid desert conditions interspersed with occasional flash floods around 230 to 180 million years ago. Upheavals in the Earth's crust tilted these rocks gently upwards to form the Edge. The mature woodlands, remnant heath and ancient mines support a wealth of plant life and wildlife, such as orchids, woodcocks, ravens, bats and masonry bees.

Protecting the Edge
In 1948 the National Trust was given around 250 acres (100ha) of the Edge so that it could protect some of the finest views and walks in Cheshire. Much of the Edge has now been designated as a Site of Special Scientific Interest (SSSI) due to its important archaeological and geological significance.

Burials and beacons
At Castle Rock, the highest point on the Edge, there is a Bronze Age burial mound. This was also the site of an Armada Beacon, one of a series of places in the landscape where fires would have been lit to warn of imminent invasion by the Spanish in 1588. The area has now gained protected status.

Top: View from the sandstone escarpment of Alderley Edge in Cheshire.
Above: Mature woodland at Alderley Edge.

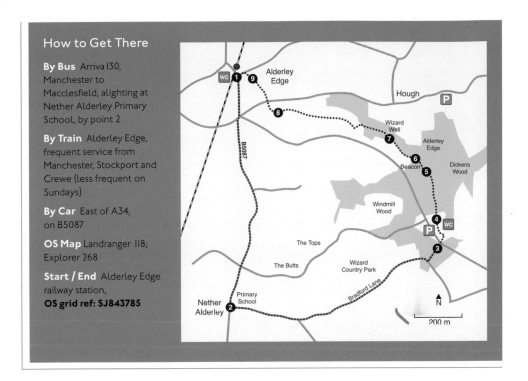

How to Get There

By Bus Arriva 130, Manchester to Macclesfield, alighting at Nether Alderley Primary School, by point 2

By Train Alderley Edge, frequent service from Manchester, Stockport and Crewe (less frequent on Sundays)

By Car East of A34, on B5087

OS Map Landranger 118; Explorer 268

Start / End Alderley Edge railway station, **OS grid ref: SJ843785**

1. From the railway station turn left towards Alderley village, where you can join the bus (130 Arriva service) that takes you to point 2 on the map, by Nether Alderley Primary School and the start of the walk. If you arrive by bus, alight at the same stop.

2. From the bus stop, turn left onto a bridleway up Bradford Lane. When the lane forks, take the left-hand route. Continue straight ahead until you reach a road just after Bradford Lodge Cottages and turn left up to Macclesfield Road (a prominent main road).

3. Take care crossing this sometimes busy road, then climb the stile which leads towards the National Trust car park and bear left.

4. Go through the squeeze stile onto the Wizard Walk.

5. Continue on the path, with the Engine Vein on your right. This is a natural fault in the rock that is rich in copper and other minerals. It was excavated by Bronze Age miners who pecked out shallow pits and hollows with simple stone hammers and oak shovels. The existence of a Roman shaft and tunnels at the vein show that it was later mined with sharper iron chisels. Where the paths cross, continue straight on towards the Armada Beacon. Take the left-hand path past the beacon and, following the stone wall, turn left at the bottom.

6. Take the steps up on your left to walk along the 'top' of the Edge. Continue onwards with a field on your left until you reach Castle Rock. There's a sheer drop here, so take care.

7. From Castle Rock head towards the road, but after a few yards take a sharp turn right. This will take you down a short set of steps; turn left at the bottom and follow the path until it forks.

Quarry Bank Mill, Wilmslow, Cheshire.

8. Take the left-hand fork and continue for a short way, passing through an exit/entrance. Turn right through the second exit/entrance at the other end of the path onto Woodbrook Road. This steep, rough road will lead you down to a T-junction where it joins Trafford Road. Turn right here, going over the crossroads with Mottram Road until you reach another T-junction.

9. Turn left here, up towards the A34. Alderley Edge railway station is on the other side of the road.

Make the Most of Your Day

After your walk, why not make your way to nearby Quarry Bank Mill, one of Britain's greatest industrial heritage sites? Inside an original eighteenth-century cotton mill, the clattering and whirring of the heritage machinery and steam engines make an astonishing noise, invoking the atmosphere of the Industrial Revolution. Here you can explore the progression of the cotton industry from the medieval era through to the nineteenth century, and enjoy a changing programme of exhibitions.

Food and Facilities

The nearest food and facilities can be found at Alderley Edge, or, for assured quality, visit Quarry Bank Mill where, sited in the historic weaving shed, the Mill Café offers a delicious range of snacks and meals. Toilets are also available at Quarry Bank Mill.

55. Discovering Dunham Massey

Explore Dunham Massey Park, home to one of the finest collections of veteran trees in England, where the oldest oak dates from the time of Henry VIII. Along the way discover a centuries-old watermill and deer barn, as well as a series of fire-damaged oak trees that, despite their gnarled appearance, are home to a rich variety of wildlife.

Dunham Massey, Altrincham
Cheshire WA14 4SJ
0161 941 1025
dunhammassey@
nationaltrust.org.uk
www.nationaltrust.org.uk/
dunham-massey

About this walk
A gentle stroll through parkland

Ancient trees up to 500 years old

Dogs welcome on a lead

Distance 2.5 miles (4km)

Time 1 hour 30 minutes

Above: The brick-built Watermill at Dunham Massey

Things to see

Gnarled oak
Small in stature, big on personality, the gnarled oak trees you pass between points 5 and 6 are full of life. Fungi, insects, birds, bats and other small mammals all live in the trees' nooks and crannies. Up to 250 years old, the trees are younger than they at first appear. Burnt, decayed, twisted and hollow, they were damaged in a bracken fire, but are still very much alive and healthy, showing the tenacity of trees to survive.

Deer barn
The deer barn you see as you walk along Charcoal Drive is where the deer herd's winter feed would have been stored. The building is thought to date from 1740, and you can

still see remnants of the hayracks today. Four colours of fallow deer now roam Dunham Massey. black, common, menil and white. The bucks grow new antlers each year, ready for the autumn rut.

Paintings of the park
A series of paintings by John Harris, dating from the 1750s, hang in Dunham Massey Hall and show the park as it appeared in the eighteenth century. These bird's-eye views give a good indication of the park's design and provide useful guides for the National Trust's restoration work.

Bird's-eye view of Dunham Massey.

How to Get There

By Train Altrincham
3 miles (4.8km); Hale 3
miles (4.8km)

By Car Off A56, leaving
M6 at junction 19 or M56 at
junction 7

OS Map Landranger 109;
Explorer 276

Start / End Dunham
Massey Clock Tower,
OS grid ref: SJ735874

1. From the clock tower, walk down the grass path towards the service road, turning left when you reach the service road itself. Dunham Massey is regarded as one of the best sites for the number and variety of its veteran trees. Veteran trees are very important for the habitat they provide for animals, such as birds and insects, and fungi. Dunham's trees are home to many rare insect species, such as the nationally scarce cobweb beetle, as well as beetle-eating bats such as the noctule.

2. Follow the service road round the corner and up the slope, passing the sixteenth-century watermill on your left. At almost 400 years old the mill is the oldest building in the park at Dunham Massey.

3. At the variegated beech tree, turn right onto Langham Grove. Walk past Old Man Pool on your left and follow the route all the way to the Langham Obelisk.

4. At the obelisk, turn left and follow the deer sanctuary log-rail barrier. Cross over Farm Walk and follow the deer sanctuary barrier past Island Pool to Middle Avenue.

5. Turn right at Middle Avenue and walk to the top of the park. When you reach the railings, go through the plantation gates on your left.

6. Follow the path all the way to Charcoal Drive, turning left at the driveway to head back towards the mansion. Along the way you will pass an old deer barn.

7. At the end of Charcoal Drive, follow the main drive down to the main entrance of the hall. On the lawn, to either side of the drive, there are pollarded lime trees, which are cut every three years.

In spring, a carpet of bluebells can be found in the gardens at Dunham Massey.

8. If you wish to extend your walk, turn right and enter the formal gardens (ticket required) to view one of the oldest oaks on the estate and the collection of ornamental trees, including cork oaks, white-stemmed birch and the handkerchief tree.

9. At the main entrance of the hall turn left, and continue back to your starting point at the clock tower.

10. To extend your walk further, continue under the clock tower, turning right to the car park. In the fenced area adjacent to the Stallion Pound is one of the oldest oak trees on the estate: at around 500 years old it predates the formal planting of the parkland. The fence was erected to protect the tree's roots from compaction.

11. Pass through the white gates and continue walking to the end of the moat path. Directly in front of you is a fabulous lime avenue planted in around 1900.

Make the Most of Your Day

After your walk, take a stroll around Dunham Massey Hall, which began life in 1616 but is largely the product of eighteenth-century remodelling. Discover the hall's role as a hospital during the First World War, and see some of the 25,000 objects amassed by the Booth and Grey families over the centuries. Durham Massey also has one of the North's great gardens, with Britain's largest winter garden, as well as a stunning new rose garden.

Food and Facilities

Whether you want a hot meal or warming pudding, afternoon tea or a slice of cake, visit the eighteenth-century stable block and treat yourself in the Stables Restaurant. Toilets are also available on site.

56. Formby Red Squirrel Ramble

Formby has an amazing and ever changing landscape, comprising glorious beaches with dramatic sand dunes, surrounded by sweeping coastal pinewoods. This delightful ramble takes you across dune grassland and through pine woodland, where you may be lucky enough to spot the elusive native red squirrel.

National Trust Formby
Victoria Road
Freshfield
Formby
Liverpool L37 1LJ
01704 878591
formby@nationaltrust.org.uk
www.nationaltrust.org.uk/formby

About this walk
The perfect place to spot red squirrels

A few short steep slopes

Dogs welcome under close control

Distance 1.8 miles (2.9km)

Time 1 hour

Above: A red squirrel at Formby in Merseyside.

Things to see

Red squirrels
Formby is part of the Sefton stronghold for the native red squirrel, one of 17 such strongholds in the north of England. The squirrels are most active in autumn and spring, but they can be seen out and about in these woodlands all year round. Have a look out for the feeders in the trees, as this is often a good place to catch a glimpse of these shy creatures.

Pine woodland
The pine woodlands were planted from the late 1800s by the Weld Blundell family, whose estate covered this area. Before the trees were planted this area would have been fixed sand dunes covered in grassland and if you look closely you can still make out the shape of the dunes underneath the trees. Over the years these trees have been a valuable windbreak for the fields used for local asparagus cultivation and the neighbouring residential area. They are most renowned as the home of the rare native red squirrel.

Nicotine Wood
The woodland known as Nicotine Wood takes its name from the area seaward of the trees where, during the 1950s and 1960s, thousands of tonnes of tobacco leaf waste were dumped by the British Nicotine Company. The waste was dumped on old asparagus fields that were no longer in production. The wood has an interesting natural as well as industrial history. The gnarled broadleaf trees that can be seen here are native black poplar, and it's thought that this is one of the most northerly places where this species can be found in the United Kingdom.

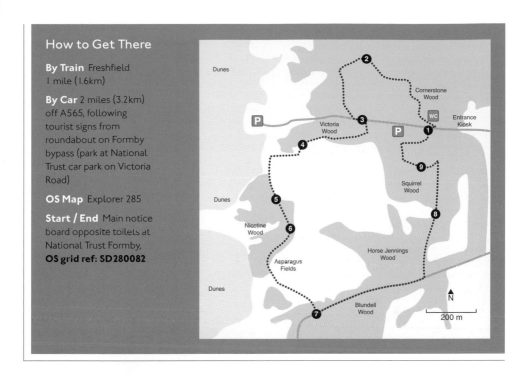

How to Get There

By Train Freshfield
1 mile (1.6km)

By Car 2 miles (3.2km)
off A565, following
tourist signs from
roundabout on Formby
bypass (park at National
Trust car park on Victoria
Road)

OS Map Explorer 285

Start / End Main notice
board opposite toilets at
National Trust Formby,
OS grid ref: SD280082

Pine woodland at Formby.

1. Cross the road and take the path (marked 'Cornerstone Path') to the left of the toilets, heading down a ramp into the woodland. Continue to follow this clear, broad path with its white and purple waymark posts through the woodland until you meet another path at a T-junction with a set of large wooden chimes on your left-hand side.

2. Turn left at the T-junction and follow Cornerstone Path for a short distance before the path forks. Here, leave Cornerstone Path and take the left-hand fork, following the path as it bends into a picnic area. Continue through the picnic area and up a ramp back to the road.

3. Cross the road into another picnic area and take the right-hand of two paths heading down a ramp into the woodland. Continue through the woods until the path reaches a fork marked by a waymark with a yellow arrow on a grey background.

4. Take the path on the left, which will lead you out of the woodland, past some wooden bollards, into an area of open dune grassland. Follow the path as it turns right, passing a bench, to a T-junction. At this junction turn left and follow the path with the sand dunes on your right and the fields on your left.

5. Continue to follow this well-defined path as it enters an area with open woodland on your right and an enclosed pine plantation on your left.

6. At the end of the enclosed pine plantation, where the path forks, take the right fork to continue through the pine woodlands with an agricultural field on your left. Follow the path as it leaves the woodland and curves to the left. At a junction where the Sefton Coastal Path breaks off to the right, keep straight ahead and after a short distance you will reach a road.

7. At the road turn left and continue for approximately a quarter of a mile (0.4km) until you can see a litter bin just into the woodland on the left-hand side. Turn left into the woodland on the path just before the bin and follow this path along and down into a dip. In the dip the path forks; take the left fork up a short steep slope before following the path as it descends into an open grassy area.

8. Cross straight across the open area and ascend a short steep slope on a well-defined path back into the woodland. Continue along this path until you reach a crossroads with a bench on your right. Turn left to go down a slope on a wide path that after a short distance becomes a boardwalk.

9. Follow this boardwalk as it curves round to the right. At the end of the boardwalk there is a T-junction. Turn right to follow a broad fenced path up the slope. After a short distance there is a fenced path off to the left; take this path to return to your starting point.

Make the Most of Your Day

The nearest National Trust property is Rufford Old Hall, to the north east on the A59. One of Lancashire's finest Tudor buildings, where history comes to life, the hall is filled with fantastic furniture, arms, armour and tapestries. Fascinatingly, the Great Hall was once a stage for a young William Shakespeare before he was famous.

Food and Facilities

Ice creams, soft drinks and coffees are served from a mobile van during peak periods. Picnic areas are also easily accessible. Toilets can be found opposite the notice board at the National Trust car park on Victoria Road. A café and toilets are also available at Rufford Old Hall.

View of the sand dunes and beach at Formby.

57. Sizergh Wildlife Walk

Sizergh Castle is a great starting point for a walk in the Lake District. The castle, still lived in by the Strickland family, is surrounded by a traditional agricultural estate with stunning views across the countryside, taking in the coast at Morecambe Bay, the Lakeland Fells and the Pennines. Discover an amazing array of natural history throughout the year in this quiet corner of the South Lakes.

Sizergh
Near Kendal
Cumbria LA8 8AE
sizergh@nationaltrust.org.uk
www.nationaltrust.org.uk/
sizergh

About this walk

Amazing views

Good for bird watching all year round

A short, steepish climb near to the start of the walk

Distance 2.5 miles (4km)

Time 1 hour 30 minutes

Above: View across the lake to the south-east front of Sizergh Castle in Cumbria.

Things to see

Special visitors

Look out for a very special visitor lurking in the trees in the car park. Hawfinches are very shy birds, best seen in winter when the trees have shed their leaves; look for them on the highest branches. Sizergh is a nationally important breeding site for these birds.

Wildflowers and ant hills

Purple swathes of field scabious and harebell, and a yellow haze of buttercups, bedstraws and cowslips fill the characteristic ant-hill fields on Sizergh Fell in early summer.

Fritillary butterflies

Fritillary butterfly species fly effortlessly through the woodland glades in summer, basking and feeding in warm open areas. Sunlight encourages the growth of food plants such as violets and cowslip on the woodland floor – these are both valuable plants for egg laying and caterpillar feeding. The trees are cut down in lines called glades, connecting valuable open feeding areas. Sheltered areas provide a rich nectaring source for adult fritillaries as they feed on brambles.

A male hawfinch.

How to Get There

By Train Oxenholme
3 miles (4.8km); Kendal
5 miles (8km)

By Car Exit M6 at
junction 36 onto A590
towards Kendal, then
take Barrow-in-Furness
turning and follow signs

OS Map Explorer OL7

Start / End Sizergh
Castle car park, **OS grid
ref: SD498878**

1. From Sizergh Castle car park, leave by the footpath gate and walk into a field at the south end, near to the coach parking bays. This field can be very wet and muddy. Walk straight on, with the wall on your left. During spring and summer buzzards and pheasants are a common sight along this stretch of footpath, as they nest in the woodland to your left.

2. Go through the next gate into another field (which can also be very muddy) and then immediately through another gate to your left, onto Sizergh Fell. Notice the difference between the two fields either side of the fence boundary, where one has been improved.

3. Wander uphill with the fence on your right and go through a field. The many bumps to be seen in this field are actually ant hills. During the summer the field is filled with magnificent wildflowers, bees and butterflies. You might even be able to spot a green woodpecker feeding on the ants.

4. As you continue uphill towards the clump of trees at the top, you pass some hawthorn trees. These are excellent for attracting nesting birds in spring and then fieldfare and redwings in winter, when they are plentiful with berries. Once you reach the top, stop to admire the amazing views out to Morecambe Bay ahead of you and the Howgills and Pennines behind.

5. From the top, walk past the clump of trees on the right-hand side. Follow the footpath with the telephone lines on your left and the stunning Lake District Fells ahead of you. Continue across the top and then downhill until you reach a gate in the wall.

6. Go through the gate and head diagonally on the path towards the left, through the field of ant hills towards the woodland in the distance. Go through the gate into the woodland glade and turn immediately right. This takes you through an area that has recently been cleared to diversify the woodland edge and enhance the butterfly populations. Look out for fritillary species here in the summer.

7. Continue with the wall on your right-hand side. Many woodland bird species can be spotted here including great spotted woodpecker, nuthatch and treecreeper.

8. Once you get to the end of the wall, turn left and walk downhill, following the wall on your right towards the road, until you reach the gate on the right-hand side. Go through the gate into the field and then continue walking downhill to the next gate, which takes you onto the tarmacked road.

9. Turn right here, and walk along the road on the right-hand side, facing the oncoming traffic, for about a third of a mile (0.5km). Pass Lane End Farm on your left – a National Trust tenanted farm. Continue along the road until you reach the big wooden gate on the right and go through onto Ashbank Lane.

10. Walk along the lane with the hedgerow full of life on your left. Walk through three more gates along the track, with the old deer park wall on your right, heading all the way back to Sizergh Castle and well-earned refreshments at the café.

Make the Most of Your Day

Make time to visit Sizergh, a beautiful medieval house owned by the Strickland family. It has many tales to tell and certainly feels lived in, with centuries-old portraits and fine furniture sitting alongside modern family photographs. Its rich and beautiful garden includes a pond, lake, a national collection of hardy ferns and a superb limestone rock garden.

Food and Facilities

The recently refurbished café has been designed to give a taste of Sizergh's history and treasures. There is also a pub and farm tea-room. Toilets are available for visitors.

The rock garden at Sizergh Castle in June.

58. Wildlife Ramble at Arnside Knott

This diverse and beautiful wildlife walk takes in four 'scapes': landscape, seascape, skyscape and… escape from life's pressures! The route takes you across Arnside Knott, a shapely 500ft (152m) limestone hill that affords stunning views of the surrounding area. The key to the Knott's diversity is its limestone landscape, which comprises a mosaic of habitats including woodland and flower-studded grassland.

Arnside Knott
Near Arnside
Cumbria
01524 702815
arnsidesilverdale@
nationaltrust.org.uk
www.nationaltrust.org.uk/
arnside-and-silverdale

About this walk
Good for spotting butterflies and birds

Breathtaking views

Steep in places, with height gain of 230ft (70m)

Dogs welcome under close control

Distance 2 miles (3.2km)

Time I hour

Things to see

Wildflowers
Grazing livestock help keep the limestone grasslands in optimum condition for wildflowers. As such, the grassland is great for orchids such as early purple varieties, which flower from late April to May, and also bird's nest and fragrant orchids. Look out for the scarce blue moor-grass with its bright grass-heads in March and April.

Insects
Nationally important butterflies such as the Scotch argus can be seen at the beginning of August in great numbers at the top of Arnside Knott. Rare butterflies like the high brown fritillary are also to be found in the summertime. Look for the caterpillars of the painted lady on nettles and purple hairstreaks on oaks. Also keep an eye out for southern wood ants, which can be seen foraging for food and even climbing trees. The warm summer evenings are great for watching glow-worms on grass stems.

Birds
Nuthatch, bullfinch, marsh tit, great spotted woodpecker and many other woodland birds can be seen in and around Red Hill Wood; the spring birdsong is superb. Also listen out for the call of marsh tits (a loud 'pitchoo' sound), and the mewing sound of common buzzards that can be heard when the birds are displaying.

Top: View from Arnside Knott over Morecambe Bay in Cumbria.
Above: A great spotted woodpecker.

How to Get There

By Train Arnside 1 mile (1.6km)

By Car Exit M6 at junction 36 on A65 towards Kendal; take B6385 to Milnthorpe then B5782 to Arnside

OS Map Landranger 97; Explorer OL7

Start / End National Trust car park at Arnside Knott, **OS grid ref: SD450774**

Map labels:
Dobshall Wood · Arnside · Red Hills Woods · Red Hills · Amside Knott · Amside Knott Wood · Silverdale Road · Hare Parrok · N · 200 m

---

1. Turn left out of the National Trust car park and after a short walk along the entrance track, climb up the bank on your right to a mountain indicator. There are great views over the estuary towards the Lake District here.

2. Keep zig-zagging up the hillside to a stone toposcope and a breathtaking panorama. The slopes here are made of frost-shattered limestone, with areas of distinctive blue moor-grass, yew and juniper.

3. Bear left on the path and climb through woodland up to open grassland (a good spot for picnics) along the crest of the ridge.

4. When you reach the highest point on the walk, at a bench, continue a short way then head right, downhill, with a wall on your left.

5. The route angles right before reaching a gate to enter Red Hills Wood. Soon after, turn left at a crossroads and tour the woodland, always following paths round to the right. This area is home to a fantastic range of trees and plants, such as dog's mercury, dog's violet and primrose. The trees are a mix of yew, holly, rowan, hazel and sessile oak. Dead and decaying wood makes an excellent habitat for fungi, hoverflies and beetles.

6. Silverdale Road appears down to your right as you emerge onto open hillside. Pass the Shilla Slopes. Only some plants such as marjoram and thyme can anchor in this rubble; both types attract butterflies.

7. Take the broad uphill track back towards the car park, going through several gates and avoiding the left-hand turns leading to Heathwaite and Copridding Wood.

Make the Most of Your Day

If you fancy visiting a country house estate after your walk, try Sizergh, 8 miles (12.8km) north en route to Kendal. See walk 57 for details.

Food and Facilities

There are a number of pubs and cafés in and around Arnside village. Otherwise, you'll find plenty of choice at Sizergh. Public toilets can be found in Arnside.

59. Exploring the Troutbeck Valley

Explore classic Lakeland scenery, farmland and architecture on this beautiful circular walk from Brockhole, near Lake Windermere, up into the Troutbeck Valley. On the way you'll be rewarded with stunning views of the surrounding fells and Lake Windermere, get to spot diverse wildlife and discover Townend, a unique seventeenth-century farmhouse.

Troutbeck
Windermere
Cumbria LA23 1LB
015394 32628
townend@
nationaltrust.org.uk
www.nationaltrust.org.uk/
townend

About this walk
Wonderful views across the Lake District

A walk of architectural interest

Crosses one stile

Distance 4 miles (6.4km)

Time 2 hours 30 minutes

Above: View across Lake Windermere in Cumbria.

Things to see

Herdwick sheep
Look out for Herdwick sheep on your walk – they can often be spotted on the Lake District's higher fells. This hardy breed is able to brave the elements in a harsh climate and is recognisable by the black fleece of the youngsters or dark grey of older sheep.

Townend House
Your walk takes you to Townend House, home for over 400 years to just one family, the Brownes. These were well-to-do farmers who passed their estate down through 12 generations until 1943 when the line died out. The money they made farming enabled them to extend and improve the house over the centuries. There is a lot of fine oak furniture here, much of which was carved by the last George Browne.

Lake Windermere
Windermere is the largest lake in England, measuring 10.5 miles (16.8km) long and 1.25 miles (2km) across at its widest point, with a depth of up to 220ft (67m). The lake is so large that it has a slight but discernible tide.

The south front of Townend House.

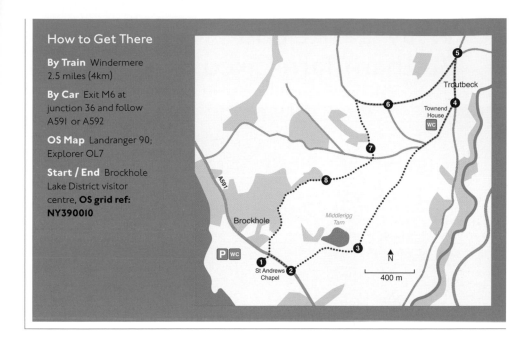

How to Get There

By Train Windermere 2.5 miles (4km)

By Car Exit M6 at junction 36 and follow A591 or A592

OS Map Landranger 90; Explorer OL7

Start / End Brockhole Lake District visitor centre, **OS grid ref: NY390010**

1. Leave Brockhole, turn right and walk along the footpath beside the A591 until you see a bridleway on the opposite side of the road.

2. Cross the road carefully and follow the track up towards Middlerigg Tarn. This track is known as Wain Lane, a tenth-century cart lane that was used by packhorses to bring slate from Troutbeck down to the lake where it could be transported by boat.

3. Follow the track past the tarn and continue along it as it veers to the left. You can see the route of the aqueduct along Wain Lane. Look out for single iron gates supported by sandstone pillars, which were used for access.

4. When the track meets a road, turn right. This will take you into Troutbeck village. You'll see Townend House to the left of the next T-junction along the road.

5. Continue along the village road past the barns and interesting houses and up towards the post office. Turn left here.

6. Follow Robin Lane, which will be joined by a bridleway on the left. Continue for about 300 yards (275m) and then turn left opposite a pillar on the right. This is an excellent spot for a view of Windermere, England's largest lake.

7. On entering the lane take the first left over a stile and follow the track down to a road. Cross over to Mirk Lane which is directly opposite.

8. Walk along Mirk Lane back down towards the A591. Carefully cross the road again to return to Brockhole.

Make the Most of Your Day
It's well worth stopping off at Townend House to explore the lives of an ordinary Lake District farming family, whose home brings to life 400 years of extraordinary stories and characters.

Food and Facilities
You'll find a café and toilets at the Brockhole Lake District visitor centre (not National Trust).

60. Wray Castle and Blelham Tarn Circuit

Wray Castle
Low Wray
Ambleside
Cumbria LA22 0JA
015394 33250
wraycastle@
nationaltrust.org.uk
www.nationaltrust.org.uk/
wray-castle

About this walk
A walk of historical interest

Several stiles

Dogs welcome on a lead
around livestock

Distance 3.5 miles (5.6km)

Time 2 hours

Passing through rolling farmland and along rough farm tracks and bridleways, this bracing walk takes you from Wray Castle to Blelham Tarn, returning via the shoreline of Lake Windermere. It combines tranquil beauty and great views with fascinating stories from the past, including tales of Iron Age swords and Victorian visionaries.

Top: View across Blelham Tarn.
Above: Wray Castle, in Cumbria, is
built in a mock-Gothic style.

Things to see

Iron Age sword
Not far from Blelham Tarn a sword from the Iron Age was found. The sword had been deliberately broken in half, possibly as part of a burial rite or a ceremony by a chieftain to claim an area of land. Finds from this period are rare in Cumbria.

Iron smelting
By the stepping stones across Blelham Beck, the ditches and hollows to the west of the beck are all that remain of a large medieval bloomer (furnace). Here, in the fourteenth and fifteenth centuries, on land owned by Furness Abbey, simple iron smelting was taking place.

Lake District champion
Hardwick Rawnsley, one of the three founders of the National Trust, was vicar at St Margaret's Church in the early 1880s. Even then he was an active campaigner to protect the Lake District landscape from damage by the quarries and railways.

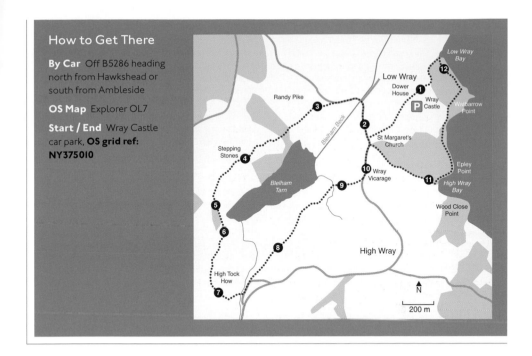

1. From the car park make your way to the road in front of the grand castle entrance and set off down the main drive, with the Dower House on the right, to the arched gatehouse. Upon reaching a public road with no pavement, watching out for traffic, turn right along the road and down the hill, passing the entrance to Low Wray Campsite. Cross the bridge over Blelham Beck towards the kissing gate on the left.

2. Go through the kissing gate and walk up by the side of the hedge, parallel to the road, for about 300 yards (275m). When you come to a metal field gate turn left onto the public bridleway towards Outgate. After about 100 yards (90m) the path forks; take the left fork, waymarked by a blue arrow, to the left of a knoll.

3. The path is grassy and indistinct. After a few yards it appears to divide and a track turns left down to Blelham Tarn. Ignore this turning and continue straight ahead, following the waymarks and keeping the tarn 100 yards (90m) to your left. After another 100 yards (90m) or so go through a gate into a wood.

4. Follow the track as it winds through the wood, crossing some marshy ground. Take the stepping stones over the stream and head up onto some more open ground, keeping the wall on your right. Continue over a stile by a gate, with the tarn away to your left.

5. At the far end of the tarn the path forks. Just before the ground rises, a wooden fingerpost points to the left, signed as a footpath to High Tock How. Take this path, with the slope (and later a wall) to your right; it can be wet underfoot here in winter. Go through a gate with a small stream and the edge of the tarn to your left.

6. Continue with the small stream on your left until you reach a small bridge; cross the footbridge and continue up the track towards a barn. Cross a squeeze stile beside a gate to the left of the barn. Go past another fingerpost signed as a public footpath to High Tock How Farm, then over a step stile beside another field gate about 30 yards (27m) away. Continue ahead with the wall on your left. High Tock How Farm can be seen over the wall to the left.

7. Continue to a footpath gate next to a field gate. Go through the gate and continue downhill along the track. This leads to another step stile beside a field gate and onto a surfaced farm drive. High Tock How Farm is to the left but turn right to a T-junction and then left. The drive drops down towards a white house. Go straight ahead, following a fingerpost signed to Wray Castle. Head through the gateway past the white house, ignoring the drive to the right and a stony track on the left. The path runs to the right of the white house and farm buildings and leads to a stone step stile beside a gate. Cross the stile and continue along the track.

8. Walk down the track, crossing another step stile next to a gate and descending to a gate next to a little stream. Continue with the stream and hedge to the right and Blelham Tarn away to the left. The path leads to a small oak-covered knoll, at which it becomes indistinct but bears left around the knoll through pasture and mixed woodland.

9. Continue through a wicket gate and across a stone-clapper bridge over a stream. Then continue straight ahead, making for the brow of the hill. The path follows the line of a hedge and leads onto the road via a gate. Turn left along the road and walk past a large house, Wray Vicarage, on the right.

10. Before Wray Castle gatehouse and the entrance to St Margaret's Church, turn right onto the public bridleway. Continue down the walled track for several hundred yards.

11. About 50 yards (45m) before it ends at a gate and the lakeshore, turn left through a gate and past a National Trust sign. Continue along the lakeshore through Wray Castle parkland, past a boathouse. With the lake on the right head towards the woodland and Watbarrow Point.

12. Continue past Watbarrow Point through the wood until you reach the two boathouses; at this point turn left by the fingerpost and follow the path by the railings back up to the castle.

Make the Most of Your Day
While you're here, visit Wray Castle, a mock-Gothic castle with turrets, towers and informal grounds. There are numerous activities to join in, including dressing up and castle-building. In nearby Hawkshead you'll find the Beatrix Potter Gallery, displaying original drawings and watercolours by the famous children's author. Here you can learn about Potter's life as a farmer and conservationist, and how her legacy helped to preserve the Lake District as the place we know today.

Food and Facilities
Wray Castle has a 'pop-up' café, run by the nearby Tower Bank Arms, where you can buy snacks, cakes and hot and cold drinks. Toilets are also available at the castle.

Figurines of Beatrix Potter characters at Wray Castle.

61. Views over Grasmere

Grasmere Shop
Grasmere
Cumbria LA22 9SW
015394 35143
allanbank@
nationaltrust.org.uk
www.nationaltrust.org.uk/
allan-bank-and-grasmere/

About this walk
Magnificent views over the
Lake District

Industrial and historical
interest

Some steep sections

Distance 3.7 miles (5.9km)

Time 2 to 3 hours

This stunning circular walk takes you from Grasmere village up onto the fells to the beautiful little Alcock Tarn. It does have some steep sections but it's worth the climb, and there are benches along the way from where you can enjoy the views, which just get better and better. The top near the tarn can be wet and boggy in winter so be sure to wear stout shoes.

Above: Alcock Tarn near Grasmere, Cumbria.

Things to see

Thirlmere pipeline
The aqueduct that crosses Greenhead Ghyll has been carrying good clean Lakeland water from Thirlmere over the hill to the north and 100 miles (160km) south to Manchester since 1894. This scheme was seen as a great engineering success when developed, and helped solve Manchester's water supply problems. The system is gravity fed and has no pumps along its route.

Greenhead Ghyll
Greenhead Ghyll, once the site of an Elizabethan lead mine, is now a scheduled ancient monument, although there is very little to see on the ground. It's difficult now to imagine the industrial nature of this quiet valley when in 1564 the Company of the Mines Royal was given permission to 'search, dig, try, roast and melt all manner of mines and ores'. Many German miners moved to the area to bring their expertise to the operation.

Coffin stone
As you descend the tarmac road towards the end of your walk, look out for a hefty boulder on your right. Before St Mary's Church in Ambleside was consecrated, coffins had to be transported 2.5 miles (4km) along the 'Corpse Road' from Ambleside to St Oswald's Church at Grasmere for burial. This stone with others along the way was used to support the coffin whilst the bearers rested.

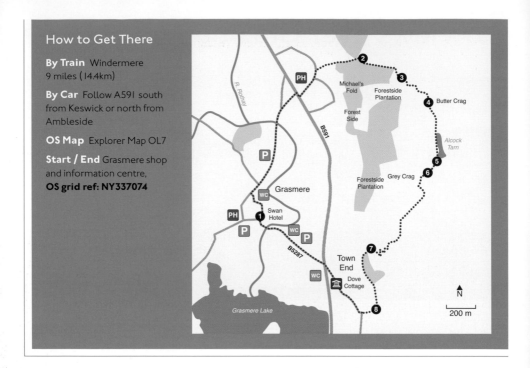

How to Get There

By Train Windermere
9 miles (14.4km)

By Car Follow A591 south
from Keswick or north from
Ambleside

OS Map Explorer Map OL7

Start / End Grasmere shop
and information centre,
OS grid ref: NY337074

1. From outside the Grasmere shop and information centre, turn left and follow the road through the village and up to the main road. Cross the main road with care and follow the minor road opposite between the car park and the Swan Hotel. After about half a mile (0.8km) turn right at the fingerpost signed 'Greenhead Gill and Alcock Tarn'. Follow the lane to the top with the stream tumbling alongside.

2. At the top of the lane, step onto the fellside and turn right and go over the bridge. Follow the path as it bends right and then left following the line of the wall. You will reach a bench from which you can take a breath and look out over the magnificent views.

3. Continue up the path following the wall, then follow it as it leaves the wall and goes up more steeply, zig-zagging up the fellside. Continue climbing up to a rocky outcrop.

4. Go left of the rocks to the cairn and then onto the flatter, often wet area until you reach a metal gate and Alcock Tarn.

5. The tarn provides a great place for a paddle to cool your feet and also a lovely spot to eat a picnic lunch. When the time comes to head down, walk along the right-hand side of the tarn and head for a gateless gap in the wall.

6. Follow the path through the gap and start the descent over a short rocky section of path overlooking the Vale of Grasmere. Take in the views as you descend. As the path goes steeply down, go through a gate past a bench and then a man-made pond (which dates back to when this area was a landscaped woodland garden).

7. At the junction in the path turn left. Continue through the metal gate and through the woods until you reach the road.

8. Turn right and follow the road, which will lead you down the hill. Turn right at the junction onto a minor road to take you past Dove Cottage and the Wordsworth Trust Museum. When you reach the A591, cross with care and follow the B5287 back into Grasmere.

Make the Most of Your Day

From here you can visit 'The loveliest spot that man hath ever found', according to William Wordsworth.

Nearby Allan Bank was once home to Wordsworth, as well as National Trust founder Canon Rawnsley. Now partially restored following a devastating fire, the house offers you the opportunity to see and touch the many layers of this home's fascinating history.

Food and Facilities

Light refreshments along with tea and coffee are available at Allan Bank, and you can buy snacks at the National Trust shop. Toilets can be found in the village (not National Trust).

Allan Bank, once home to William Wordsworth.

62. Cruising Coniston Water

This Lake District walk starts and ends with a trip on Coniston's famous steam-powered yacht *Gondola*, providing a perfect opportunity to view the area's spectacular scenery from the water. Having disembarked, the route continues on foot, taking you through mixed woodland, open fell and past two fascinating old buildings. Rich in both flora and fauna, this is a photographer's paradise.

Coniston Pier
Lake Road
Coniston
Cumbria LA21 8AN
01539 432733
sygondola@
nationaltrust.org.uk
www.nationaltrust.org.uk/
gondola

About this walk
Sailings are seasonal and charges apply (check online)

Stiles and a steep climb

Dogs welcome on a lead around livestock

Good footwear and equipment including a map recommended

Distance 4.6 miles (7.4km)

Time 2 hours 30 minutes

Above: The steam yacht *Gondola* cruises on Coniston Water in Cumbria.

Things to see

Low Parkamoor Farm and Lawson Park
Low Parkamoor Farm is a remote, sixteenth-century Grade II listed farmhouse, set in a spectacular location some 650ft (198m) above Coniston Water. Recently restored by the National Trust, it is now used as a residential resource and retreat by Grizedale Arts. Lawson Park dates from the 1300s, and now forms the headquarters of Grizedale Arts.

Steam yacht *Gondola*
Built for Sir James Ramsden, a director of the Furness Railway Company, the steam-powered *Gondola* was launched in 1859 to take tourists on pleasure trips on

Coniston Water. The original boat has been completely rebuilt by the National Trust, giving passengers the chance to sail in her sumptuous upholstered saloons once again.

Brantwood House
Brantwood (not National Trust) was home to the Victorian artist, critic and social revolutionary John Ruskin from 1872 until his death in 1900. Here, Ruskin was visited by many eminent Victorians, including Charles Darwin and Kate Greenaway. It is both a treasure house of historical importance and a lively centre for contemporary arts and the environment.

Boarding the *Gondola*.

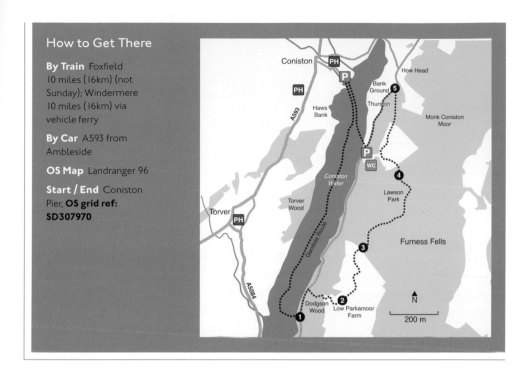

1. Take the trip across Coniston Water to Parkamoor Jetty on the steam yacht *Gondola* (charges apply). On leaving the jetty, turn left and follow the lane to the car park at Dodgson Wood. Turn into the car park and exit from the rear left-hand side – this is where all the hard work has to be done! Take your time and enjoy the tranquillity and delightful woodland surroundings. Follow the broad track as it swings to the right, leaving the small barn to your left before starting to climb. Pass over a stile and on through the wood, with a stream to your right-hand side. At the white waymark post bear left; cross the beck and shortly after bear right at the next waymark post. Again cross another small beck and ignoring the gate and stile to your left continue on a narrow path. Pass through a single gate and carry on up the path with the wall to your left. Keep climbing on to a major track where you turn left, passing through a gate and on to Low Parkamoor Farm.

2. Leaving the farm on your left, pass through a gate into a field and follow a grassy path with a fence to your left until you reach the next gate. Passing through

the gate the path becomes stony, and a steady but gentle climb follows. Be aware, this path is shared with mountain bikers who may descend at speed. Pass over the crest where stunning views will have you reaching for your camera. Descend to the viewpoint, a grassy ledge on the left just before you enter the forest (six flat slates confirm you have reached this magic spot).

3. Leave the viewpoint and pass through the gate onto a narrow track with forest on either side. Again, this undulating path is popular with bikers so stay alert. After about 15 minutes, and upon reaching a major forest track, turn left at the sign for High Cross and Moor Top. Ignore the first track to the left for Coniston and likewise the footpath going left at the foot of the hill. Just before the crest you will reach the Lawson Park bridleway. Turn left off the forest track and follow the rocky, and often muddy, firebreak through the pines and down to Lawson Park.

4. Turn right, leaving the farm behind you to your left, and descend on a narrower track and through a gate with more open country on your left. Away to your left is a fine view of the Coniston Fells and a tiny barn that you will shortly pass by. Pass through another gate and, still descending, cross another beck. After a short climb, pass the barn and soon afterwards a seat of considerable interest. Still descending, pass Brantwood Estate gates (the first are metal, the second wooden), and enjoy the long gentle stroll through lovely woodland to the road.

5. Turn left onto the lane (it's narrow so beware of the occasional car) and pass the entrance to Low Bank Ground, followed by Black Beck Cottage and Thurston. Brantwood House, former home of John Ruskin, now comes into view on your left. Rejoin *Gondola* by crossing the road and passing through the lower gardens to the Brantwood Jetty (OS grid reference: SD311958).

Make the Most of Your Day

Finish your walk with a tour around Brantwood House (not National Trust), or visit Hill Top in nearby Hawkshead, a seventeenth-century farmhouse that was home to the children's author Beatrix Potter. A time capsule of Potter's life, full of her favourite things, this house and its surroundings provided the inspiration for many of the author's books.

Food and Facilities

Visit the Jumping Jenny coffee house and licensed restaurant by Brantwood House where you can enjoy a well-deserved treat. Or wait until you get back to Coniston, where there is a selection of cafés. Toilets are available for patrons of the Jumping Jenny Café and at Coniston Pier.

View across Coniston Water towards Coniston village and the surrounding landscape.

63. Eskdale Ramble

This classic river walk along the River Esk takes you through an intimate landscape of crags, waterfalls, woods and fields. The area forms part of the Wasdale, Eskdale and Duddon estates, a vast area of open country, valleys, mountains, rivers and lakes owned by the National Trust, lying at the foot of Scafell Pike, England's tallest mountain.

Eskdale
Holmrook
Cumbria CA19 1TT
01946 726064
wasdale@
nationaltrust.org.uk
www.nationaltrust.org.uk/
wasdale-eskdale-and-duddon

About this walk
A scenic Lake District walk

Site of industrial interest

View a waterfall en route

Option of taking heritage railway to starting point

Distance 3.5 miles (5.6km)

Time 2 hours 30 minutes

Things to see

St Catherine's Church
This chapel was built to serve a large area that included Wasdale. Before the construction of the church at Wasdale Head the dead were transported over the fells to St Catherine's. This route is known today as the 'coffin route'.

The railway in Eskdale
The Ravenglass and Eskdale Railway opened for the purpose of ferrying iron ore from workings near Boot to the coast. After a turbulent history the line closed for industrial traffic in 1953 when granite quarrying at Beckfoot closed; this industrial heritage is still visible in the landscape. The line is now run as a heritage railway with steam-powered locomotives.

Doctor's Bridge
Originally a packhorse bridge, the so-called Doctor's Bridge is now a road bridge. Probably dating from the seventeenth century, it was widened in 1734 for a surgeon named Edward Tyson to accommodate the width of his trap.

Top: Beautiful Eskdale in the Lake District, Cumbria.
Above: The 'Doctor's Bridge' over the River Esk.

By Train Ravenglass
8 miles (12.8km), adjacent
to the Ravenglass and
Eskdale Heritage Railway,
which runs to Dalegarth

By Car Off A595,
following signs from
Gosforth for Eskade
and Boot

OS Map Landranger 89
and 90

Start / End Dalegarth
railway station (near
Boot) pay and display
car park, **OS grid ref:
NY 173007**

1. Leave Dalegarth Station and turn left along the road towards Boot. At the crossroads adjacent to the pub turn right and head south down the track.

2. After passing through Esk View Farm and associated buildings you'll see linear stone walls, which are the remains of the railway line for the quarries.

3. The track passes St Catherine's Church and the stepping stones across the river Esk. From the church follow the river upstream along a pitched surface.

4. Continue along the path until you reach a gate. At this point there are two paths that are close together and run parallel: a well-defined lower path that crosses the Esk and an upper path that is not well defined and can be easily mistaken for a grass strip. Take the lower path to the old railway bridge.

5. At the bridge you can see Gill Force, a small rocky waterfall on the Esk. From here, go back along the path until you reach the point where the path split. Take the path leading to the right, heading up a slight gradient following the river upstream. Continue along

this path through various gates and thin woody areas until you reach a small hump-back bridge known locally as Doctor's Bridge.

6. Cross the Esk at Doctor's Bridge and follow the river downstream, heading away from Penny Hill Farm. At Low Birker Farm follow the bridleway through the property and continue along a well-defined walled track. This track eventually leads to a small footbridge over a ford and through a gate.

7. Continue through the gate and towards Gill Force along a path through open ground lined by gorse and bracken. Follow the earthen path through a wood until you get to a gate exiting the woodland. Continue out of the wood until you reach a corner in a dry stone wall where the path bends to the left across a ford. Continue along the track until you reach a gate and enter a plantation.

8. Once you pass through the gate you drop into a plantation and cross the beck with a ford and footbridge. At this point you have the opportunity to visit Stanley Force waterfall or continue on the route.

View of Scafell Pike, England's tallest mountain.

9. Head towards the gate and exit the plantation, following the bridleway across the field. Upon exiting the field turn right onto the track and follow it towards the minor road. On the way you pass a car park and bridge.

10. At the road junction turn right by the old school and war memorial, and head towards the station and car park.

Make the Most of Your Day

Make your way back to Santon Bridge and head up the road to Wastwater, England's deepest lake, which lies at the foot of the country's highest mountain, Scafell Pike. Here you can admire the stunning scenery and paddle in the lake or, for the adventurous, take a canoe out onto the water, from where you get a very special perspective on the surrounding landscape.

Food and Facilities

A fully licensed café can be found at Dalegarth Station; toilet facilities can also be found here (not National Trust).

64. Octavia Hill Walk at Brandelhow

This is an easy lakeside amble along the quiet side of Derwentwater, leading you through the tranquil parkland at Brandelhow, birthplace of the National Trust in the Lake District. Octavia Hill, one of the founders of the Trust, planted a tree at the official opening to the public of Brandelhow in October 1902. Combine your walk with a scenic boat trip across the lake.

Brandelhow Park
Borrowdale
Keswick
Cumbria CA 12 5UP
017687 74649
borrowdale@
nationaltrust.org.uk
www.nationaltrust.org.uk/
borrowdale

About this walk
Take launch from Keswick to avoid limited parking

Rich in wildlife and fungi

Site of historic significance

Dogs welcome, kept under close control during lambing

Distance 3.6 miles (5.7km)

Time 1 hour 30 minutes

Things to see

Brandelhow Park
Octavia Hill campaigned passionately for the protection of Brandelhow. Bought with money raised through public subscription, it became the first piece of the Lake District to be safeguarded by the Trust from development. The hands sculpture, entitled *Entrust*, was commissioned in 2002 to celebrate the first 100 years of the National Trust in the Lake District.

Fungi in the woods
Brandelhow is a great place in the autumn for discovering fungi. The mixture of woodland and parkland creates a good environment for encouragement of biodiversity, and the woods support many species of fungi.

Wildlife at Brandelhow
As Brandelhow is on the 'quiet' side of Derwentwater, away from the roads, it's rich in wildlife. This walk offers you a good chance of seeing kingfishers, woodpeckers, nuthatches, roe deer, red squirrels and, if you're very lucky, perhaps even an otter.

Top: Dawn at Derwentwater in Cumbria.
Above: *Entrust*, by Rosalind Rawnsley.

By Train Keswick Launch from Keswick Lakeside to Hawes End Jetty

By Car B5289 south from Keswick. Parking is limited at site, so it's recommended you park at Keswick Lakeside car park (just south of A66) and catch launch to Hawes End Jetty

OS Map Explorer OL4

Start / End Hawes End Jetty, Derwentwater, **OS grid ref: NY250213**

1. From Hawes End Jetty, turn left and head south along the wide track that runs parallel to the lakeshore for half a mile (0.8km). (The Keswick Launch Company runs boats in both directions around the lake throughout summer. In winter, it runs a restricted timetable – see their website for details.)

2. The wide track is joined from the right by another track. Continue through the park with trees on your left, through a narrow band of trees and on towards the lakeshore and Low Brandelhow Jetty.

3. At the jetty, keep heading south (to your right) and follow the lakeshore path. The path takes you past the hands sculpture, and gets a little rougher and muddier as it follows the lakeshore towards High Brandelhow Jetty.

4. At the jetty make a sharp U-turn onto the upper track in the wood, passing under the line of large Douglas fir trees. Follow this upper path all the way back to the Hawes End Adventure Centre.

5. As you walk back through the woods, ignore side paths to left and right and stay on the main path. You'll get glimpses of the lake, and pass by a traditional stone barn. Out of sight to your left, close to the road below Cat Bells, is where commemorative trees were planted by Princess Louise and National Trust founders Octavia Hill and Canon Rawnsley in 1902.

6. Pass beside Hawes End Adventure Centre and come onto a road, then look for a track to your right signposted 'Hawes End Jetty'. This will take you back to the jetty at the start of the walk.

Make the Most of Your Day
Swimming in Derwentwater is very popular in the warmer summer months but beware boat traffic. There are some quieter areas – between Lord's Island and the shore is a no-boat area.

Food and Facilities
Visit one of the nearby cafés or the Flock Inn at Roshthwaite (not National Trust). Public toilets are available at Keswick.

65. Aira Force Waterfall Walk

Follow in the footsteps of William Wordswoth and his sister, and discover why Aira Force inspired the romantic poets to pick up their pens. This walk leads you towards the thunderous roar of the waterfalls, before emerging from the confines of the gorge to afford expansive views over Ullswater from the summit of Gowbarrow.

Ullswater
Near Watermillock
Penrith
Cumbria CA II
017684 82067
ullswater@
nationaltrust.org.uk
www.nationaltrust.org.uk/
aira-force-and-ullswater/

About this walk

Superb views over Ullswater

Some narrow parts with steep drops and flights of steps

Dogs welcome on a lead near livestock

Distance 4.5 miles (7.2km)

Time I hour 30 minutes to 3 hours

Things to see

Aira Force
The most famous of the Lake District waterfalls, Aira Force drops an impressive 65ft (20m) down into the gorge, and is surrounded by pretty woodland. This is the place where Wordsworth was inspired to write many of his poems. Look out for rainbows when the conditions are right.

Gowbarrow trig point
Impressive views all around can be enjoyed from the trig point at the summit of Gowbarrow Fell. It was on the west side of the fell in 1802 that Dorothy Wordsworth

noticed wild daffodils growing. Her observations later inspired her brother William to write his famous poem 'Daffodils'.

Gowbarrow Park
Gowbarrow Park was once home to a large herd of deer, and evidence of old shooting boxes and stalkers' huts can still be seen here today. The deer have since been replaced by low numbers of hardy traditional sheep such as Herdwick to help restore heather and tree cover to the fell. Judging by the purple haze in summer, this tactic appears to be working.

Top: Walking through the woodland near Aira Force in Cumbria.
Above: Aira Force waterfall.

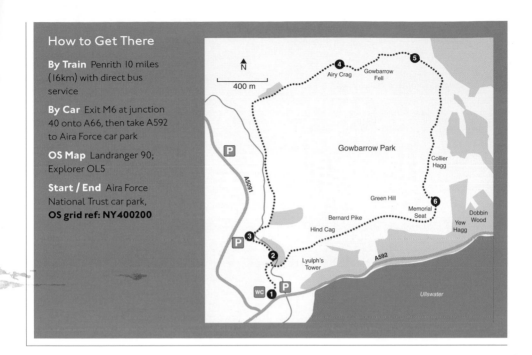

1. Take the arched gate out of the top end of the car park and go through a metal gate. Follow the path and head through a gateway in the wall into a grassy area known as the Glade.

2. Take the left-hand path through the arboretum and follow the path up to a little wooden gate on your left (which has superb views out over Ullswater to the left). The specimen trees in the arboretum were planted in 1846 and now include some of the tallest and stoutest trees in Cumbria. Don't go through the gate but follow the path to the right, dropping down a long steep flight of steps to the viewing platform at the base of the waterfall. Continue over the bridge and climb the steep steps on the left.

3. At the top of these steps bear left to the upper bridge for a view down Aira Force. Rejoin the main path and walk upstream, keeping the river on your left as you go. Keep going until the path takes you through a gap in the wall and then through a gate onto open farmland.

4. Before you get to the next gate in the wall ahead turn right up the field and take the permissive path to the fell gate. Keeping the wall on your left continue up the fellside on a good stone-pitched path maintained by the Fix the Fells project. This offers a fine opportunity for a breather as you take in the views.

5. Once the path flattens out and bears away from the wall, follow it up to the trig point on the summit of Gowbarrow, from where you have fine views all round. Look south to Place Fell and Red Screes over to Kirkstone, with the bulk of Helvellyn beyond. Blencathra, Bannerdale and Carrock Fell can be seen to the north-west, with the Pennines to the north-east. Martindale and High Street are to the south-east.

6. On leaving the summit continue along the path, keeping parallel with the wall on your left. Follow the path down, bearing right until you reach the ruin of an old shooting lodge. Keeping right, continue up and around the eastern flank of Gowbarrow.

7. From here a good path takes you to the brow of the hill then down to an obvious cairn over a fence stile to the superb vantage point marked on the map as Memorial Seat. Go back over the stile and bear left, staying on the path down towards the woodlands.

Aira Beck thunders over the rocks towards the waterfall.

8. At the bottom of the slope you will see across the field a building known as Lyulph's Tower (private), built as a hunting lodge by the Howard family in the eighteenth century. It was designed to look like a grand castle from the lake – from the land it appears a little more modest. Just before the wood take the left-hand fork and pass through a gate to rejoin the footpath bearing left back to the Glade and car park.

Make the Most of Your Day

Why not go on a tree-hunting expedition? Visit Glenamara Park where you'll find some intriguing veteran trees that have grown into weird and wonderful shapes. The land here is grazed by cows, which has allowed the trees to grow big and old. Or head down to Skelghyll Woods, near Stagshaw Gardens at Ambleside, where some of the country's tallest trees grow.

Food and Facilities

Refreshments can be found at the Aira Force tea-room (not National Trust), by the car park. Or head south on the A592 for the Side Farm tea-room at Patterdale. Toilets are available at the Aira Force car park.

66. Acorn Bank Heritage Walk

Temple Sowerby
Near Penrith
Cumbria CA10 1SP
017683 61893
acornbank@
nationaltrust.org.uk
www.nationaltrust.org.uk/
acorn-bank

About this walk
Through the foothills of the Pennines

Several stiles

Boggy at certain times of year

Dogs welcome on a lead

Distance 3.2 miles (5.1 km)

Time 1 hour 30 minutes

Enjoy this peaceful backwater and discover Acorn Bank's surprising industrial heritage. A great stopping off point close to the M6, the estate is a haven for wildlife, perhaps best known for its collection of over 300 varieties of herbs and its traditional fruit orchards. The walk affords panoramic views across the Eden Valley to the Lakeland mountains.

Things to see

Acorn Bank House
Acorn Bank House nestles in the foothills of the Pennines, with the brooding mass of Cross Fell (the highest peak in the Pennine range) rising up beyond.

Crowdundle Beck
Part of a Special Conservation Area, Crowdundle Beck is a tributary of the River Eden and forms the old county boundary between Westmorland and Cumberland. Look out here for otters, crayfish, salmon, kingfishers, herons and dippers. The Eden Rivers Trust is dedicated to conserving the river, its tributaries and surrounding countryside.

Settle to Carlisle Railway
The Settle to Carlisle line passes right through the walk and was the last railway to be built by hand, employing an enormous number of navigators. Hundreds of men died from smallpox or injury while constructing it. The railway passes over the impressive Crowdundle

Top: Acorn Bank House, Cumbria, dates back to the sixteenth century.
Above: Crowdundle Beck in the spring.

viaduct, which you walk under just before point 3 of the walk. Built in 1873, the viaduct is 55ft (17m) high and 86 yards (78m) long

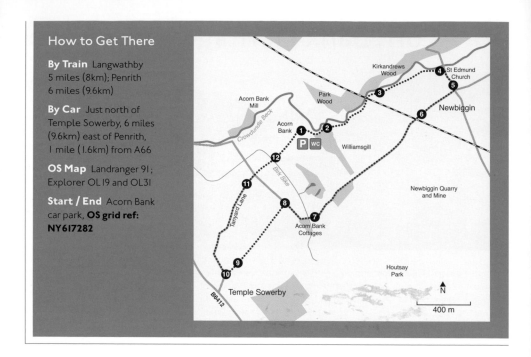

How to Get There

By Train Langwathby
5 miles (8km); Penrith
6 miles (9.6km)

By Car Just north of
Temple Sowerby, 6 miles
(9.6km) east of Penrith,
1 mile (1.6km) from A66

OS Map Landranger 91;
Explorer OL19 and OL31

Start / End Acorn Bank
car park, **OS grid ref:**
NY617282

(Map labels: St Edmund Church, Kirkandrews Wood, Park Wood, Newbiggin, Acorn Bank Mill, Crowdundle Beck, Acorn Bank, Williamsgill, Birk Sike, Newbiggin Quarry and Mine, Tanyard Lane, Acorn Bank Cottages, Houtsay Park, Temple Sowerby, B6412, N, 400 m)

1. Leave Acorn Bank car park and take the woodland footpath to the right downhill until you come to a wooden step stile with a dog gate. Cross the stile into the field – it can be very boggy here in wet conditions.

2. Follow the riverbank through the field (beware of riverbank erosion after periods of flooding). Pass through the empty gateway in the fence into the next field (note: the gateway may since have been replaced by a stile). Continue under the viaduct ahead, following the river on the left into another field.

3. From this point you can see in the distance at Great Dun Fell the Civil Aviation Authority's air traffic control radar with its great 'golf ball' on top. In spring there is an abundance of primroses in the woodland on the other side of the riverbank. Look out for an old walled garden on your left.

4. When you arrive at the old barn, go over a stile and turn right onto a tarmacked road. The church of St Edmund is on your left.

5. Continue down the road into the centre of Newbiggin – this village is just one of a number of Cumbrian hamlets that bear this name. At the crossroads turn right and walk towards Temple Sowerby, walking on the right-hand side to face the oncoming traffic. The farmhouse at the crossroads features a datestone from 1695.

6. Continue on the road under the railway bridge. Further on, through the hedge, look out for the 'swallow holes' in the fields, where the ground has caved in from the old mine workings. Next on your right you will see the prefab building that used to be the engine house for the gypsum mines at Acorn Bank.

7. Cross the bridge over Birk Sike, a drainage ditch dug in the eighteenth century to drain the land for agriculture. After the road turns right, look out for a kissing gate on the left into Borough Fields.

8. Go through and follow the fence line on the right, then through another kissing gate into the next field, which was once part of the old strip field system of farming. Look back now for the best view of the Pennines to the north-east. The conical hills are Dufton and Knock Pikes.

9. Go through the next kissing gate and down the alley with the walled garden to your left. This brings you straight into the village of Temple Sowerby, a traditional Westmorland village arranged around a village green. Often referred to as the 'Queen of Westmorland', it once belonged to the Lords of the Manor at Acorn Bank.

10. Turn right onto the tarmacked road. As you leave the village by Tanyard Lane (known locally as 'The Tanny'), you will see a newly-converted long building on your right, which is an old tannery. Temple Sowerby was a tanning village during the eighteenth century and would have been very smelly.

11. At the T-junction you will see Acorn Bank ahead, nestling under Cross Fell. Go straight ahead, through the kissing gate into the parkland and follow the old approach to the manor house. This would have been oak woodland back in 1600 and is how Acorn Bank got its name.

12. Cross the bridge over Birk Sike again. Passing through the kissing gate into another field you soon come to a metal gate beside the cattle grid. Cross the main drive into the property and go through the next gate back into the car park.

Make the Most of Your Day

Take time to visit the glorious gardens at Acorn Bank. The seventeenth-century walls shelter the National Trust's largest collection of medicinal and culinary plants, while the traditional orchards are carpeted with wildflowers and surrounded by herbaceous borders. The watermill at Acorn Bank has been restored and brought back to life by a team of dedicated volunteers and it is now producing flour again after a gap of more than 70 years.

Food and Facilities

Finish off your walk by indulging yourself at the tea-room, where culinary herbs and fruit from the garden are used daily in soups, salads and puddings. Toilets are available in the garden courtyard.

The traditional orchard at Acorn Bank bears a rich harvest of fruit in autumn.

67. Whitehaven's Hidden Gems

This dramatic cliff-top walk starts at Whitehaven's historic seventeenth-century harbour, passing the town's industrial archaeology to join Wainwright's Coast to Coast Path. Experience wild, secluded beaches and discover a series of hidden gems such as Saltom Pit, the Haig Colliery Mining Museum and Fleswick Bay. It's a linear walk so catch the bus or train back.

The Beacon
Whitehaven
Cumbria CA28 7LY
017687 74649
buttermere@
nationaltrust.org.uk
www.nationaltrust.org.uk/
buttermere-ennerdale-and-
whitehaven-coast

About this walk
A fascinating coastal walk in search of hidden gems

Some narrow sections with short but steep climbs

Dogs welcome under close control around livestock

Distance 7 miles (11.2km)

Time 4 hours

Things to see

Colourful Coast project
The National Trust is working with various partners to conserve this wonderful stretch of coastline,

A chough in flight.

in a project named the Colourful Coast in recognition of the mass of wildflowers that bloom along the cliff-tops in spring. The project partners have reclaimed former industrial land for wildlife and access, and have worked with local farmers to improve habitats for farmland birds.

Saltom Pit
Saltom Pit was the first under-sea coal mine in England. It stands just 20ft (6m) above the beach, and the shaft was dug by hand in 1725. The Colourful Coast project has stabilised the building and restored the path down to it.

Guillemots, puffins and chough
St Bees Head is an RSPB nature reserve featuring three secure viewing areas on the cliffs near the lighthouse. From May to July it's possible to get stunning views of the nesting seabirds. The cliffs of St Bees provide the only nesting site in England for the black guillemot. Although rarely seen, ten pairs of puffins are also believed to nest here. Additionally the Colourful Coast project is working to improve habitats to encourage chough back to nest here, for the first time in over a 100 years.

Top: A view over Whitehaven Harbour, Cumbria. The Candlestick stands sentinel over Wellington Pit.

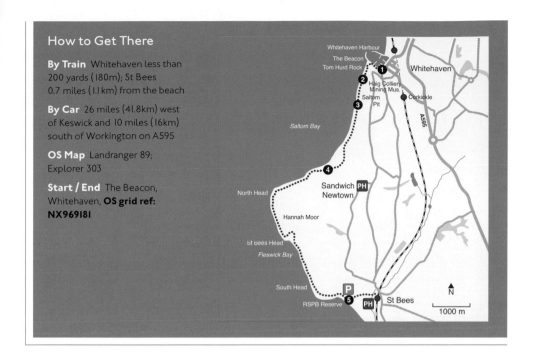

How to Get There

By Train Whitehaven less than 200 yards (180m); St Bees 0.7 miles (1.1 km) from the beach

By Car 26 miles (41.8km) west of Keswick and 10 miles (16km) south of Workington on A595

OS Map Landranger 89; Explorer 303

Start / End The Beacon, Whitehaven, **OS grid ref: NX969181**

1. Start by Wellington Terrace at Whitehaven Harbour, just past the Beacon Museum. Follow the waymarks up to the Candlestick (the imposing chimney of Wellington Pit), then continue to the Haig Colliery Mining Museum. On the cliff-top, join the wagon way where trucks full of coal used to be shunted down to the harbour. With Georgian alabaster mines, sandstone quarries, a twelfth-century priory, England's first under-sea coal mine and a top secret Second World War radar station, this coastline has fascinating stories to tell. The Beacon, Haig Colliery Mining Museum and St Bees Priory tell them well, and are well worth visiting to find out more.

2. Just after the museum, follow the side path to the right to an information board above Saltom Pit. There's a path here down to the ruined winding house if you want to explore further, or continue along the cliff path.

3. Follow the path for a short distance until you come to another junction. Here, the wagon way continues on to the left, while the narrower footpath runs along the cliff-top to the right. Take this right-hand path, which soon becomes a field-edge path. Follow this until it comes to a concrete track. Cross this track and follow the path straight ahead. You will join an incline sloping up the cliffside towards the sandstone quarry. Here you can choose to drop down to Barrowmouth Bay, another hidden gem. Fleswick, Barrowmouth and Saltom bays are wild and tranquil places, and it's worth a bit of a scramble to get down to them. Semi-precious stones hide among the shingle at Fleswick, and it's thought the caves there were used by smugglers.

4. At the quarry follow the waymarked path on the seaward side of the quarry gates. At the far side of this quarry you will finally emerge onto the St Bees coastal path, which you can now follow all the way to St Bees. At first there is only one path, running along the top of the cliffs, but for most of the route there is also the option of walking in the fields to the left.

Rosebay willowherb adds splashes of colour to Whitehaven's Colourful Coast.

5. This path brings you to the lighthouse, RSPB viewing points, Fleswick Bay and eventually to the beach at St Bees – hidden gems one and all. To reach the railway station next to St Bees Priory, take the road running out of the car park behind the beach. Where the main road curves to the left, turn right onto a side road and then onto a footpath that crosses a field towards the priory. The station is about 200 yards (180m) to the right of the priory.

Make the Most of Your Day

Take time to visit the Haig Colliery Mining Museum (not National Trust) while you are in Whitehaven, to find out more about this area's rich mining heritage. Or head north to explore Wordsworth House and Garden in Cockermouth. This lovely Georgian townhouse was the birthplace and childhood home of romantic poet William and his sister Dorothy, and provides visitors with a unique opportunity to experience late eighteenth-century life at first hand.

Food and Facilities

Pubs and cafés can be found in Whitehaven and St Bees, where public toilets are also available. Or try the cosy café at Wordsworth House, where you can treat yourself to potted shrimps, homemade soups and tasty scones.

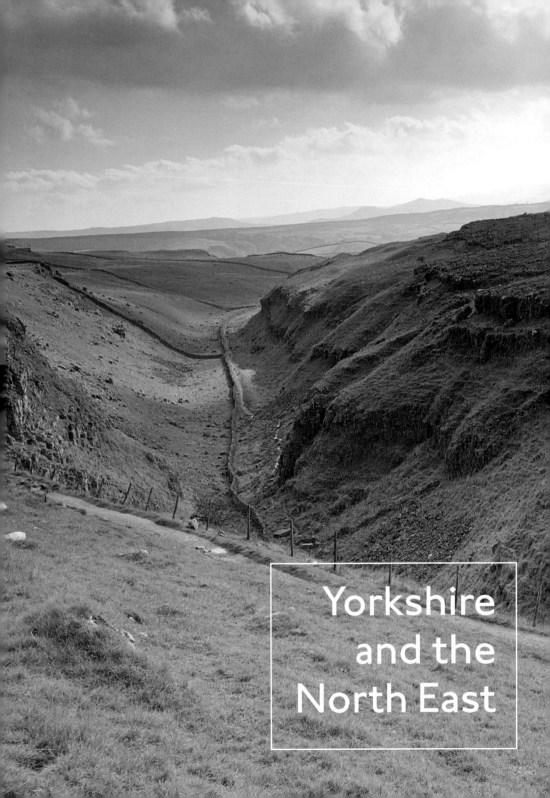

Yorkshire
and the
North East

68. Marsden Moor Heritage Hike

Uncover the past and discover Marsden Moor's rich history – from Neolithic man through to the Industrial Revolution – on this bracing walk, part of which runs along the Pennine Way. On your way, look out for some of the moorl and plants and birds that make this area internationally important, and take time to stop and admire the magnificent open moorland views.

The Old Goods Yard
Station Road
Marsden
Huddersfield
West Yorkshire HD7 6DH
01484 847016
marsdenmoor@
nationaltrust.org.uk
www.nationaltrust.org.uk/
marsden-moor

About this walk
Rich in industrial history

Several stiles

Sturdy walking boots recommended

Dogs welcome on a lead during lambing and nesting season

Distance 8 miles (12.8km)

Time 4 hours 30 minutes

Things to see

A long history
The moorland around you has been used by people for thousands of years, from early hunter-gatherers ambushing prey to traders taking goods to market along the packhorse roads. The walk takes you past reservoirs and conduits supplying water to the people of Yorkshire, feeding the Huddersfield Narrow Canal.

Birds and plants
Marsden is host to an array of moorland bird species such as curlew, grouse, golden plover, dunlin, merlin, short-eared owl and even the rare twite. Look out for common upland plant species such as heather, bilberry, crowberry and a variety of grasses; if you are lucky, you may even come across the carnivorous sundew.

Moor restoration
The National Trust carries out important restoration work on Marsden Moor to help conserve the area for the future. Work includes gully blocking using wooden dams and heather bales to keep the peat wet and stable and prevent it from being washed away. The Trust also revegetates bare peat with cotton grass and heather to prevent erosion and provide food and shelter for birds.

Sunrise over Marsden Moor.

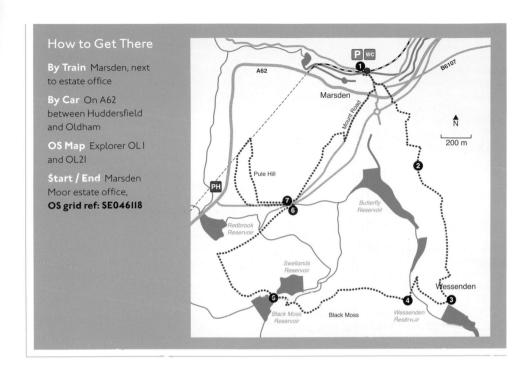

How to Get There

By Train Marsden, next to estate office

By Car On A62 between Huddersfield and Oldham

OS Map Explorer OL1 and OL21

Start / End Marsden Moor estate office, **OS grid ref: SE046118**

1. From the estate office, head down Station Road through Marsden and cross the A62. Walk through the park, past the handstand to come out on Carrs Road. Cross the road and take the path at the end of the row of cottages. Follow the path past a newly renovated house behind the other houses, keeping the wall on the left; after a short distance, turn right. Head uphill and over a stile until you arrive at a house and stables. Turn left, then go over another stile and follow the path behind the house. Keep right until you reach a choice of three gates. Take the left-hand gate to head up the slope, where you cross a stile that takes you onto a track. Turn left and head past Upper Acre Farm to meet the Deer Hill Conduit. Turn right and follow the conduit until you reach waymark number 9. Here you can take in the view of Marsden and its mills and appreciate how important the mills were to the local economy.

Opposite top: A wooden signpost indicates the route along the Pennine Way as it crosses Marsden Moor in West Yorkshire.

2. Continue along the conduit to reach waymark number 10 and take in the fine views over the Butterley and Blakeley reservoirs. Keep walking along the conduit, crossing over a stile. Just before you get to the next stile, head down the field boundary to the corner stile and take the path behind Wessenden Lodge.

3. When you meet the main Wessenden track, turn right and follow the path in front of the lodge and continue down this track for about 800 yards (730m). Follow the Pennine Way steeply down into the bottom of the valley and then even more steeply back to the top to meet waymark 11. Here is a good point to catch your breath and admire the views of the Wessenden Valley and a former shooting lodge.

4. Follow the Pennine Way to the right, along Blakely Clough and up steps onto the moor to reach the Black Moss and Swellands reservoirs. More information can be found on the interpretation panel here.

5. Cross the dam wall and follow the path left towards Black Moss's other dam wall, then head right and follow the path northwards through one of the

National Trust sheep enclosures. The area you are walking through was once very badly eroded, but by eliminating grazing and spreading heather brash and seeds the plot has recovered. Keep walking along this path until you meet the Pennine Bridleway. Turn right and walk along the bridleway to meet Mount Road where you will find an information board about the turnpikes.

6. If you fancy getting some stunning views of the estate from the top of Pule Hill, follow Mount Road left/westwards until you come to a signpost on your right pointing out the Standedge Trail, which contours around Pule Hill. This path is very boggy to begin with, but soon dries out. Continue to follow the route around Pule Hill until you come to the path that leads you up past the quarries where you can turn back on yourself to walk along the edge to the summit and waymark number 14. When you've admired the view, walk straight back down to join Mount Road and retrace your steps to the information board.

7. Carry on past the information board until just before the cattle grid where you turn left onto Old Mount Road. Follow the footpath along a track

towards Hades Farm until you reach waymark number 15. The path leading off the track leads down to meet up with Old Mount Road where you turn left and head back down into Marsden. Cross the A62 again and walk past St Bartholomew's Church to Station Road and back to the car park.

Make the Most of Your Day

There's lots going on at Marsden Moor all year round, from navigation courses and photography workshops to family events and plant sales (to find out more visit the website). Sites and activities not to be missed include having a picnic at Eastergate Bridge or watching the paragliders at Buckstones.

Food and Facilities

During the summer months there is an ice-cream vendor at Buckstones car park on the A640. Otherwise, visit one of the pubs in Marsden village. The nearest toilet (not National Trust) is also located in Marsden village.

Looking north from Pule Hill over the snow-covered landscape.

69. Exploring Hardcastle Crags

This lovely walk takes you into Hardcastle Crags, a famous beauty spot in the South Pennines with more than 400 acres (162ha) of unspoilt woodland. The route passes through a steep-sided valley alongside tumbling streams, heading towards Gibson Mill, a former cotton mill transformed into a visitor centre that explores the valley's history over the past 200 years.

Hardcastle Crags
Near Hebden Bridge
West Yorkshire
01422 844518
hardcastlecrags@
nationaltrust.org.uk
www.nationaltrust.org.uk/
hardcastle-crags

About this walk
Natural history and industrial heritage combined

Bluebells in spring

Uneven and steep in places

Dogs welcome under close control

Distance 3 miles (4.8km)

Time 1 hour

Things to see

Hebden Water
Water from Hebden Water kept the many mills that once operated in the valley running. The dams, weirs and millponds you see today are all that remain of this thriving industry, with the exception of Gibson Mill. Look out for dragonflies hovering over the ponds in spring and summer.

Flora and fauna
The woodland and streams attract many types of birds including dipper, jay, woodpecker, grey wagtail, heron, goldcrest and nuthatch. The damp, shaded conditions are perfect for many species of fern, moss and lichen. Lichens are especially sensitive to pollution so their presence indicates good air quality. Bluebells cover the woodland floor in spring, while autumn sees hundreds of varieties of fungi emerge. The woods are also home to the northern hairy wood ant.

Gibson Mill
The nineteenth-century former cotton-spinning and weaving mill that lies at the heart of the valley is now championing sustainable technology. Gibson Mill is completely cut off from the National Grid, so it has to generate all its own power as well as recycle all its waste. It uses solar panels and water-powered turbines, and even the lift works via green technology.

Top: A stepped path through Hardcastle Crags, Yorkshire.
Above: Gibson Mill.

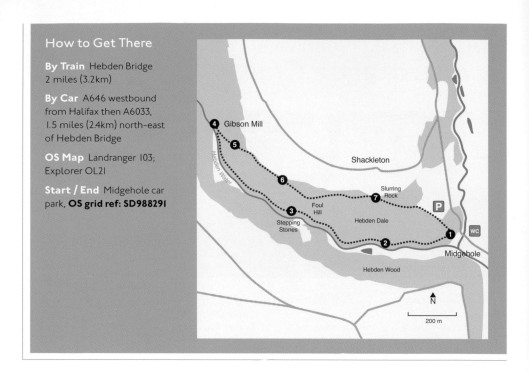

How to Get There

By Train Hebden Bridge 2 miles (3.2km)

By Car A646 westbound from Halifax then A6033, 1.5 miles (2.4km) north-east of Hebden Bridge

OS Map Landranger 103; Explorer OL21

Start / End Midgehole car park, **OS grid ref: SD988291**

1. From the information point at Midgehole car park turn left down the hill and then immediately right following the path to the picnic area. The cotton industry left its mark on the landscape, from millponds to packhorse trails. In the early twentieth century workers from neighbouring towns and villages would visit Hardcastle Crags, walking from as far as Littleborough for tea and a dance at Gibson Mill.

2. Follow the path upstream along the river and into the woods, looking for signs of the valley's industrial past as you pass millponds and weirs.

3. Continue along the riverside path, then climb a flight of steps before dropping back down to the river by a set of stepping stones.

4. Continuing along the riverside path you will come to Gibson Mill.

5. Leave the mill on the main track, heading back towards the car park. After a short distance, at the top of the slope, take the path leading off to the left up into the woods. According to National Trust Warden Ian O'Leary, 'The ferns and mosses carpeting the woodland floor and the majestic trees create an inviting, yet at times eerie, landscape.'

6. After a short while the path leads down through a conifer plantation. Look out for signs of the northern hairy wood ant before joining the main track through the estate.

7. Follow the waymarked route back up the valley to reach Slurring Rock. This is where children used to slide down the rocks in their clogs. Continue past the rocks and drop down onto the old packhorse route that takes you back to the car park.

The riverside walk at Hardcastle Crags is awash with colour during autumn.

Make the Most of Your Day

Take time to explore the visitor centre at Gibson Mill, which tells the story of the people who lived, worked and played in the valley, with interactive displays, dressing up activities and dancing. The National Trust also puts on tours, exhibitions and special events throughout the year, so there's always plenty to see and do (visit www.nationaltrust.org.uk for details).

Food and Facilities

The Weaving Shed Café at Gibson Mill is perfect for a light lunch or tea and cake, the latter baked locally by traditional family bakers. The room itself, originally built as a weaving shed, was used as a roller-rink in the heyday of Hardcastle Crags as an entertainment emporium. Toilet facilities are also available at the Mill.

70. Malham Tarn Archaeology Walk

Malham Tarn
Settle
North Yorkshire BD24 9PT
01729 830416
malhamtarn@
nationaltrust.org.uk
www.nationaltrust.org.uk/
malham-tarn-estate

About this walk
Rich in wildlife and
archaeology

One short steep uphill
section

Dogs welcome on a lead
around livestock

Distance 5.5 miles (8.8km)

Time 3 to 4 hours

This outstanding area of ancient limestone pastures, upland hill farms and flower-rich hay meadows provides a marvellous setting for this fascinating walk. Explore the beautiful Malham Tarn, a popular beauty spot in the Yorkshire Dales, and discover archaeological remains in a landscape that has been used by man since the Mesolithic era.

Things to see

Top: View across wildflower meadows on the Malham Tarn Estate, North Yorkshire. Above: Malham Tarn.

Middle House Farm
New Middle House Farm, with its steeply pitched roofs, was built in the sixteenth century in the distinctive style used by former Malham Moor Estate owner, Walter Morrison, who was a generous benefactor to the local community. Tarn House was Morrison's favourite home.

Monks' Road
The old Monks' Road follows the edge of the fellside above the wall line down to Arncliffe. Part of an important long-distance route for Fountains Abbey, this section connected the sheep pastures on Malham Moor with the grange at Kilnsey, where the sheep would be taken for clipping. The wool was then sold on the Continent.

Malham Tarn
This permanent source of fresh water has long formed a focus for human activity. Flint artefacts dating from the Mesolithic to the Bronze Age indicate that this area was an important seasonal hunting ground. The tarn has been used as a fishery since medieval times, when the monks of Fountains Abbey stocked it with fish. It's still used today for fishing, although there's now a strict catch and release policy.

How to Get There

By Train Settle 7 miles
(11.2km); Skipton 19 miles
(30.5km)

By Car A65 from Skipton,
then follow signs from
Gargrave to Malham; take
Malham Rakes road to car park

OS Map Explorer OL2 and
OL41; Landranger 98

Start / End Street Gate car
park, **OS grid ref: SD905657**

1. Pass through the gate and follow the wall on your right along Mastiles Lane to the Roman camp. The location of this legions' temporary marching camp was perfect for marshalling and manoeuvring troops. At the end of a day's march the soldiers would dig a ditch with a bank inside and place wooden stakes on top as a palisade.

2. Turn left, taking the footpath across the north-east corner of the Roman camp, and following it towards Middle House Farm. After you've crossed Gordale Beck, look to your right – the tops of the fells were full of settlements during the Iron Age.

3. From Middle House Farm you can wander up the hill to the left of the farm to look at the sixteenth-century farmstead of Old Middle House (point 4 on the map) or head along the old Monks' Road to point 5. Old Middle House, now derelict, was a typical early Dales settlement, with lambing crofts and a few closes for hay and sheepfolds. It was built on the site of a much older building that housed shepherds for the Fountains Abbey Estate.

4. Return down the hill, pass through the gate and then follow the path to your right.

5. Follow the Monks' Road to Malham Tarn. Much of the land on Malham Moor was used by Fountains Abbey to rear sheep, hence the name Fountains Fell.

6. When you reach the shores of Malham Tarn turn left and then take the left fork onto a grass track that goes beneath Great Close Hill, away from the Tarn.

7. Pause at Great Close Plantation and take a look around you. This was the site of the great cattle fairs of the eighteenth century. Drovers from Scotland would bring up to 20,000 cattle over the summer to trade here, enabling local farmers to supply nearby towns and cities with meat and dairy produce.

8. After Great Close Plantation, bear right to join the track and return to Street Gate car park.

Make the Most of Your Day

While you're in the area, don't miss the Queen of the Fairies. The beautiful waterfall at Janet's Foss is a magical place to visit, only a short walk from Malham village. The walk is particularly memorable in springtime when the woodland is a mass of wild garlic. The National Trust also arranges special events at Malham Tarn, from pond-dipping to geocaching, so look online for details. For more information about this area, visit the National Park Centre in Malham (not National Trust).

Food and Facilities

Refreshments and toilet facilities can be found in Malham village, with a larger choice in Skipton.

The dry stone walls on the Malham Tarn Estate.

71. Yorkshire Dales Wildlife Walk

Upper Wharfedale
Yockenthwaite
Near Skipton
Yorkshire BD23 5JA
01729 830416
upperwharfedale@
nationaltrust.org.uk
www.nationaltrust.org.uk/
upper-wharfedale

About this walk
Links three (or four) villages

Optional extension to
Buckden

One steep climb

Dogs welcome on a lead

Distance 6 miles (9.6km)
or longer option of 9 miles
(14.4km)

Time 3 hours

Above: The River Wharfe near
Yockenthwaite, in Upper Wharfedale.

Starting at the village of Yockenthwaite, this wonderful wildlife walk
takes you through an area of classic Yorkshire Dales countryside. Here,
the characteristic dry stone walls and barns of the Dales, flower-rich hay
meadows, limestone pavements and beautiful wooded valleys combine
to create a haven for exploring all that nature has to offer.

Things to see

Woodland flora
The limestone pavement in Strans
Wood is made up of blocks (clints)
and cracks (grikes). Wild thyme,
limestone bedstraw and bird's-
foot trefoil inhabit the clints, and
shade-loving plants such as hart's-
tongue fern and trapped tree seeds
grow in the grikes. The roadsides
bloom with wildflowers such as
the aniseed-scented sweet cicely
and pink bistort. Summer sees
blue meadow crane's-bill, fragrant
meadowsweet and yellow rattle
(it's said that when the seeds rattle,
it is time to cut the meadow), bird's-
eye primrose, blue moor-grass and
carnivorous common butterwort.

Dry stone walls
Dry stone walls are typical of the
Dales landscape. The hay
meadows enclosed within them
can be spectacular in late spring
and summer when the wild
flowers blossom.

Birds and aquatic creatures
The meadows are important for
breeding yellow wagtail. Look out
for wading birds such as curlew
and lapwing by the River Wharfe in
spring; ducks, goosander, kingfisher
and grey wagtail may also be seen.
Dippers perch on boulders in fast-
flowing streams preying on aquatic
invertebrates. Below the water's
surface, lurking beneath a stone,
there may be bullhead (a small fish)
and crayfish; brown trout, eel and
grayling are also present, indicating
clean water.

How to Get There

By Train Skipton 12 miles (19.3km)

By Car Yockenthwaite 3 miles (4.8km) north-west of Buckden, off B6160

OS Map Landranger 98

Start / End Yockenthwaite Bridge, **OS grid ref: SD904790**

1. Start at Yockenthwaite Bridge and follow the footpath signposted to Scar House. Turn right off the farm track at another footpath sign, going through Strans Wood and emerging onto the open hillside.

2. In 1652, George Fox, the founder of the Quakers, stayed at Scar House and converted the farmer; the house later became a Quaker meeting place. A small enclosure with five trees marks the site of an old burial ground. Continue towards Cray, keeping the woodland boundary on your right. (For a shorter walk, turn right at Scar House and follow the track into Hubberholme.) Enjoy the view down Wharfedale's glaciated valley with its wide floor and ice-carved steep sides.

3. Walk across Crook Gill and carry on through the hay meadows to Cray. Enjoy the wildflowers and lots of birds throughout spring and summer. Hay is a valuable crop for farmers and it can suffer if trampled by too many feet, so please walk in single file here.

4. Drop down to your right when entering Cray and follow a footpath along Cray Gill to a road. (For a longer walk, see point 6). Turn right and walk along it for about 400 yards (365m) until you reach Hubberholme. The common blue butterfly flies from May to October and is often seen over the grassland here. It's particularly associated with the plant bird's-foot trefoil, which provides food for the caterpillars. Also look out for tiny craven door snails on old walls and moist shaded rocks, and butterflies such as the northern brown argus (associated with common rock rose) and the green-veined white.

5. Return to Yockenthwaite via a footpath behind Hubberholme Church and follow this route beside the River Wharfe all the way back.

6. There are lots of other interesting places to discover around here. With an optional extra 3 miles (4.8km) on this route you can visit Buckden, where you'll find an exhibition on the area's history at the National Trust's Townhead Barn. Take the fellside path from Cray to get there, then follow the riverside route from Buckden over to Hubberholme to rejoin the walk at point 5.

Make the Most of Your Day

Take time to visit the exhibition at Townhead Barn in Buckden, where you can find out how climate change is affecting us. The National Trust also organises a range of activities in Wharfedale, from gill scrambling to geocaching, den-building to photography workshops (see the website for details).

Food and Facilities

Cafés and pubs can be found in villages along the way, offering toilet facilities to patrons. Public toilets are also available in Buckden.

The meadows along this route are an important habitat for breeding yellow wagtails.

72. Buckden Pike Summit

Upper Wharfedale
Buckden
Near Skipton
North Yorkshire BD23 5JA
01729 830416
upperwharfedale@
nationaltrust.org.uk
www.nationaltrust.org.uk/
upper-wharfedale

About this walk
Through classic Dales scenery

Site of industrial
archaeological interest

Some stiles and a steep climb

Dogs welcome under close
control

Distance 5 miles (8km)

Time 2 to 3 hours

Discover remnants of the lead-mining industry set within the beautiful landscape of Upper Wharfedale. From the village of Buckden, this strenuous walk takes you through fields and hay meadows, along unmade tracks and across the open fellside to the summit of Buckden Pike, from where you get far-reaching views across the Yorkshire Dales.

Above: View over Upper Wharfedale in the Yorkshire Dales.

Things to see

Buckden Lead Mine
The mine shafts of Buckden Lead Mine twist and climb to follow the narrow mineral veins. The mine was first mined in 1697, under the ownership of the Earl of Burlington. The ore was smelted at Buckden High Smelt Mill until 1706 when Buckden Low Mill took over. After 1843 the ore was smelted at Starbotton Cupola; the flue ran over 1,000ft (300m) up the hill to a chimney in Cam Pastures. Thirty years later most of the mines had closed due to a drop in demand and cheap imports.

Hay meadows
The hay meadows can be seen along the valley bottom in June and July, where they attract wildlife such as butterflies and insects. The National Trust encourages traditional farming methods to maintain the rich variety of wildflowers that are so much a part of the Dales landscape. Meadows are cut for hay in July, when the flowers have set seed. The application of manure and only a limited amount of fertiliser prevents the grass outgrowing the wildflowers and smothering them.

Polish war memorial
In 1942, a Wellington bomber crashed during bad weather on Buckden Pike, killing five men. The only survivor followed a set of fox tracks in the snow, which led him down to the village of Cray. He later arranged for the building of the Polish war memorial that stands at the top of Buckden Pike.

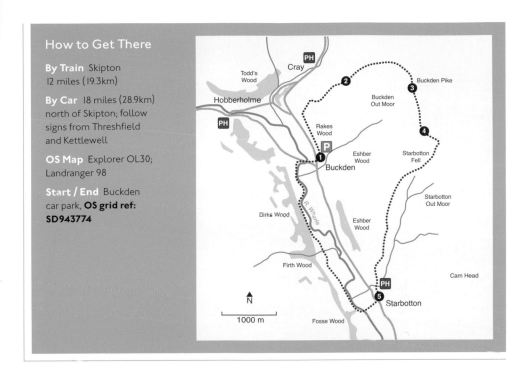

By Train Skipton
12 miles (19.3km)

By Car 18 miles (28.9km)
north of Skipton; follow
signs from Threshfield
and Kettlewell

OS Map Explorer OL30;
Landranger 98

Start / End Buckden
car park, **OS grid ref:**
SD943774

1. Leave the car park through the bridleway gate, heading away from Buckden village. Immediately turn right at the sign to Buckden Lead Mine and take the path to a stile. Cross the stile and continue to a track.

The meadows at Upper Wharfedale are strewn with wildflowers in summer.

Turn right and follow the track to reach the sheep pens on your right. Cross the beck and follow the sign to the lead mine.

2. Above the steep and strenuous section of the Centenary Path, the route approaches a wall then doubles back on itself. Continue following the signs to the lead mine. The orange hue of the Buckden Lead Mine spoil heap can clearly be seen as you approach. The building at the base of the spoil was Buckden High Smelt Mill. Please don't enter the mine: it's a valuable habitat for shade-loving ferns and mosses and provides an important roost site for bats. It can also be very hazardous.

3. At the lead mine, walk around it to the left and head up to a wall above you. Follow the wall up the fellside to the summit ridge and cross a ladder stile at the corner of the wall. Keeping the wall on your right, make your way towards the trig point.

4. Before you reach the trig point you can take a detour to visit the Polish war memorial: turn right instead of left at the summit and follow the path to the memorial.

View across the landscape at Buckden, with mist hanging over the valley and sheep grazing in the lower pastures.

5. Follow the bridleway signs back down into Buckden, taking care on the level section below the summit as this can be quite boggy at times. Look out for field barns along the way. These were used for over-wintering cattle, which were fed on hay stored in the loft above. Dung was forked outside through the muck hole, where it remained until spring and was then spread on the fields. Today, few barns are used this way.

Make the Most of Your Day
Take time to visit the exhibition at Townhead Barn in Buckden, where you can find out how climate change is affecting us. The National Trust also organises a range of activities in Wharfedale, from gill scrambling to geocaching, den-building to photography workshops (see www.nationaltrust.org.uk for details).

Food and Facilities
Stop for a bite after your walk at one of the pubs in Buckden, where you can take advantage of their toilet facilities. Public toilets are also available in Buckden.

73. Fountains Abbey Amble

Set in 800 acres (324ha) of beautiful countryside, Fountains Abbey and Studley Royal are a World Heritage Site that offers visitors an unparalleled opportunity to appreciate the range of England's heritage. This circular walk takes you through the medieval deer park and past a range of architectural and landscape features such as St Mary's Church and the Valley of the Seven Bridges.

Fountains Abbey and
Studley Royal
Ripon
Yorkshire HG4 3DY
01765 608888
fountainsabbey@
nationaltrust.org.uk
www.nationaltrust.org.uk/
fountains-abbey

About this walk
Through beautiful parkland

Points of architectural interest

A chance to spot three
species of deer

Distance 5 miles (8km)

Time 2 hours 30 minutes

Above St Mary's Church, Studley
Royal, North Yorkshire.

Things to see

Deer at Studley
There are three species of deer living on the estate: red, fallow and sika. Red deer are the largest and the stags have impressive pointed antlers. Fallow bucks have flat, palmate antlers and are a tan colour with white spots. Sika deer are the only non-native species in the park and are generally smaller than the red and fallow deer. They also have white spots so it can be difficult to tell them apart from the fallows from a distance.

Studley Royal House and stable block
The house began life as the manor house of the medieval village of Studley Magna, and subsequently

underwent many alterations. In the 1750s, William Aislabie remodelled the façade to create a fashionable Neo-classical front. A century later, the Marquis of Ripon renovated the house again and laid out the formal gardens in the 1860s. Sadly, the house was completely gutted by fire in 1946 and was pulled down. All that remains is the stable block, which is now a privately owned house.

Valley of the Seven Bridges
William Aislabie created this area of the eighteenth-century landscape in a picturesque style, in contrast to his father John's more formal landscape in the Water Gardens. He also created one of the first

Above: One of the seven bridges in the Valley of the Seven Bridges.

Chinese landscape gardens here, though sadly little remains of it.

How to Get There

By Bus Service 36 Harrogate to Ripon, then Ripon Roweller 139 to Fountains Abbey (limited service, see online for details)

By Train Harrogate 12 miles (19.3km)

By Car 4 miles (6.4km) west of Ripon off B6265; 12 miles (19.3km) north of Harrogate off A61

OS Map OS Explorer 298 and 299

Start / End Fountains Abbey visitor centre, **OS grid ref: SE272687**

---

1. Leave the visitor centre and follow the signs for St Mary's Church. Follow the well-defined bridlepath that runs parallel to the main drive until you reach the large gates on your right that give access to St Mary's Church and the deer park. Go through the pedestrian gate and proceed down the roadway, with the church and a stone obelisk on your left. The obelisk was erected in 1815, replacing an earlier wooden version and stone pyramid. It was intended as a monument to John Aislabie, the designer of the eighteenth-century water gardens.

2. Pause a moment to admire St Mary's Church on your left, a masterpiece by the Victorian Gothic architect William Burges. You are now in the deer park. Studley Royal was developed as a hunting ground for deer in the late Middle Ages. Today, the park supports about 550 deer of three different species.

3. Continue down the roadway, noting how the driveway aligns St Mary's Church with the Cathedral in Ripon, a clever piece of landscaping.

4. When you reach a small crossroads, take the left turn and continue along the road, past the large converted stable block on your left. Continue for

about 50 yards (45m) then take the grass track that veers off to the right, passing by a large beech tree on your left.

5. Follow the path down a slight slope and cross the stone bridge at the bottom known as Rough Bridge. Where the track splits into two, take the right-hand path up a slight incline and follow it as it bends to the left and continues east between two lines of trees. At the top of the rise, follow the path as it bends sharply to the right.

6. About 300 yards (275m) down the path there is a gate in the wall on the left; go through the gate and follow the path to Studley Roger village. This path brings you out in the middle of the village onto the road. Turn right and follow the road past the entrance to Fountains Abbey. Continue straight forwards and take the road and track that leads up an incline, keeping the entrance gates on your right.

7. Continue up the rise past a farm and Plumpton Hall on your right. Take the opportunity here to look at the views to your left, which include Ripon Cathedral in the distance.

8. Continue along the path and pass through the Green Man gate. Follow the path as it bears right through a wood. You will see the River Skell on your right.

9. Follow the path as it comes out of the woods and ends in front of a large metal gate that leads to the Valley of the Seven Bridges. Go through the gate heading west and follow the path as it crosses and re-crosses the river over a number of small stone bridges.

10. Look up to your right for the feature marked on the map 'Devil's Chimney'. This curious building originally had four pinnacles, and was a scaled down copy of a classical Roman monument called the Tomb of the Horatii. Its dimensions are deliberately small, creating the impression that it is being viewed from a far greater distance than is actually the case. Continue to follow the path until you reach the lake and, on the far side, the Victorian tea-rooms.

11. From here take the roadway up to the lower car park. Cross the car park and head for a small path at the rear signposted 'St Mary's Church 500yds Visitor Centre 1 mile'. The path rises and goes through trees bending to the right.

12. The path climbs steadily and you will soon see St Mary's Church in front of you. Where the path splits in two, take the left-hand path heading west to the main gates of the deer park. Go through the pedestrian gate and turn sharp left to follow the footpath back to the visitor centre and main car park.

Red deer at Fountains Abbey,

Make the Most of Your Day
There's so much to see at Fountains Abbey and Studley Royal that a day is hardly enough. A visit to the abbey is a must, being the most complete Cistercian abbey remains in the country. Fountains Hall is an elegant mansion dating from the early seventeenth century, and partly built from stone from the ruined abbey. Studley Royal Water Garden was the breathtaking vision of John Aislabie and his son William, who designed one of England's most spectacular Georgian water gardens.

Food and Facilities
You'll be spoiled for choice, with Fountains Restaurant serving hot breakfasts and lunches, and the Studley and Abbey tea-rooms offering light bites, teas, coffee and cakes. Toilets are available at the visitor centre as well as the restaurant.

74. Brimham Rocks Ramble

Brimham Rocks
Summerbridge
Harrogate
North Yorkshire HG3 4DW
01423 780688
brimhamrocks@
nationaltrust.org.uk
www.nationaltrust.org.uk/
brimham-rocks

About this walk
A site of geological interest

Stunning views

Some stiles and stepping stones

A great spot for picking bilberries

Distance 5 miles (8km)

Time 3 hours

Take a ramble through moorland and meadows, taking in the surrounding countryside adjacent to Brimham Rocks, a series of dramatic rock formations in the North Yorkshire landscape. From here you can enjoy the magnificent long-distance views – on a clear sunny day you may even be able to see York Minster.

Things to see

Bilberry picking
Bilberries thrive on the acid soil of the high ground and heathland at Brimham. Look out for their pinkish flowers and cup-shaped petals. You have to be eagle-eyed to spot the tiny fruit. The best time to pick bilberries is from the end of July until the beginning of September; the crop is at its most abundant for about two weeks after the berries have turned dark blue.

Brimham Rocks
The most unusual rock formations have been named after their fantastic shapes – look out for the markers as you explore. Spot the Dancing Bear, the Eagle and the Gorilla, crawl through the Smartie Tube and balance on the Rocking Stones. Then see if you can come up with alternative names for Idol Rock or the Druid's Writing Desk.

Wild-growing cotton grass
In summer months, the fields at point 7 are abundant with wild-growing cotton grass. They make for a great landscape shot with the giant balls of Menwith Hill in the background.

Top: The fantastically shaped rock formations at Brimham Rocks, North Yorkshire.
Above: Wild-growing cotton grass.

How to Get There

By Train Harrogate 11 miles (17.7km)

By Car 11 miles (17.7km) from Harrogate off B6165: 4 miles (6.4km) from Pateley Bridge off B6265

OS Map Explorer 26

Start / End Brimham Rocks car park, **OS grid ref: SE206650**

Map labels:
Warsill
Hare Heads — 9
Brimham Rocks
10 — WC — 8
Summer Wood House — 7
High Woods — P — 1
Brimham Moor
Stepping Stones — 6
Riva Hill — Riva Hill Farm
2
5
Braisty Woods
Fiddler's Green
3
4
N
400 m

---

1. Leave the car park via the main entrance. Turn right along the private road, signposted to Druids' Cave Farm. After about 100 yards (90m) turn left and follow the grassy pathway to the main road. Cross over the road with care and follow the public footpath signposted to Riva Hill. As you approach the National Trust boundary cross over the stile and follow the path passing Riva Hill House farm on your left. Go through the gate and walk about 30 yards (27m) to the rusty gate on the right-hand side.

2. Go through the gate, heading upwards through ferns until you reach the elderflower tree on the crest of the hill. Take a moment to admire the 180-degree vista: looking south you can see Menwith Hill, Knabb's Head wind farm and Harrogate. Follow the path towards the left but heading for the green barns. (Watch out for any livestock in the field – as an alternative route, you can retrace your steps down the hill and take the bridleway along the Nidderdale Way, rejoining the walk at point 4.) When you reach

the stile in the stone wall, go over and through the wooded area, exiting almost immediately. Go over two wooden stiles into the meadow and follow the path, keeping the fence on your right.

3. Cross over the next stile onto the concrete path and continue towards the barn. Turn left at the barn, following the path through the fields towards the gate and stile ahead. Go over the stile and continue along the well-trodden path across the field, keeping the hedgerow on your left. Head for the corner of the field. Cross the wooden stile and turn left along the bridleway (Nidderdale Way). Carry on until you reach the road.

4. Turn left, following the Nidderdale Way, with meadows on either side. At the end of the track turn left and continue along Nidderdale Way through the farmyard, passing between two barns. Take the track down the hill, passing through an avenue of trees. Leave the Nidderdale Way and head towards Park House Warsil Pass through the farmstead.

5. After about 200 yards (180m), take the gate on right through the meadow and go through the gate on the other side. Follow the slim path to the metal gate; pass through this and though another gate. Beckside Farm is on your left-hand side. Continue on the cinder track, bearing right at the end onto the farm driveway. Bear left, following the blue waymark arrow up to and through the houses until you reach the bridleway.

6. Turn left along the bridleway until you reach the cattle grid. Cross the grid and stream and head up the concrete drive. Turn right through the woodland and follow the path for about 300 yards (275m) until you reach a stream. Cross the stream with care via the stepping stones. There is now a steady climb onwards and upwards until you reach a wooden gate that leads you into a meadow. Follow the footpath on the left side.

7. Bear left through the wooden gate, passing through Summer Wood House along its driveway and over the cattle grid. Cross another cattle grid that, at the same time, passes over the National Trust boundary. Continue up the drive to the main road.

8. Cross over the main road onto the National Trust moorland. Bracken-clad paths lead towards the rocky outcrops beyond. Continue on to the top and take the path to the right, which meanders this way and that across the heather and bracken moor, passing the rocky outcrops.

9. Head towards the very large rocks and bear left along the ridge. Head right from the moor towards the large outcrop of rocks, then bear left then right. Beware of the cliff edges as you follow the undulating path, taking in the magnificent views over Nidderdale.

10. Approach a wooded area and emerge to find Brimham Rocks in all their wonderful splendour. You can now return at your leisure down one of the many paths that meander through the rock formations, taking you back to the car park.

Make the Most of Your Day

There's lots to do and discover at Brimham Rocks, from rambling and climbing to photography and bouldering. Children's events include Easter egg trails, family climbing days and llama walks around the rocks. Further afield lies Fountains Abbey and Studley Royal Water Gardens (see walk 73 for more details).

Food and Facilities

There is a refreshment kiosk near the visitor centre, and toilets 600 yards (550m) from the car park.

Left and opposite: Visitors exploring Brimham Rocks in North Yorkshire.

75. To the Top of Roseberry Topping

Roseberry Topping, Cleveland
Newton-under-Roseberry
North Yorkshire TS9 6QR
01723 870423
roseberrytopping@
nationaltrust.org.uk
www.nationaltrust.org.uk/
roseberry-topping

About this walk

Spectacular views

Good for bluebells in spring

Steep sections and
uneven terrain

Walking boots recommended

Distance 2 miles (3.2km)

Time I hour

This short but challenging walk takes you to the summit of Roseberry Topping, one of the most beloved landmarks in the Tees Valley area. Its distinctive shape was caused by the combination of a geological fault and a mining collapse in 1912. You'll find it a fascinating place to explore, for its human and geological history as well as its abundant wildlife.

Above: Roseberry Topping viewed from Little Roseberry, North Yorkshire.

Roseberry Topping rising up above Newton Wood, with a carpet of bluebells in the foreground.

Things to see

Odin's Hill
At the start of the walk, take time to appreciate Roseberry Topping from afar. Its distinctive shape has been a source of awe for mankind for centuries. The Vikings, who first named the hill, believed it was sacred and dedicated it to their god, Odin. In more recent times there has been a long history of mining here. The hill's distinctive profile, partly due to the collapse of an ironstone mine in 1912, earned it the nickname of the Yorkshire Matterhorn.

Inspiring views
As a boy Captain Cook lived at Airey Holme Farm and regularly climbed Roseberry Topping to enjoy the spectacular views across the Cleveland plain and beyond. These adventures are said to have provided the inspiration for him to become an explorer.

The folly
The origins of the folly to the south-west of Roseberry are something of a mystery. Most historians believe it was built as a summer-house where Victorian walkers could rest, rather than a shooting box as the plaque suggests.

How to Get There

By Train Great Ayton
1.5 miles (2.4km)

By Car On A173 between
Guisborough and Great
Ayton

OS Map Landranger 93;
Explorer OL26

Start / End Newton-
under-Roseberry car park,
OS grid ref: NZ570128

1. Follow the tarmac path from the toilet block and turn right up Roseberry Lane.

2. Climb the steps at the end of the lane and enter Newton Wood through the kissing gate. Turn immediately left to follow the bottom edge of the woods. Newton Wood is probably the best example of semi-natural oak woodland in the Cleveland area. There's plenty of wildlife to spot at any time of year, including roe deer and woodpeckers.

3. Turn right to climb the stone path that follows the edge of the woodland. As George Tweddell said in his sonnet of 1870, 'We may roam far and wide before we see, A finer sight than here from Rosebury'.

4. Follow the stone path as it turns left through a gate onto Roseberry Common. The rocks that form Roseberry Topping were laid down during the Jurassic period. Every step you take towards the summit represents around 5,000 years in geological time. Look out for fossils in the rocks as you climb.

5. After enjoying the view from the summit, descend on the stone path on the opposite side of the hill from where you came up.

6. At the fence turn right and continue through a gate to the folly.

7. Continue on the grassy path between the gorse and pass through the gate back into Newton Wood.

8. Turn left, then immediately right, down a steep path through the wood.

9. Continue straight on at the clearing to the path that follows the bottom edge of the wood, back to the gate at the end of Roseberry Lane.

10. Go through the gate and return down the lane to the car park.

Make the Most of Your Day
When you've finished exploring Roseberry Topping, make your way to Ormesby Hall just outside Middlesbrough, an intimate Georgian mansion with a fascinating Victorian kitchen.

Food and Facilities
Refreshments can be found in Newton-under-Roseberry, or at Ormesby. Public toilets are available in the car park at Newton-under-Roseberry.

76. Allen Banks Woodland Walk

Allen Banks
Northumberland
01434 888321
allenbanks@
nationaltrust.org.uk
www.nationaltrust.org.uk/
allen-banks-and-staward-
gorge

About this walk
A relatively flat riverside walk

Bluebells in spring, fungi in autumn

Some narrow sections with steep drops to the side

Distance 2.5 miles (4km)

Time 1 hour

Explore the woods and see what wildlife you can spot on this gentle riverside walk that takes you through the steep-sided valley of the River Allen, a tributary of the south Tyne. Allen Banks is the largest area of ancient woodland in Northumberland and has been here since at least medieval times. This long history has helped make it a fantastic home for flora, fauna and fungi.

Above: Allen Banks, Northumberland.

Things to see

Wildflowers

A carpet of bluebells and ramsons, commonly known as wild garlic, covers the woodland floor in spring and early summer. During warm weather and when crushed the latter has an unmistakably pungent aroma. Many of the plants here are characteristic of ancient woodland and soil types help dictate which species grow where. Woodruff, ramsons and dog's mercury are found on the richer brown earths, while greater woodrush dominates in poorer and drier soils.

Wildlife

This ancient woodland is host to an array of wildlife ranging from common birds to the elusive and rare dormouse. April to July is a great time to see birds – over 70 species have been recorded on the estate, including species in decline such as wood warbler and pied flycatcher. The River Allen provides a feeding ground for heron, goosander, dippers and, more rarely, kingfishers. Other animals include red squirrels, roe deer, bats, badgers and even the occasional otter, plus a world of bugs and insects.

Fungi

Allen Banks is one of the best places in the North East for fungi, with 181 species recorded here. Autumn's the best time to see mushrooms and toadstools. Deathcap, destroying angel and panthercap fungi are deadly poisonous with no known antidote; all can be found in the woodland here. The deathcap is reputed to have been used to murder the Roman emperor Claudius – some say it was added to his favourite mushroom dish by his wife!

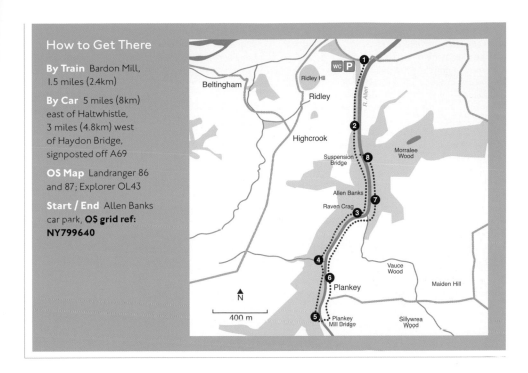

1. Starting at the car park, follow the main footpath into the woodland. Take the lower left-hand fork in the path and the River Allen comes into view.

2. The path drops close to the waterside and the woodland opens out. The river is rocky and fast flowing here, a prime spot for birds such as dipper and grey wagtail.

A female pied flycatcher.

3. At a bend in the river, under Raven Crag, the river becomes deeper and slows to create a flat pool where, on summer evenings, Daubenton's bats skim just above the water, feeding on insects. There are 17 species of bat indigenous to Britain; the National Trust's three-year Bat Life project aims to find out how many species are found at Allen Banks.

4. Decaying fallen trees on the banks above you are part of the life cycle of the woodland. Insects and fungi feed on and break down the rotting timber, returning vital nutrients to the soil. Woodpeckers and other birds then feed on the insects and create nests in the standing deadwood.

5. After crossing the Kingswood Burn, turn left and cross the Plankey Mill Bridge over the River Allen. Walk right, towards the farm buildings, and join the public road which travels left for about 100 yards (90m). Take the track to the left of this road, heading down to a kissing gate near the river and some old ruins.

6. Walk through the meadows along the river bank. Alder trees with lichen-covered stems and branches line the river. Lichens require clean air so are good indicators of pollution-free areas. During the summer, keep a look out for wildflowers such as field pansies, orchids and yellow rattle near the river and in the hay fields here. They make it a great habitat for a wide range of butterflies.

7. Enter the woodland opposite Raven Crag and soon take to a higher-level path.

8. Unfortunately, the suspension bridge has suffered flood damage so to get back carry on past it and follow the footpath alongside the river, leaving the woodland and making your way through two fields. Follow the path under the road bridge and through a gate leading onto the road, then head back across the bridge to the car park.

Make the Most of Your Day

When you've finished exploring this beautiful valley, head north to Hadrian's Wall where you'll discover Housesteads Fort. The wall has 16 permanent bases of which Housesteads is one of the best preserved. Excavations at the fort revealed a turreted curtain wall, three barrack blocks and well-preserved latrines.

Food and Facilities

There's no café on site at Allan Banks so why not pack a hamper and use one of the picnic benches? Alternatively, Housesteads visitor centre is just a stone's throw away. Here, you can buy a variety of refreshments, both hot and cold, as well as some treats for afterwards. Toilets are also available at Housesteads.

Housesteads Fort, one of the 16 permanent bases on Hadrian's Wall.

77. Gibside Family Trail

Gibside
Near Rowlands Gill
Burnopfield
Gateshead
Tyne and Wear NE16 6BG
01207 541820
gibside@nationaltrust.org.uk
www.nationaltrust.org.uk/
gibside

About this walk
Lots of fun for all the family

A walk through beautiful parkland

Suitable any time of the year

Distance 3.5 miles (5.6km)

Time 2 hours to all day

Discover the fun side of Gibside with this action-packed walk through West Woods, taking in the park's top family highlights, including the Strawberry Castle Adventure Play Area, the Low Ropes Challenge, the Nature Playscape and Mini-Gibside Hall. It's all pushchair-accessible and there's plenty of opportunity to spot wildlife along the way.

Things to see

Strawberry Castle
This adventure play area is inspired by a mystery from Gibside's past. It's known that 200 years ago there was a place called Strawberry Castle at Gibside, but no one knows what it was or where it was. Families helped the National Trust to design this adventure play area so, if the original one can't be found, at least children can enjoy this make-believe version.

Low Ropes Challenge
More adventurous kids will love Gibside's low ropes course where they can use their skills to swing, balance, climb and scramble their way from one end to the other without touching the ground. Located in an old quarry near a little stream, this also makes the perfect spot for a picnic off the beaten track.

Den-building
You'll be amazed by what can be constructed from the branches, twigs and leaves that are just lying about on the woodland floor.

With a little help from an adult, kids can construct their own dens and get huge enjoyment sheltering under cover in their own self-built natural palace.

Top: The portico of the Chapel at Gibside, Tyne and Wear.
Above: Den-building in the woods.

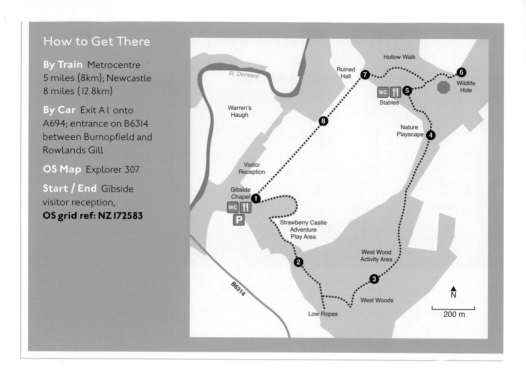

How to Get There

By Train Metrocentre
5 miles (8km); Newcastle
8 miles (12.8km)

By Car Exit A1 onto
A694; entrance on B6314
between Burnopfield and
Rowlands Gill

OS Map Explorer 307

Start / End Gibside
visitor reception,
OS grid ref: NZ 172583

1. Join the pushchair-friendly footpath from visitor reception, around the side of the Sun Dial Garden to the back of Gibside Chapel. Here you can pick up the new trail to Strawberry Castle Adventure Play Area. With Park Fields on your left and woodland on your right, keep a look out for sheep, cows or wild birds.

2. When the kids have had their fill of swings, slides and zip wires, find the new footpath on the far side of the Strawberry Castle Adventure Play Area. It continues to skirt around Park Fields before winding downhill into West Wood. At a crossroads of paths, cross over the main track and take the narrow footpath directly in front of you. After about 100 yards (90m) fork off to the right for the Low Ropes Challenge. The West Woods are a great place to hunt for bugs. Try lifting a fallen log or pile of leaves to see what's hidden beneath.

3. Leave the Low Ropes Challenge by following the little stream-side trail back to the narrow footpath you turned off earlier. Turn right and continue uphill deeper into West Woods. When you reach the main track, turn left and continue until you reach the West Wood activity area in among the trees on your left-hand side. It's the perfect spot to build a den from fallen twigs, branches and leaves.

4. After the kids have completed their den, continue along the main track and after 10 or 15 minutes you'll find the Nature Playscape on your left-hand side. It's well hidden in the undergrowth so listen out carefully for noisy children and rustling leaves. Here kids can practice their balancing and climbing skills on fallen logs and a wooden climbing wall, or squeeze through the tree-trunk forest and much more.

5. After all this exploring, continue downhill from the Nature Playscape to the stables; this large stone building with huge doors is hard to miss. Inside, in the Discovery Room, you'll find the Mini-Gibside Hall, a two-floor Wendy house with a difference, where little ones can imagine life centuries ago. Children can have a go at milking Daisy the cow, too.

6. Leave the stables courtyard the same way you came in through the archway and great double doors. Turn left and continue straight ahead on the main track. Don't take the track that heads downhill to your left. Ignore the second track downhill to your left, but turn off on the third footpath to your left (signposted 'Column to Liberty'). After a short walk, the wildlife hide appears on your left. Try to keep everyone quiet if you pop in so you don't scare away any birds or animals.

7. When you've all finished trying to spot woodland birds, red kites, deer or maybe just sheep, leave the hide and turn right, returning the way you came and on to the main track. Ignore the first track downhill to your right, but take the second track downhill instead of walking back towards the stables. At the bottom of the hill you'll see a big dip called the Hollow Walk on your right. This provides a great opportunity for kids to roll down a hill.

8. After they've had a good roll down the hill and clambered up to the path again, go up the slope onto Gibside's beautiful tree-lined avenue. If you've come prepared, Green Close Field on your right (a large open space with a lump in the middle, just passed the ruined hall) is an ideal spot to fly a kite. If not, follow the avenue back towards the chapel and visitor reception.

Make the Most of Your Day

There's so much to see and do at Gibside you'll have no problem spending a whole day here. Gibside is a Georgian 'grand design' on a spectacular scale. The vision of coal baron George Bowes, the Palladian chapel is an architectural masterpiece, the stable block is a vibrant learning and discovery centre, and the once grand hall is now a dramatic shell.

Food and Facilities

Stop off at the stables for light refreshments in the coffee shop or find time for an ice cream and a cuppa in the Potting Shed café and tea-room, renowned for its homemade scones and soups. Toilets are also available on site.

The Column to Liberty dominates the skyline at Gibside.

78. Around Nelly's Moss Lakes

Cragside
Rothbury
Northumberland NE65 7PX
01669 620333
cragside@nationaltrust.org.uk
www.nationaltrust.org.uk/cragside

About this walk
A charming lakeside ramble
Site of historic significance
Rich in wildlife

Distance 1.5 miles (2.4km)

Time 1 hour

This lovely lakeside walk takes you around Nelly's Moss North and South lakes at Cragside. These lakes supplied water for the turbine that powered the house's lighting system, making Cragside the first house in the world to be lit by hydroelectricity. On your way round look out for the wildlife that inhabits the lakes, or see if you can spot Nelly's ghost!

Things to see

Nelly's Moss
The north and south lakes are named after Nelly, who, according to local legend, was a witch reputed to have been burned at the stake here in the Middle Ages. The truth of Nelly's story is unclear, but she is said to haunt this area at night. Moss is the name given to a wet, boggy area – a very appropriate name as the size of Nelly's Moss South Lake varies so much in size. In winter it can fill the area, lapping at the rocks, but in summer it can shrink to a puddle, revealing the boggy area or moss.

Water birds
Herons can sometimes be seen standing in the shallow water of South Lake, particularly when the water level is low. They stand very still, sometimes using their wings to cast shade, enabling them to see the fish more clearly. Many water birds nest and feed on North Lake, including mallard, coot, tufted duck, goldeneye, pochard and moorhen.

An engineering first
The Victorian engineer Sir William Armstrong was so fascinated by water that his family joked he had water on the brain. Indeed, the success of his manufacturing business was driven by the development of hydraulic lifting gear. In the 1870s Armstrong used the various water courses at Cragside to experiment with creating hydroelectricity, eventually installing a water-driven Siemens dynamo to power the

Top: View along Nelly's Moss South Lake at Cragside, Northumberland.
Above: Male mallard ducks.

electric lamps in the library. This was the first household use of hydroelectricity in the world.

By Train Morpeth 15 miles
(24.1 km)

By Car On B6341, 15 miles
(24.1 km) north-west of
Morpeth off A697

OS Map Landranger 81;
Explorer 325 and OL42

Start / End Crozier car park,
OS grid ref: NU070617

1. Begin your walk by going back to the estate drive and turning right.

2. A little way along the road, just before reaching the bridge, take the stone steps on the left.

3. After walking down the steps, follow the path across some steeply sloping rocks.

4. Follow the path along the lakeside until you come to a small green hut at a junction, where you continue straight on.

5. Carry straight on at the next junction at a boat house. You are now at Nelly's Moss North Lake.

6. Once again, follow the path alongside the lake. Eventually you will come to a small wooden bridge; continue around the lake. The path now leads around the opposite side of North Lake, then down the side of South Lake.

7. Between the two lakes runs a dam, built by Cragside's owner Sir William Armstrong in the nineteenth century. The dam keeps the level of North Lake constant.

8. The path alongside the South Lake is signposted 'Nelly's Moss South Lake' and cuts through the rhododendrons.

9. Follow the path alongside the lake until you come to a small car park and the estate drive. Turn right along the road, taking care to watch for vehicles.

10. The road here passes along another dam. On the right at the roadside is a plant known locally as fairybell.

11. Follow the road over the bridge and back to Crozier car park.

Make the Most of Your Day
While you're here, be sure to visit the house, with its dramatic yet cosy interior and fine examples of Arts and Crafts workmanship.

Food and Facilities
Take a break at the popular tea-room. Toilets are available at the visitor centre and up near the play area.

79. Dunstanburgh Castle Ghost Walk

For a spooky ghost walk in an isolated setting, look no further than the Northumberland coastline, which is dominated by the magnificent ruin of Dunstanburgh Castle. Some believe that the ghost of a sixteenth-century knight still haunts the ruins. Watch out for wading birds such as oystercatcher, dunlin and redshank along the way.

Dunstanburgh Castle
Craster
Northumberland NE66 3TT
01665 576231
dunstanburghcastle@
nationaltrust.org.uk
www.nationaltrust.org.uk/
dunstanburgh-castle

About this walk
Site of historical interest

A lovely coastal walk

Fine views of the
Northumberland coast

Dogs welcome in on a lead at
castle

Distance 3 miles (4.8km)

Time 1 hour 15 minutes

Above: View across the Northumbrian coast to Dunstanburgh Castle in the late afternoon light.

Things to see

Dunstanburgh Castle
Just north of Craster, the ruins of Dunstanburgh Castle stand around 100ft (30m) above the sea on a rocky headland, boldly looking out over the North Sea. The castle is thought to have been a defensive site in the Roman and Dark Ages. The remains you can see today date back to the fourteenth century. The castle fell into disrepair after the Wars of the Roses.

The spooky tale of Sir Guy the Seeker
One stormy night in the sixteenth century, a gallant knight named Sir Guy is said to have taken shelter in the castle. A hideous spectre appeared and told him of a beautiful lady who needed saving. The knight followed the figure to where the maiden lay sleeping and was told to choose between a sword and a horn. Sir Guy blew the horn and suddenly 100 knights in white appeared and charged towards him. When he regained consciousness he was lying beneath the ruins in the gatehouse. He spent the rest of his life searching in vain for the maiden. Some say his harrowing cries can still be heard on stormy evenings!

Embleton Bay
The concrete bunkers on the sand were built during the Second World War. Marram and lyme grass grow on the sand dunes, providing a more stable environment that enables other plants to grow. Look out for colourful wildflowers such as purple bloody crane's-bill along the route.

Dawn breaks over the sands of Embleton Bay, Northumberland.

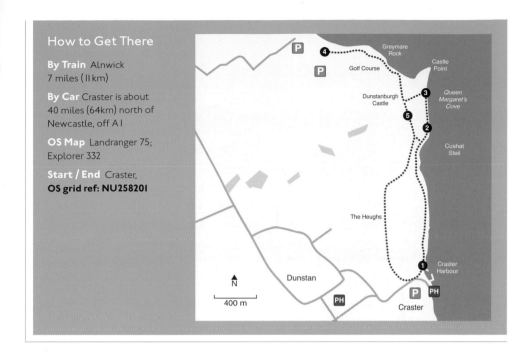

How to Get There

By Train Alnwick
7 miles (11 km)

By Car Craster is about
40 miles (64km) north of
Newcastle, off A1

OS Map Landranger 75;
Explorer 332

Start / End Craster,
OS grid ref: NU258201

1. From Craster, walk north towards Dunstanburgh Castle, passing the harbour. The path takes you through farmland with the rocky shoreline to your right.

2. Soon you reach the castle, where, in summer, roosting swallows swirl overhead and among the ruined chambers and staircases. It's easy to imagine why this atmospheric castle is said to be haunted. If you want to explore further, entrance is free to National Trust and English Heritage members.

3. After edging around the base of the castle, note the peculiar cliff formation to your right. The Greymare Rock was formed by volcanic pressure that folded the limestone. From April to August it is a breeding spot for kittiwake and fulmar.

4. Continuing along the path, you pass a golf course on your left and descend onto the beach. Stroll to the far end of Embleton Bay and cross Embleton Burn as it trickles into the sea. If you haven't already, you may want to take your shoes and socks off and have a paddle here.

5. Return from the beach and head back on the same path towards the castle. Once past the castle, climb up to your right onto a higher-level track back to Craster.

Make the Most of Your Day
Why not go rock-pooling? The rock pools that dot the rocky reefs are full of sea creatures. Look for sea urchins, starfish and other aquatic animals exposed at low tide. The National Trust hosts a wide range of events along the Northumberland coast, from outdoor theatre to whale spotting (check websites for details).

Food and Facilities
Pubs and cafés can be found in Craster, and there are public toilets beside the tourist information centre.

80. Farne Islands Bird Experience

The Farne Islands are one of the natural highlights of the Northumbrian coast. Famed for providing sanctuary to St Cuthbert in the seventh century, Inner Farne is now renowned as a summer haven for nesting seabirds. For a unique wildlife experience, visit between April and July, or explore a more tranquil, historic island after the breeding season has finished.

Inner Farne
Near Seahouses
Northumberland
01665 720651
farneislands@
nationaltrust.org.uk
www.nationaltrust.org.uk/
farne-islands

About this walk
One of Britain's top wildlife experiences

An ideal walk for little legs

Boardwalk slippery when wet

Accessible by boat from Seahouses harbour

Distance 0.5 miles (0.8km)

Time 1 hour

Above: Bird watching on Inner Farne, Northumberland.

Things to see

Breeding seabirds
There can be as many as 50,000 birds on Inner Farne during the breeding season, including three different types of tern, puffin, shag, guillemot, razorbill, fulmar, eider duck and waders such as oystercatcher and ringed plover. They arrive in spring to lay their eggs, hatch their chicks and care for their young, before departing in late summer to spend the rest of the year out in the North Sea or on migratory journeys across Europe and Africa. The Arctic tern travels furthest of all, flying tens of thousands of miles to spend the summer months in the Antarctic, only to fly back again the following year.

Grey seals
The Farne Islands are home to one of the biggest grey seal colonies in the British Isles. The seals have been here for at least 800 years, but were hunted for oil and skins for most of that time. Now they're protected and you can see them peeking out of the water or huddling together lazily on rocks.

Puffins
Puffins can be seen between April and early August. They dig burrows underground where they lay their eggs. You may spot adults, mouths filled with sand eels, but the young stay well hidden to avoid being eaten by gulls.

A lone puffin on the Farne Islands, Northumberland.

How to Get There

By Boat Seahouses harbour to Inner Farne, daily service April to September, weather permitting

By Train Alnmouth 17 miles (27.3km)

By Car Off A1, north of Alnwick; park in car park in Seahouses car park (not National Trust) and take boat

OS Map Landranger 75; Explorer 340

Start / End Island Jetty, **OS grid ref: NU230370**

1. Taking care, step off the boat onto the jetty and climb up the boardwalk. The small stone building on your left is the fish house. It stands on the site of the medieval guesthouse where visiting monks would stay. From April to July this is the first place you meet breeding Arctic terns. They nest near the path and can be very defensive of their eggs or chicks. Expect to be dive-bombed, but don't panic; just slowly wave a hand above your head to discourage them.

2. Visit St Cuthbert's Chapel, see the Pele Tower and check out the information centre while you're here, or go left to start your circuit of the island immediately. Again, this is an Arctic tern nesting zone in early summer and chicks could be dotted around the cobbles, so watch where you step and be sure not to run, or you'll disturb the birds.

3. Look left here, as this is the one spot on Inner Farne where sandwich terns cluster together to breed.

4. Walk up the island to the lighthouse. Before it was built in 1825, a beacon would be lit on top of the Pele Tower to warn off ships. Turn left to the Lighthouse Cliff viewpoint; you can see Dunstanburgh Castle in the distance on a clear day. These are the tallest rock faces on the island and the cliff-tops are home to thousands of breeding guillemot, shag and kittiwake in the summer months.

5. Return to the lighthouse and turn left past the picnic area. There used to be two more cottages here where the lighthouse keepers and their families lived.

6. Follow the boardwalk through an area filled with puffin burrows and take a quick detour left to the Quarry viewpoint. The dramatic outline of Bamburgh Castle can be seen straight ahead of you on the mainland.

7. On your left is a large expanse of rocky foreshore. If there's a large sea swell, you might see the Churn Blowhole spout water up to 90ft (27m) into the air.

Daily boat services carry visitors between the mainland and Inner Farne from spring to late summer.

8. Return to the information centre, passing the monks' old vegetable garden on your left, and await your return boat.

Make the Most of Your Day

There's so much to explore along this fabulous stretch of coast, where the unspoilt coastline boasts quaint fishing villages, deserted beaches with white sands and blue seas, and excellent rock pools. For an extra special experience, visit nearby Lindisfarne, a romantic sixteenth-century castle renovated by Edwardian architect Edwin Lutyens, with an enchanting walled garden by Gertrude Jekyll.

Food and Facilities

Pubs and cafés can be found in Seahouses, and toilet facilities are available on Inner Farne.

Wales

81. Pen y Fan and Corn Du

Pont Ar Daf
Brecon Beacons
Powys
01874 625515
brecon@nationaltrust.org.uk
www.nationaltrust.org.uk/
brecon-beacons-central

About this walk
Spectacular views

Steep climbs

Dogs welcome under close control

Distance 4 miles (6.4km)

Time 2 hours 30 minutes

This strenuous mountain walk on well-made footpaths takes you to the summit of Pen y Fan, southern Britain's highest mountain, and on to Corn Du, the second highest peak in the Brecon Beacons. Rising 2907ft (886m) above sea level, Pen y Fan offers extensive panoramic views of the surrounding countryside, making it well worth the climb.

Above: The footpath between Corn Du and Pen y Fan in the Brecon Beacons National Park.

Things to see

Footpaths in the Brecon Beacons
As you climb uphill towards Bwlch Duwynt look out for the different methods of footpath construction used on the Brecon Beacons. The gullies on the uphill side of the path take the water flowing downhill to suitable crossing points where culverts have been constructed; this keeps most of the water off the footpath and prevents erosion. Some of the footpath has been stone pitched. This method of creating a hardwearing surface predates Roman times, but is costly and very time-consuming.

Pen y Fan and Corn Du
The cairn on the summit of Pen y Fan was a Bronze Age burial chamber. When it was excavated in 1991 a bronze brooch and spearhead were found inside the chamber. The cairn on Corn Du was also a Bronze Age burial chamber. The summit here was once covered in peat and grass. The Neuadd Valley and Reservoir stretch away towards the south.

Legend of Llyn Cwm Llwch
A legend tells the story of an enchanted island invisible from the lakeside, which could only be reached via a door onto a

passageway that opened once a year on May Day. Those who had the courage to pass through the doorway would find themselves in a beautiful garden inhabited by fairies, but they were warned never to take anything from the island. One May Day, a visitor placed a flower in his pocket. When he emerged from the rock the flower vanished and he lost all his senses. Since that day, the legend goes, the door to the island has never opened.

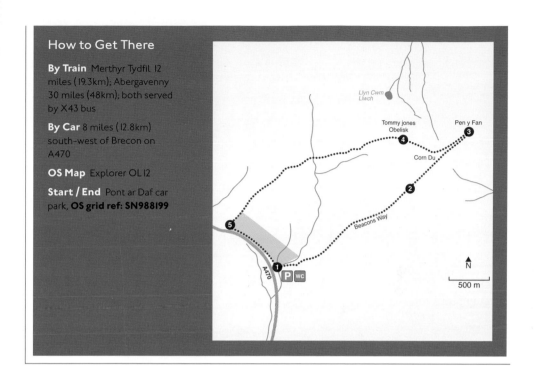

How to Get There

By Train Merthyr Tydfil 12 miles (19.3km); Abergavenny 30 miles (48km); both served by X43 bus

By Car 8 miles (12.8km) south-west of Brecon on A470

OS Map Explorer OL 12

Start / End Pont ar Daf car park, **OS grid ref: SN988199**

At Pen y Fan and Corn Du, special construction methods are used to drain the footpaths and prevent soil erosion.

1. Take the footpath through the woods at the southern end of the car park. Pass through the kissing gate and cross the wooden footbridge over the river. From here, follow the footpath uphill towards Bwlch Duwynt.

2. Once you reach Bwlch Duwynt (which means 'Windy Pass' in Welsh), take the footpath to your left (positioned at about 11 o'clock), which leads across the southern slope of Corn Du. You'll soon reach the saddle between Corn Du and Pen y Fan. From here there are spectacular views to the south, down the Neuadd Valley to the reservoirs above Merthyr Tydfil. Continue along the footpath for the last push to the summit of Pen y Fan.

3. The views from the top are spectacular when weather permits. To the north, the town of Brecon can be seen and on a particularly good day the summit of Cadair Idris is just visible. Looking east you can just make out the Sugar Loaf in the far distance, and to the south-west the Bristol Channel at Porthcawl can be seen on a bright day. Once you've finished taking in

Spectacular views can be had from the saddle between Corn Du and Pen y Fan.

the views, retrace your steps to the saddle in between Pen y Fan and Corn Du, and make your way up the pitched footpath to the summit plateau of Corn Du.

4. Looking north-west from here into the Cwm Llwch valley is Llyn Cwm Llwch (Llyn meaning 'lake'). On the ridge line you'll see the Tommy Jones Obelisk, a memorial to a five-year-old boy who died after getting lost on the Beacons in 1900. Leave Corn Du from the northern end and climb down the steep section to reach the pitched path below, which heads towards the obelisk. After about 300 yards (275m) the path divides; take the permissive path to the left that heads down towards the stream, Blaen Taf Fawr. Once across the stream, head upwards following the path to the gate on the Gyrn. Y Gyrn has a considerable amount of heather on it due to grazing by sheep and ponies, which helps to promote a healthy habitat for upland birds such as red grouse.

5. Keep following the path and descend down to the A470 at Storey Arms. The old coach road is still visible on the right as you reach the gate. Turn left and follow the road back to Pont ar Daf car park.

Make the Most of Your Day

Take time out to visit the Henrhyd Falls, southern Britain's highest waterfall, tucked away on the western edge of the Brecon Beacons. Plunging 90ft (27m) into a wooded gorge, Henrhyd waterfall is a spectacular sight and the surrounding Graigllech Woods are a haven for wildlife. The falls occur on a geological fault on the river Nant Llech and have retreated up the valley by 165ft (50m) since the last Ice Age.

Food and Facilities

Refreshment vans can be found at Storey Arms and at Pont ar Daf most weekends and in many lay-bys on the A470. Toilets are available at Pont ar Daf car park (not National Trust).

82. Henrhyd Falls Woodland Walk

Henrhyd Falls
Near Coelbren
Brecon Beacons
01874 625515
brecon@
nationaltrust.org.uk
www.nationaltrust.org.uk/
brecon-beacons-central

About this walk
Visit to the Brecon Beacons'
highest waterfall

Can be wet and uneven

Some steps and steep drops
to the side

Distance 3.5 miles (5.6km)

Time 2 hours 30 minutes

This walk takes you to the spectacular Henrhyd Falls, the highest waterfall in South Wales. From here, you go down the Nant Llech valley, passing the site of a landslide and a disused watermill. Along the way, look out for woodland birds such as woodpeckers, tree creepers, warblers and wrens. Dippers and wagtails can also be seen hunting for insects along the river.

Things to see

Henrhyd Falls
At 90 feet (27m), Henrhyd Falls are the highest waterfall in the Brecon Beacons National Park. The falls occur on a geological fault on the River Nant Llech and have retreated up the valley by up to 165ft (50m) since the last Ice Age. When the river is in full spate, the spray from the waterfall travels over 300ft (91m) down the valley. Trout can sometimes be seen trying to jump the smaller, lower falls at Henrhyd.

Woodland wildlife
The heavily wooded gorge where Henrhyd Falls tumbles down into the Nant Llech is a haven for water-loving wildlife. Graigllech Wood, which surrounds the Nant Llech and Henrhyd Falls, is a broadleaved semi-natural woodland rich in locally rare and scarce ferns and a variety of mosses and liverworts, including species that are nationally scarce and threatened in Europe.

River Tawe
The River Tawe rises in the Black Mountains to the north and travels 30 miles (48km) down the Swansea Valley to the coast at Swansea, where it flows into the Bristol Channel. The Nant Llech is just one of its tributaries – the main ones are the Afon Twrch and the Upper and Lower Clydach rivers.

Top and above: Views of Henrhyd Falls in Powys.

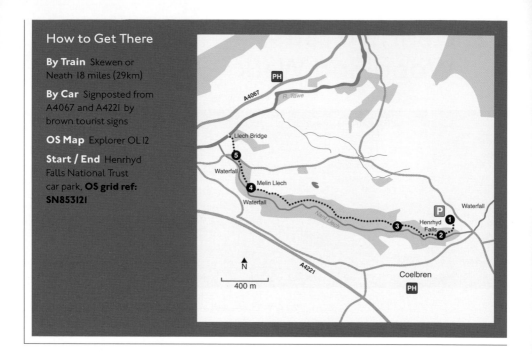

How to Get There

By Train Skewen or Neath 18 miles (29km)

By Car Signposted from A4067 and A4221 by brown tourist signs

OS Map Explorer OL 12

Start / End Henrhyd Falls National Trust car park, **OS grid ref: SN853121**

1. Start your walk from the National Trust car park and pass through two gates, following the footpath down the slope to a track junction at the bottom. Turn left and cross the wooden bridge, walking up the staircase to the footpath at the top. This bridge and staircase was built in 2001 by National Trust staff and volunteers following a landslide. Continue along the footpath to the waterfall. Take care here as the spray from the falls can make the ground slippery. Once you've taken time to enjoy the spectacular waterfall, retrace your steps back across the bridge to the track junction.

2. Go straight ahead, following the footpath with the Nant Llech on your left-hand side. The trees that cling to the steep sides of the valley are mainly sessile oak and ash, although you can also find small-leafed lime, alder and wych elm. Keep following the footpath and just after you cross a boardwalk the smaller waterfall can be seen on your left.

3. Keep following the footpath until you pass through a gate that marks the end of National Trust land. Then cross a small bridge and continue to follow the path down the valley. After about 15 minutes, you'll reach the site of a large landslide were the path narrows and negotiates its way through the debris.

4. Continue along this path until you reach the site of the disused watermill – the Melin Llech. (Please don't enter the buildings as they're private property.) From Melin Llech, don't cross the bridge on the left but follow the track uphill for about 25 yards (23m) where you join the footpath on your left. Continue along the path to a kissing gate and minor road; cross the road and turn right to another kissing gate on your left. Follow the path for another two minutes and the River Tawe will come into view. The River Tawe flows all the way to Swansea. You have now reached the mid-way point of the walk.

5. Return to the minor road by the path you've just followed. Once at the minor road, you can either follow the path that brought you down the Nant Llech back to the car park, or return along the minor roads via Coelbren.

Make the Most of Your Day

A trip to Aberdulais Tin Works and Waterfall, near Neath, makes for a fascinating afternoon. Here you can trace the 400-year history of tin mining in the area and explore industrial features such as the water wheel, chimney stack, tramway bridge and tinning house. An interactive exhibition at the Old Stables tells the story of tinplate and the lives of the men, women and children who worked here in Victorian times.

Food and Facilities

Seek out the local pubs in and around Coelbren for refreshments and toilet facilities. If you make it to Aberdulais, the Old School House Café offers a mouthwatering selection of light bites and beverages.

The waterwheel at Aberdulais Tin Works, Neath and Port Talbot.

83. Rhossili: Serpents, Seascapes and Shipwrecks

Rhossili
Swansea
Glamorgan
01792 390707
rhossili.shop
@nationaltrust.org.uk
www.nationaltrust.org.uk/
rhossili-and-south-gower-
coast

About this walk
Stunning views across an
iconic beach

A disabled access track

Dogs welcome under close
control around livestock

Distance 2 miles (3.2km)

Time 1 hour

Rhossili Bay on the Gower Peninsula is one of the gems of the Welsh coastline. This lovely walk along iconic cliffs affords breathtaking views over the golden sands of Rhossili to the rugged limestone rocks of the Worm's Head. The area is rich in flora and fauna, so look out for the red legs and beak of the local chough and maybe even a grey seal or two.

Above: View across Rhossili Bay on the Gower Peninsula, Glamorgan.

Things to see

Rhossili Beach
With its golden sands stretching for 3 miles (4.8km) along the coastline, Rhossili is one of the best beaches in Wales and a haven for people who want to enjoy the coast – walking, surfing, swimming or just building sandcastles. Visible on the beach at low tide are the remains of the *Helvetia*, a ship wrecked in 1887.

Worm's Head
The Worm's Head is a tidal island, accessible for approximately two half-hour periods either side of low tide. The coastguard lookout has tide tables available and will offer advice as to the best time to cross. When the tide is out, the adventurous can cross the rocky causeway to the island, where grey seals can be seen lazing on the rocks below.

Serpents
The name Worm's Head comes from the Nordic word 'wurm', which means 'serpent' or 'dragon'.

The Worm's Head.

How to Get There

By Train Swansea I
8.5 miles (29.7 km)

By Car A4118 and B4247
from Swansea (note: the
car park is privately owned
and a fee will be charged)

OS Map Landranger 159

Start / End Rhossili,
OS grid ref: SS413881

1. With your back to the bus stop, turn right and walk along the road, continuing between the car park and the Worm's Head Hotel. The National Trust shop is a little further on your left.

2. The shop is in one of the former coastguard cottages. The powerful tides and shifting sands at Rhossili have caused many shipwrecks.

3. Continue to follow the route through the gateway on the surfaced track.

4. To the right of the path there is a series of mounds. These are the remains of an Iron Age fort. The magnificent views from here meant the inhabitants of the fort could see their enemies for miles around.

5. As you continue along the surfaced track you will see fields and hedge banks that formed part of a medieval open-field strip system. The Normans introduced this system of farming in the twelfth century.

6. Where the surfaced track bears sharp left, walk straight on, following a wide grass path towards the coastguard lookout where you will have a spectacular view of the Worm's Head.

7. The coastguard lookout was built in Victorian times and is now manned by volunteers.

8. Once you have reached the coastguard lookout and admired the view, retrace your steps to take you back to your starting point.

Make the Most of Your Day
Don't forget to visit the exhibition room above the National Trust shop, where you'll find information about the Gower Peninsula. The National Trust also holds wildlife event days, guided walks, green events and national beach events at Rhossili, so check online before you set out to see what's on.

Food and Facilities
There is a pub opposite the car park, and a café in the village (neither National Trust). Toilets are located between the car park and the Trust shop.

84. Cwmdu Wildflower Meadow Walk

Take a wander through the flower-rich meadows around the picturesque village of Cwmdu in Carmarthenshire, where in mid-summer you'll see orchids, ox-eye daisies, bright-eyes and yellow rattle. The abundance of these flowers means the meadows are alive with insects, too. Look out in particular for the pretty ringlet butterfly that flourishes here.

Cwmdu
Near Llandeilo
Carmarthenshire SA19 6RT
01558 824512
dinefwr@nationaltrust.org.uk
www.nationaltrust.org.uk/
dinefwr

About this walk
Perfect summer walk for wildflower enthusiasts

Some stiles

Dogs welcome on a lead around livestock

Distance 1 mile (1.6km)

Time 30 minutes

Above: Rhyderonnen Terrace in Cwmdu, Carmarthenshire.

Things to see

Yellow rattle, a classic meadow wildflower.

Rhyderonnen Terrace
Rhyderonnen Terrace in the village of Cwmdu was created in the early 1800s when the cottages, with their 'blind' windows, were built onto the existing inn and shop. Comprising a pub, post office, chapel and vestry, it represents a rural Welsh village of the past. The terrace is a National Trust property and contains a holiday cottage.

Wildflower hay meadows
The hay fields have escaped the modern agricultural 'improvements' of deep ploughing, re-seeding, chemical fertilisers and herbicide treatments. If you look out over to the farmland in the distance you'll see the marked difference in the landscape between conservation and intensive agriculture.

The old school
Now the chapel vestry, this building probably started life as a cottage. In the mid-1800s it was extended and used as the village school until 1908, when a purpose-built school was added to the hamlet.

How to Get There

By Train Llandeilo
6 miles (9.6km)

By Car Take B4302 from
Llandeilo, turning left at
Halfway and following
lane into village

OS Map Explorer 186

Start / End Cwmdu
Inn car park, **OS grid ref:
SN263230**

N

100 m

1. Walk along the lane between Rhyderonnen Terrace and the pub garden. The box hedge is over 200 years old. Just past the chapel, turn right up the track towards Gwaunforfydd and follow the narrow path to the right of the yard. Go through the gate at the end and follow the fence line on to the stile behind the stone building. Cross the stile into the field. Follow the ridge up the field and listen for the sound of water. One of the many streams that criss-cross the area flows in a gulley down the steep bank, through the beech trees.

2. Go through the field gate into the first of the two wildflower meadows.

3. Carry on up the field into the second meadow. It's worth stopping for a while to see how many different types of flowers and insects you can spot. Whorled caraway, the flower emblem of Carmarthenshire, grows here, along with several varieties of orchid.

Look out for the red 'lollipops' of great burnet. It flowers from June to September in meadows such as these that have been undisturbed for years.

4. Cross over the stile, leaving the unimproved pasture. You'll see few flowers in this field, though bluebells and primroses grow under the hedges in spring. Follow the hedge line to the gate and turn right down the farm track. The hedges on either side are quite old and varied. A different range of flowers grows here, from primroses and violets in the spring to knapweed and meadowsweet in late summer.

5. As you follow the track to the cattle grid look behind you at the string of farmsteads on the hillside. The field boundaries here have hardly changed for over the last 100 years. Go through the gate to the right of the cattle grid and walk up the track to rejoin the lane. Turn right and go back down the hill to the car park, passing the old school on your right.

The Dolaucothi Gold Mines, near Llanwrda, give a fascinating insight into an ancient industry.

Make the Most of Your Day

Head south to check out Paxton's Tower, a neo-Gothic folly erected in honour of Lord Nelson, situated on a hilltop near Llanarthney in the Towy Valley (no access or facilities on site). Or, if you've got time, head 16 miles (25.7 km) north to the Dolaucothi Gold Mines, where you can try your hand at gold panning, experience the frustrations of searching for gold or take an underground tour. The only Roman gold mines in Britain, they were abandoned for hundreds of years after the Romans left. Mining resumed in the nineteenth century, however, finally ending in 1938.

Food and Facilities

For refreshments and toilet facilities, visit the Cwmdu Inn, run by the community with support from the National Trust. A tea-room and pub can be found at Dolaucothi.

85. Discovering Stackpole's Wildlife

Stackpole
Pembrokeshire
SA71 5DQ
01646 661359
stackpole@
nationaltrust.org.uk
www.nationaltrust.org.uk/
stackpole

About this walk
Through a beautiful designed landscape

Great for spotting dragonflies and otters

Long flights of steps

Dogs welcome on a lead

Distance 6 miles (9.6km)

Time 4 hours

This walk takes in some of the finest wildlife habitats in Pembrokeshire: grassy limestone cliffs with breeding seabirds, sandy beaches, dunes and freshwater lakes. The famous Bosherston Lakes were created 200 years ago to provide a backdrop to Stackpole Court. They have evolved into a wildlife haven famous for otters, water birds and dragonflies.

Things to see

Stackpole
Stackpole is a designed landscape, created by the Cawdor family as a backdrop to their grand house, Stackpole Court, which was demolished in 1963. Between 1780 and 1860 the family planted many thousands of trees and created the Bosherston Lakes. The house may be gone but thankfully the landscape still survives.

Stackpole Head
The headland and arch reached after point 3 of the walk mark the most spectacular section of the coastline. The ledges are packed with guillemots in early summer. One day the arch will collapse into the sea, leaving an offshore stack.

Bosherston lily ponds
These shallow lakes are famous for their water lilies in summer, but are also important for their beds of rare stonewort below the surface. An impressive 24 species of dragonfly have been recorded at Stackpole. These man-made lakes were created as part of Stackpole Court's designed landscape.

Top: Barafundle Beach, Stackpole, Pembrokeshire.
Above: Bosherton lily ponds.

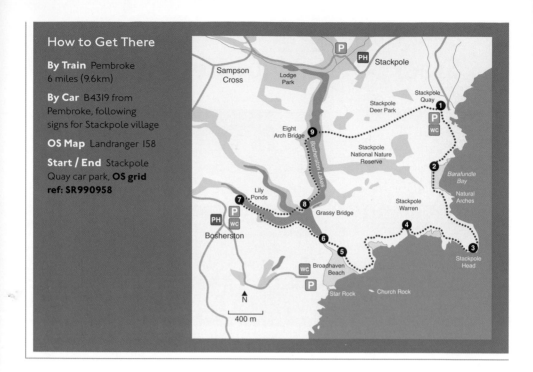

How to Get There

By Train Pembroke
6 miles (9.6km)

By Car B4319 from
Pembroke, following
signs for Stackpole village

OS Map Landranger 158

Start / End Stackpole
Quay car park, **OS grid
ref: SR990958**

Sampson
Cross

Lodge
Park

PH Stackpole

Stackpole
Quay

Stackpole
Deer Park

Eight
Arch Bridge

Stackpole
National Nature
Reserve

Bosherston Lakes

Barafundle
Bay

Natural
Arches

Lily
Ponds

Stackpole
Warren

Grassy Bridge

PH

Bosherston

Broadhaven
Beach

Star Rock

Church Rock

Stackpole
Head

N
400 m

1. From Stackpole Quay car park, follow the coastal path to Barafundle Beach. Pause at the top of the steps to look down on Stackpole Quay, and at the change from limestone to old red sandstone to your left.

2. When you reach Barafundle, go down the steps to the sands. Cross the beach and climb the steps through the woodland on the far side.

3. Follow the coastal path towards Stackpole Head, pausing on your way to admire Lattice Windows, the natural stone arches below you. On Stackpole Head in spring and summer look for breeding seabirds on the ledges.

4. Continue along the coastal path, with the expanse of Stackpole Warrens grassland on your right. In spring and summer this is rich in wildflowers and butterflies.

5. Several possible routes take you down to the shore of the Bosherston Lakes. Aim for the lake outlet at the back of Broadhaven Beach. The narrow fringing reed-

bed is a great place for watching breeding birds in the summer and bitterns and water rails in winter.

6. Cross the tiny stone bridge over the spillway and follow the Western Arm path towards Bosherston.

7. Cross the Bosherston Causeway, climb over the limestone bluff and cross the Central Causeway. These are the famous lily ponds – look for water lilies from June to September. Follow the path down to the Grassy Bridge.

8. Don't cross the Grassy Bridge, but turn left and follow the Eastern Arm footpath up to the Eight Arch Bridge. The bridge was built in 1797 to connect Stackpole Court to Stackpole Quay. You can see the terrace of the former court further up the lake – walk there if you've time. The bridge is the best place to look for otters.

9. Cross the Eight Arch Bridge and follow the deer park track back to Stackpole Quay.

The cliffs at Stackpole Head, where the different strata in the rocks are clearly visible.

Make the Most of Your Day

There's so much to see and do at Stackpole, from bird watching, fishing and climbing to kayaking, diving and snorkelling. The National Trust also has an exciting calendar of events, including concerts and plays, and dawn chorus walks, so before you come check out the website to see what's on.

Food and Facilities

Finish your walk at the Boathouse tea-room for some traditional Pembrokeshire fayre. Or, if you're looking for a quick snack, then the courtyard kiosk serves local Pembrokeshire pasties, ice creams, tea, coffee and cold drinks. Toilets can be found at the Stackpole Quay car park and the Bosherston Lily Ponds car park.

86. Lawrenny Wildlife Walk

Upstream from the busy port of Milford Haven lies a world of drowned wooded valleys with a wide expanse of salt-marshes and mudflats. This scenic circular walk takes you through the steep-sided ancient oak woodland of Lawrenny, overlooking the Daugleddau Estuary, and along the tidal creeks of Garron Pill and the River Cresswell.

Lawrenny
Pembrokeshire
01437 720385
st.davids@
nationaltrust.org.uk
www.nationaltrust.org.uk/
cleddau-woodlands

About this walk

A great walk in any season

Migrant ospreys in autumn

Some stiles

Dogs welcome under close control

Distance 3 miles (4.8km)

Time 1 hour 45 minutes

Above: Lawrenny Wood is a haven for tawny owls.

Things to see

Lawrenny Wood
Lawrenny Wood is one of the last fragments of ancient oak woodland to survive in Pembrokeshire. Perched on a bank overlooking the River Cleddau and the Daugleddau Estuary, the stunted and gnarled oak trees occupy land that was always too steep and rocky to farm. The ancient trees provide plentiful nest sites for hole-nesting birds, from redstarts and blue tits to jackdaws and tawny owls. The waters of the Daugleddau Estuary may be seen far below you through the gaps in the trees.

Garron Pill birdlife
Garron Pill is a tidal creek notable for its huge numbers of autumn migrants and wintering wildfowl. Look out for wigeon, greenshank, curlew and little egret.

Woodland and salt-marsh
The National Trust woodland and salt-marsh at West Williamston may be seen from point 7 on the map, across the Cresswell River. Limestone was formerly quarried from the tidal channels here. The estuary is rich in wildfowl and shorebirds and in autumn you may even glimpse the occasional migrant osprey hunting for grey mullet.

A little egret.

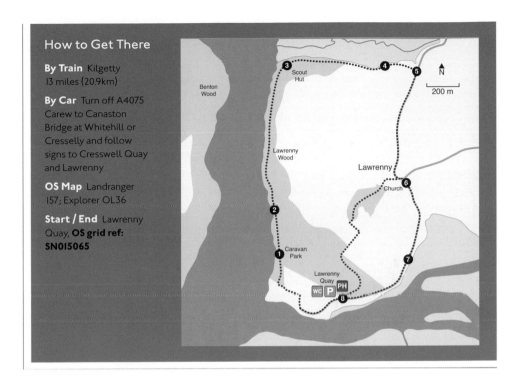

How to Get There

By Train Kilgetty
13 miles (20.9km)

By Car Turn off A4075
Carew to Canaston
Bridge at Whitehill or
Cresselly and follow
signs to Cresswell Quay
and Lawrenny

OS Map Landranger
157; Explorer OL36

Start / End Lawrenny
Quay, **OS grid ref:**
SN015065

Benton
Wood

3 Scout
Hut

4

5

N

200 m

Lawrenny
Wood

Lawrenny

6
Church

2

1 Caravan
Park

Lawrenny
Quay

WC P PH

8

7

1. From Lawrenny Quay turn left, passing the Quayside tea-room on your left. Follow footpath signs through the boatyard and into the trees, passing the caravan site on your right. Cross a National Trust stile into the ancient woodland. The path threads through the gnarled oak trees, providing glimpses down to the estuary below.

2. In spring, see if you can spot or hear the redstart, a bird that breeds in old oak woodlands. A few small, scattered wild service trees grow in the shrub layer below the path, a good indication that this is ancient woodland.

3. The path swings to the right, passing a scout hut. The point at the corner of the wood is a good place to scan the mudflats opposite. The village of Llangwm can be seen across the river to the north-west.

4. After about 500 yards (460m) the path descends to the shore of Garron Pill and continues along the high-tide line. Ancient oak trees, their roots partly

undercut by the tide, overhang the shore. At low tide the deep channels in the mud are used by feeding shorebirds.

5. Joining the road, walk uphill towards Lawrenny village. Pass a youth hostel on your right before descending to the centre of the village and the church.

6. Bear right through the village to rejoin the road to Lawrenny Quay. For an alternative route, take the signposted footpath across the field below the church and site of Lawrenny Castle. Beyond the castle site (with fine views across the estuary) the path enters National Trust woods and descends to the road near the hotel.

7. With woodland either side of the road once more – now mixed broadleaf – return to Lawrenny Quay.

8. On the way, look across the mudflats (or water, depending on the state of the tide) to West Williamston in the east, where a system of narrow rocky creeks gives way to salt-marsh and mudflats. Look out for ducks and waders here.

Make the Most of Your Day

When you've had your fill of bird watching, make your way to nearby Tenby where you can visit the Tudor Merchant's House and imagine what life was like for a successful merchant and his family 500 years ago. This unaltered three-storey building has been furnished with exquisitely carved replicas and brightly coloured wall hangings to re-create the atmosphere of an early way of life.

Food and Facilities

The award-winning Quayside tea-room at Lawrenny has an idyllic waterside setting and serves fine local Pembrokeshire produce, including wild mushrooms, lobster and crab (not National Trust). Toilets are available for customers only. Public toilets can be found at Tenby and Pembroke Dock.

The Tudor Merchant's House at Tenby gives a good idea of what life was like 500 years ago.

87. Marloes Peninsula Ramble

Marloes
Haverfordwest
Pembrokeshire SA62
01437 720385
marloesands@
nationaltrust.org.uk
www.nationaltrust.org.uk/
marloes-peninsula

About this walk
Stunning coastal views
Site of archaeological interest
Some gradients and steps

Distance 5 miles (8km)

Time 2 hours

Above: View across Marloes Sands in
Pembrokeshire.

Explore the very edge of Pembrokeshire with this heathland walk along the beautiful Marloes Peninsula. You'll be rewarded with amazing views over the Pembrokeshire coast and discover a landscape teeming with wildlife, including seals, seabirds and porpoises. Look out for the remains of an Iron Age coastal fort along the way.

Things to see

Birdlife
The peninsula is a great place for spotting seabirds such as puffins and gannets. Guillemots, puffins and razorbills breed in huge colonies on the island of Skomer, and Grassholm is one of the largest gannetries in the world. Wooltack Point is a good vantage point for watching seabirds fishing during the spring and summer. This area is also a very popular breeding ground for the distinctive chough (with its red legs and beak), which can be seen all year round.

Seals and porpoises
About 50 Atlantic grey seal pups are born each year on the beaches around the peninsula, making the cliffs above the beaches excellent for cliff-top seal watching. Seal pups can be spotted on the small beaches at the west end of the deer park in late summer, and Jack Sound is a popular haunt for porpoises.

Managing the heathland
Look out for Welsh mountain ponies in the deer park. Their grazing is essential for keeping the coastal heathland vegetation in good order. Heathland plants, such as heather and gorse, need nutrient-poor acidic soils to grow, but modern farming practices have increased soil fertility by applying lime, manure and fertiliser. Trehill Farm aims to provide more favourable conditions for heathland plants by stripping the topsoil and adding sulphur to speed up the re-acidification process.

Guillemots gather on a cliff-top.

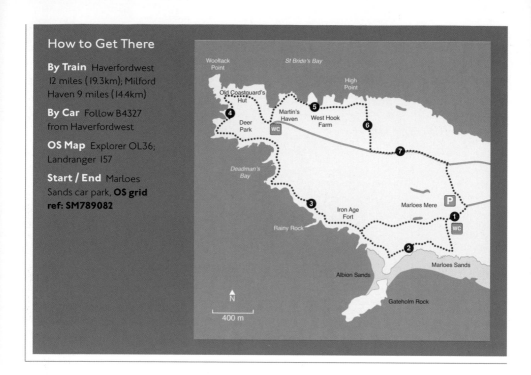

How to Get There

By Train Haverfordwest
12 miles (19.3km); Milford
Haven 9 miles (14.4km)

By Car Follow B4327
from Haverfordwest

OS Map Explorer OL36;
Landranger 157

Start / End Marloes
Sands car park, **OS grid
ref: SM789082**

1. From the south end of Marloes Sands car park turn right by the emergency phone, following signs to the YHA youth hostel and toilets. A short distance past the toilets, take a path to the left through a self-closing gate signposted to the beach. At the next self-closing gate the islands of Skokholm and Gateholm come into view.

2. On reaching the coastal path you'll see Marloes Sands to your left. Turn right and continue towards Gateholm Island. As you come level with Gateholm, Skokholm is ahead of you with Skomer coming into view on the right. Just before the earth ramparts of the Iron Age coastal fort, a fingerpost points back towards Marloes Mere and the youth hostel; this makes an alternative short walk of 1.8 miles (2.9km). The fort marked on the map has long since been lost to the sea, but the earth ramparts that protected people from land attacks can still be seen along this walk.

3. Continue along the coastal path and through the Iron Age fort, enjoying the dramatic sedimentary rock formations. Skomer Island and Midland Isle gradually come into view. Grassholm, white with gannets in summer, can be seen on the horizon from the Iron Age fort.

4. At a footbridge, shortly before a white cottage, take the left fork towards more Iron Age ramparts and follow the path round the coastline of the deer park (so-named after a failed attempt to establish a deer park here at the turn of the twentieth century). The treacherous waters of Jack Sound lie between the deer park and Midland Isle, while Wooltack Point offers spectacular views across St Bride's Bay. There are wonderful panoramic views from the former coastguard hut, which is now used by the National Coastwatch Institute. Take time to explore the deer park and, when you're ready, leave by the path down through the ramparts and the gate.

5. Turn left towards Martin's Haven and the Skomer embarkation point. Just before the beach follow the coastal path right and up the steps. The path continues east, with St Bride's Bay to the left and West Hook Farm to the right. Enjoy the magnificent views across St Bride's Bay towards Newgale, the Solva Coast, St David's Peninsula and Ramsey Island.

A cliff-top view at Marloes Peninsula looking towards the deer park.

6. After just over a mile (1.6km), leave the coastal path, turning right through a self-closing gate and past a West Hook Farm National Trust omega sign, then cross three fields to the road.

7. Turn left and walk along the road past Trehill Farm. Just over 400 yards (365m) past the farm, turn right by two semi-detached cottages and down the track leading back to the car park. (Alternatively, about 100 yards (90m) past the turning, a track to the right leads to the hides overlooking Marloes Mere.)

Make the Most of Your Day

Take time to explore Marloes Mere, a wetland well known to bird watchers for its rich birdlife. The track runs along the south side of the mere and there are two hides. The area is important for its breeding, migrant and wintering birds. Look out for ducks, migrant songbirds, and marsh and hen harriers.

Food and Facilities

Refreshments and public toilets are available at Haverfordwest. Or visit nearby Marloes village where you'll find a pub and café.

88. Exploring St David's Head

Explore Pembrokeshire's most spectacular coastal headland, situated only a couple of miles north-west of Wales' smallest city, St David's. Look out across an island-dotted seascape, set against the steep backdrop of Carn Llidi, and explore prehistoric monuments and a rich array of coastal wildlife on this rugged circular walk.

St David's Head
Whitesands
Near St David's
Pembrokeshire
01437 720385
st.davids@
nationaltrust.org.uk
www.nationaltrust.org.uk/
st-davids-peninsula

About this walk
Fabulous coastal views

Great for watching gannets
dive-bombing into the sea

Site of archaeological interest

Some rocky area, slopes and
steps

Distance 3.75 miles (6km)

Time I hour 30 minutes

Above: View towards St David's Head and Carn Llidi on the Pembrokeshire coast.

Things to see

Coastal heath
Heather and gorse turn St David's Head a bright shade of purple and gold in late summer. They also provide a home for butterflies, moths and beetles, plus birds such as the stonechat and linnet. Up to 50 Welsh mountain ponies graze St David's Head. They keep the vegetation open and maintain the right conditions for the coastal heath plants like heather, gorse and the rare hairy greenweed to thrive.

Cliff-top birds
A range of birds breed on the cliffs at St David's Head each summer, including peregrine falcon, raven, swift and chough. St David's Head is about 15 miles (24.1 km) from Grassholm, one of the largest gannetries in the world, where there are about 39,000 breeding pairs of gannets. You can often see gannets plunging dramatically into the sea off St David's Head as they feed on mackerel.

Coetan Arthur
Coetan Arthur is a Neolithic burial chamber dating from about 4000BC. It has a huge capstone almost 20ft (6m) wide, supported by a single side stone over 3ft (0.9m) tall, and was almost certainly built this way, mimicking the shape of Carn Llidi behind it. This coastline has a rich prehistoric past. There are also remains of ancient field patterns, enclosures and defensive banks dotted all around.

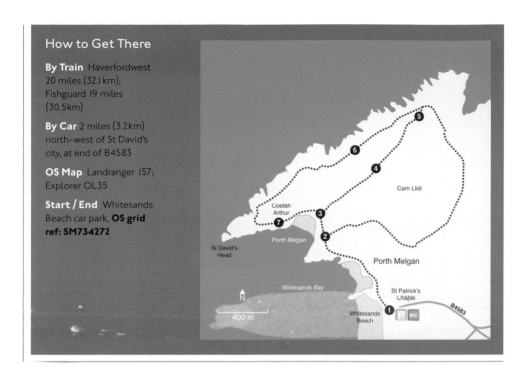

1. From Whitesands Beach car park, go through a gap in the wall on passing the site of St Patrick's Chapel. Climb a sandy slope up onto the cliff path and, after about half a mile (0.8km), you reach a kissing gate and National Trust sign. Continue to the crest of the hill.

St David's Head, Pembrokeshire.

2. From here you can see the burial chamber Coetan Arthur silhouetted against the sky. St David's Head is forged of very old volcanic rock, some of it dating back almost 500 million years. This geology is best represented by Carn Llidi, the towering jagged outcrop, or tor, and in the rocky islands of Ramsey, Bishops and Clerks several miles out to sea. The main walking route follows the coast, descending into the valley ahead via broad steps to a spring above the tiny cove of Porth Melgan. Alternatively, you can branch right and head gently uphill round the back of Carn Llidi with fine views to the east, rejoining the route at point 5 on the map.

3. If you stuck to the coastline, cross the stream by a bridge and turn right to walk up this valley. This area can be slippery and muddy in winter.

4. To your right is a marshy area with the typical 'dinosaur egg' shapes of purple moor-grass or 'rhos pasture', green in summer and earthy coloured in winter. Higher up, on the flanks of Carn Llidi, you can see ancient field patterns. Look out for birds such as stonechat, meadow pipit and skylark in clumps of reed-bed and willow. The rare Dartford warbler has also been seen in recent years.

5. At the highest point here, the peak of Pen Beri and the expanse of Cardigan Bay can be seen in the distance. Two headlands away is the winking lighthouse of Strumble Head with the peak of Garn Fawr above it. Descend to rejoin the coastal path and turn left towards St David's Head.

6. On the plateau a remarkable rockscape opens up. Jagged erratic rocks are mirrored by the rugged profile of Ramsey Island out to sea. North of Ramsey are the little islets of 'Bishops and Clerks', one of which is home to a big lighthouse. Offshore, you might be lucky enough to spot porpoises or dolphins playing in the waves.

7. The route eventually passes Coetan Arthur and descends to an Iron Age coastal fort at the end of the peninsula. Continue on the coast path, returning to Porth Melgan. Retrace your route from here back to Whitesands Beach.

Make the Most of Your Day

Make your way to the National Trust's St David's visitor centre and shop in St David's High Street, where you can find out about the Trust's special places in Pembrokeshire using their interactive technologies. One such place is Cilgerran Castle, a striking thirteenth-century castle perched overlooking the spectacular Teifi Gorge that has inspired many artists, including Turner.

Food and Facilities

There is a café on Whitesands Beach serving light refreshments, and toilets can be found in the car park (not National Trust).

The wide expanse of Whitesands Beach, Pembrokeshire, looking towards St David's Head.

89. Cwm Tydu Butterfly Walk

Cwm Tydu
New Quay
Ceredigion
01545 570200
llanerchaeron@
nationaltrust.org.uk
www.nationaltrust.org.uk/
llanerchaeron

About this walk
Good for butterflies in spring
and summer

One short steep section and a
longer modest ascent

Dogs welcome on a lead

Distance 3 miles (4.8km)

Time 2 hours

This circular route takes you along the cliffs from the little bay of Cwm
Tydu to Cwm Soden, one of the few sites for the pearl-bordered fritillary
butterfly in Wales. The walk offers opportunities to spot a variety of
other insects such as the bloody-nosed beetle, the Welsh chafer, and the
giant lacewing that lives along the shady stream.

Above: Cwm Tydu, Ceredigion..

Things to see

Wildlife between points 1 and 3 on the map

Along the first stretch, between points 1 and 2, you'll find Wall Brown during May to August, and Small pearl-bordered fritillary in May and early June in the more inland sections. Look and listen out for chough and see spring squill in abundance in the short turf in spring. After point 2, watch out for common blue and wall brown in spring and late summer. The Welsh chafer beetle can be abundant here in high summer, and overhead you may see fulmars, gannets and guillemots and the occasional peregrine falcon.

Wildlife between points 3 and 5 on the map

Between points 3 and 4 is the main area for dark-green, pearl and small pearl-bordered fritillaries, especially over the more inland bracken areas. Also look out for green hairstreak on the gorse and dingy skipper, common blue and marbled white in the meadow. Beyond point 4 look out for silver-washed fritillary in July and August, and plants such as common knapweed, bird's-foot trefoil and early purple orchid. The stream is frequented by grey wagtail, giant lacewing and the huge gold-ringed dragonfly.

Wildlife beyond point 5

Between points 5 and 6 on the map you'll see a variety of wildlife including Speckled Wood butterflies in the shady lanes, plus common blue, meadow brown and small copper butterflies. Beyond point 6 you're now back in chough country. Look out for the Welsh mountain ponies that live here, helping to create good conditions for the chough. As you walk along, keep an eye out for two conspicuous beetle species on the sandy paths – the beautiful bloody-nosed beetle or the rare violet oil beetle.

How to Get There

By Car Off A487, between Pentregat and Synod Inn

OS Map Explorer 198

Start / End Cwm Tydu Beach car park, **OS grid ref: SN356575**

Map labels: Afon Soden · Castell Bach Settlement · Pen Y Graig House · Cwm Tydu · 200 m · N

1. Facing seaward at Cwm Tydu, bear right and take the footpath up the cliffs, via the kissing gate. The first bit is the worst. The path then zig-zags up the steep slope before veering seaward. Follow this main coastal footpath, keeping an eye out for cetaceans, especially porpoises and dolphins, in the sea below.

2. Go through the second kissing gate and continue to follow the coastal footpath, past the remains of a cliff-top Iron Age hill fort, along and then down to the mouth of Afon Soden at Cwm Silio.

3. Explore the stony storm beach, which seals sometimes use, then cross the wooden footbridge over the stream. Initially bear left to explore the maritime grassland on the cliffs, where there is abundant thrift, bird's-foot trefoil and kidney vetch. Then head inland, past the fingerpost and along the main footpath that runs across the lower slope. The bracken stands here are managed specifically for fritillary butterflies. Descend into the small pocket of meadowland appearing on your right.

4. Walk over the bridge. Here you have two options: option one is to follow the path straight on and turn right after the second bridge; option two is to turn left, signed 'Nanternis', and follow the path into another flowery meadow, at the end of which bear right into a third meadow. Follow the path down through this third meadow, into a fourth small meadow. It will return you to the second bridge.

5. Turn right after the second bridge and head up the wooded lane, following signs for Cwm Tydu, until you reach a field gate. Go through the gate and keep to the hedge on the seaward side, where you walk up the hill through a wonderful wildflower meadow. In the top right-hand corner, you reach a kissing gate leading onto a short dirt track – turn right at the end of this onto the surfaced lane. When you come to Pen Y Graig House, go through the kissing gate to your right next to the farmhouse, and you'll find yourself back on the cliff-top above Cwm Silio.

6. After the farmhouse gate, bear immediately left, following the footpath over a minor plank bridge heading along and down towards the Castell Bach settlement. You should now recognise where you are – just bear left and retrace your steps along the coastal footpath to the car park at Cwm Tydu.

Make the Most of Your Day

Take time to visit Llanerchaeron, a rare example of a self-sufficient eighteenth-century Welsh estate of the minor gentry that has survived virtually unaltered. The villa, designed in the 1790s, is the most complete example of the early work of John Nash. It has its own service courtyard with a dairy, laundry, brewery and salting house, and walled kitchen gardens. The pleasure grounds and ornamental lake and parkland provide peaceful walks.

Food and Facilities

Look for cafés in New Quay or head for Llanerchaeron, where the café makes the most of the fresh and seasonal produce on its doorstep. Here you can taste some of the Trust's local farm and garden produce or their traditional homemade cawl, bara brith or Welsh cakes. Toilets can be found in New Quay and at Llanerchaeron.

A pearl-bordered fritillary.

90. Exploring Snowdonia's Industrial Past

The walk starts in Nantmor village, in Snowdonia National Park, and takes in a wealth of industrial archaeology relating to the old copper mines of Cwm Bychan and Llyndy. Along the way you'll see stunning views of the mountains of Snowdonia, a wealth of plants and wildlife, and indicators of the farming history of the area.

Craflwyn
Beddgelert
Gwynedd
01766 510120
eryri@nationaltrust.org.uk
www.nationaltrust.org.uk/
craflwyn-and-beddgelert

About this walk
Site of industrial archaeological interest

Steep in places with some steps

Dogs welcome on a lead

Distance 4.5 miles (7.2km)

Time 2 hours 30 minutes

Above: View across woodland to Cwm Bychan, south of the village of Beddgelert, Gwynedd.

Things to see

Industrial heritage
Four pylons from the valley's original ore-transporting aerial ropeway, built in 1927, are still in existence, along with the concrete bases of others. Historical accounts show that the system wasn't a complete success, with buckets often hitting the ground and spilling their loads. The remains of the ropeway add to the other features seen across the whole valley, with spoil heaps and buildings harking back to the area's industrial past.

Llyndy copper mine
This was a relatively successful mine in the first half of the nineteenth century. To the left of the path, as you pass by, you'll see a large paved area. In 1839, 20 girls were employed to work on this 'cobbing' floor to break the ore. The manager at the time was quoted as describing the girls as 'the cheapest thing we have on the mine and without them it is hardly possible to know what we should do'.

Glaslyn River
The copper sulphate of the surrounding hills gives the Glaslyn River its distinctive turquoise tinge. The spray from the river and the coolness of the gorge provides ideal conditions for ferns, mosses and liverworts. The river itself is home to otters, salmon, kingfishers and dippers. Until the early nineteenth century, when William Maddocks built the cob at Porthmadog, the sea came into within a few yards of the Aberglaslyn Bridge.

How to Get There

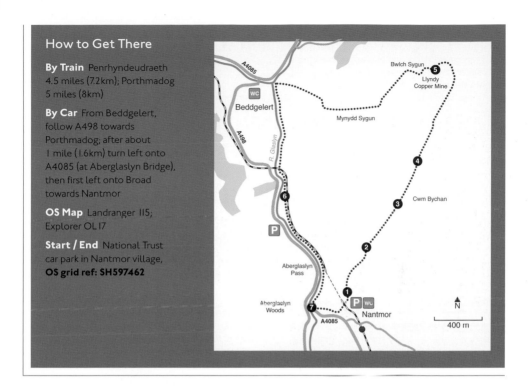

By Train Penrhyndeudraeth
4.5 miles (7.2km); Porthmadog
5 miles (8km)

By Car From Beddgelert,
follow A498 towards
Porthmadog; after about
1 mile (1.6km) turn left onto
A4085 (at Aberglaslyn Bridge),
then first left onto Broad
towards Nantmor

OS Map Landranger 115;
Explorer OL17

Start / End National Trust
car park in Nantmor village,
OS grid ref: SH597462

Remains of the Cwm Bychan ropeway, Beddgelert.

Stay Safe The area is dotted with tunnels,
spoil heaps and pits so, for safety's sake, it's
recommended you keep to the path.

1. Go through the gate to the left of the facilities
in the car park and follow the sign for Cwm Bychan,
passing underneath the old railway bridge. The
mines of Cwm Bychan were in their heyday between
1782 and 1802 and were worked intermittently until
1930. You'll notice two huge concrete circles known
as 'buddles'; these were designed to provide a
mechanical way of panning copper ore in the valley.
Make your way up the valley through the woodland.

2. Dotted around you'll see several trees that
seem alien to the landscape. They probably derive
from nearby estate gardens that were planted in
Victorian times. The Lawson cypress now seen on
these slopes were most likely brought here by birds
carrying their seeds.

3. Here you'll see here the remains of traditional farming methods. Pwll Golchi Uchaf (Upper Washing Pool) was created by damming a nearby stream and was used by the local farmers for washing their sheep. Up until the 1960s it was common for farmers to wash their sheep before shearing to ensure a higher price for their fleece.

4. As you climb higher up the valley along the path you'll notice several pylons within the landscape. These are the remains of the aerial ropeway built to carry ore from the upper end of Cwm Bychan down the valley to Nantmor.

5. At the crossroads turn left and soon you'll come across Llyndy copper mine. After seeing the site and crossing the stile, turn immediately left and follow the path towards a steep descent. At Bwlch Sygun keep to the ridge until you reach a large cairn on Mynydd Sygun. From here, start heading downwards, passing through a kissing gate; a wooden gate marks the end of your descent. Wind your way to Beddgelert village green and the footbridge over the River Glaslyn. At this point you can take a well-earned break, taking advantage of the facilities in the village. Otherwise, turn left immediately before the footbridge along the bank of the river.

6. Pass another footbridge on your right and go through the gate to cross over the railway line. Follow the path that runs between the railway and the river. The Welsh Highland Railway originally opened in 1922, only to be abandoned as a commercial failure in 1936. The line has recently been restored as a heritage railway. The building on your left is a former sheep-dipping bath, now used to share information about Aberglaslyn. Continue along the path near the river, following it along the side of the gorge. Great care should be taken when negotiating this part of the path, especially the stone buttress above the river, where you can use the handles provided for extra security.

7. You're now in the Aberglaslyn Pass. After crossing the wooden bridge, climb away from the river into mature oak woodland high above the gorge. Turn left up the steps and follow the path through the woodland back to the car park at Nantmor.

Make the Most of Your Day

Explore Beddgelert village while you're here, taking time to look at the National Trust's unique Tŷ Isaf shop, a Grade II listed building brimming with character that dates back to the late seventeenth century. Then seek out Gelert's Grave on the west bank of the River Glaslyn. Legend has it that the thirteenth-century Prince Llywelyn killed his faithful hound Gelert in the mistaken belief he had killed his young son, only to realise too late that Gelert had in fact saved his son's life by killing a predatory wolf.

Food and Facilities

Cafés can be found in Beddgelert village, and toilets are available in the car park at Nantmor.

A sign points the way to Gelert's Grave.

91. Tŷ Mawr Wybrnant and the Welsh Bible

This family-friendly walk explores the social history of a typical Welsh upland valley in Snowdonia National Park. At its centre lies Tŷ Mawr Wybrnant farmhouse, the birthplace of Bishop William Morgan, who translated the Bible into Welsh. The walk highlights several elements of this historic landscape, from wildlife to historic buildings and fields.

Tŷ Mawr Wybrnant
Penmachno
Betws-y-Coed
Conwy LL25 0HU
01690 760213
tymawrwybrnant@
nationaltrust.org.uk
www.nationaltrust.org.uk/
ty-mawr-wybrnant/

About this walk
Across open fields and forestry tracks

Site of historical and social significance

Dogs welcome on a lead

Distance 3 miles (4.8km)

Time I hour 30 minutes

Above: A wooden sign points the way.

Things to see

Wildlife
The area around point 5 on the map was once a large conifer plantation; nonetheless, you can see that several varieties of habitat have survived. The rock faces are great places for the navelwort or pennywort. In wetter areas look out for sphagnum moss, which is easily identified by its spongy texture.

Herben
A map of the valley from 1838 shows that the field you cross at the start of your walk was exactly as it is today. It's just over 2 acres (0.8ha) in size and is known as 'herben', meaning 'arable'. The building near the south-east corner was used for cattle in winter and the snaking hedge towards the stream marks the parish boundary between Dolwyddelan and Penmachno.

The drovers' road
At one point you'll come to a section of the old drovers' road, running between stone walls; this was the road along which locally raised cattle were driven to market. This ancient path to Dolwyddelan was the main route between the Machno and Lledr valleys. Prior to the railway opening in 1879, the cattle were shod at Dolwyddelan before leaving on foot for England, where they provided the main source of beef. Porthmyn (drovers)

Tŷ Mawr Wybrnant, Conwy.

led the cattle to the Midlands, Essex or Kent, walking hundreds of miles to get there.

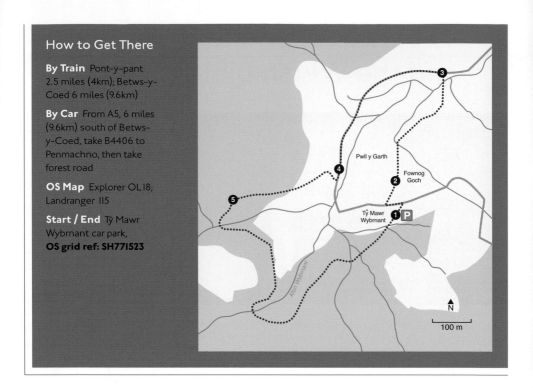

How to Get There

By Train Pont-y-pant
2.5 miles (4km); Betws-y-
Coed 6 miles (9.6km)

By Car From A5, 6 miles
(9.6km) south of Betws-
y-Coed, take B4406 to
Penmachno, then take
forest road

OS Map Explorer OL18;
Landranger 115

Start / End Tŷ Mawr
Wybrnant car park,
OS grid ref: SH771523

Pwll y Garth

Fownog
Goch

Tŷ Mawr
Wybrnant

Afon Wybrnant

N

100 m

1. Walk to the entrance of the car park and turn left. After going through the gate, turn right and walk across the field towards the gateway and ruined building.

2. Walk through to the next field and follow a fairly obvious path on the right-hand side, aiming for the far left corner. This field is called Fownog Goch on a map of 1838. It's wet and ploughable and would have been used for rough grazing. The sunken areas in the lower parts of the field are turbaries, or peat diggings. Peat was the main source of fuel in upland areas. It was cut into slabs in April and May and left to dry. The soft rush seen here, known in Welsh as 'canhwyllfrwynen' ('candle rush'), was used until the latter half of the nineteenth century as a form of candle. The light produced by this plant was much poorer than the wax candles we recognise today. Rush candle holders and candle-making equipment can be seen at Tŷ Mawr Wybrnant.

3. Make your way to the northernmost corner of the field. Pass through the gate and over the Wybrnant stream on the clapper bridge. Turn left along the road to Tŷ Mawr Wybrnant, a traditional stone-built upland farmhouse dating from the sixteenth century. It was here that William Morgan was born in 1545.

4. When you reach the wooden gate just before Tŷ Mawr Wybrnant, turn sharp right and follow the waymarks uphill. Pass through a small gate before turning left past a large smooth rock on your right-hand side. Keep the dry stone wall on your left.

5. Walk along the drovers' path until you come to the junction with the forestry path, where you turn left. You'll soon reach seats overlooking the Wybrnant Valley, so take time to stop here and admire the view. When you're ready, continue along the forestry road, keeping left until you arrive back at the car park.

View across the valley from Tŷ Mawr Wybrnant.

Make the Most of Your Day

Find time to visit Tŷ Mawr Wybrnant, where you can explore centuries of Welsh living. Copies of Bishop William Morgan's translation of the Bible, as they were first published in 1588 and 1620, are also on display, along with a small, but significant, collection of family Bibles and religious works in Welsh. There is also a growing collection of Bibles in about 200 different languages, donated by visitors from across the world, who have come to see Morgan's birthplace.

Food and Facilities

There is no café at Tŷ Mawr Wybrnant, but you can bring your own picnic and relax by the stream. Otherwise you will find cafés and restaurants in nearby Betws-y-Coed. National Trust toilets are located at Tŷ Mawr Wybrnant.

92. Family Fun at Plas Newydd

Plas Newydd
Anglesey LL61 6DQ
01248 714795
plasnewydd@
nationaltrust.org.uk
www.nationaltrust.org.uk/
plas-newydd

About this walk
Spectacular views of
Snowdonia

An ideal walk for little legs

Some steps, with an
alternative route for buggies

Dogs not permitted in the
grounds of Plas Newydd

Distance 1 mile (1.6km)

Time As long as you like

This short walk around the grounds at Plas Newydd gives a delightful insight into the way the Marquess of Anglesey's family entertained themselves in the 1930s. Today, families can enjoy the backdrop of Snowdonia and the Menai Strait, and there is plenty along the way to keep the children happy, including a tree house and a great adventure playground.

Top: Plas Newydd on the shores of
the Menai Strait, Anglesey.
Above: View across Plas Newydd
towards Snowdonia.

Things to see

Plas Newydd House and Snowdonia
As you walk through the garden from the old dairy block, the house will be hidden from your view. You'll have to wait in anticipation to catch a glimpse of the home of the Marquess of Anglesey. Be prepared to turn a corner and come face-to-face with a stunning view towards Snowdonia.

Adventure playground
You can end the walk in style with a visit to the adventure playground. Hidden among the trees in Dairy Wood, this area is open all year. You don't have to visit the garden to enter the playground and it's a great place to come with the family.

Different parts of the playground suit different ages – have fun!

Plas Newydd's 'West Indies'
The area known as the 'West Indies' is a great place for the kids to run free and explore. Look out for the new tree house. The original was built in 1963 for Lady Amelia but unfortunately became unsafe and had to be taken down. The Marquess's children loved to play here – try to imagine what kind of games they would have played in the 1930s.

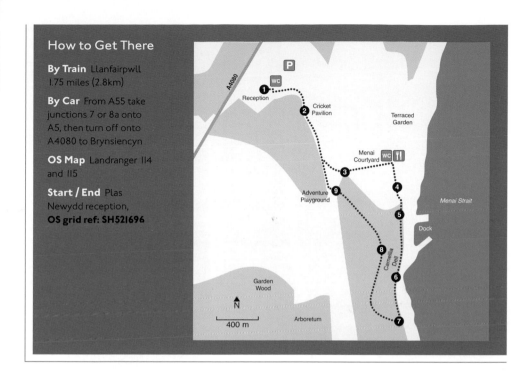

How to Get There

By Train Llanfairpwll
1.75 miles (2.8km)

By Car From A55 take
junctions 7 or 8a onto
A5, then turn off onto
A4080 to Brynsiencyn

OS Map Landranger 114
and 115

Start / End Plas
Newydd reception,
OS grid ref: SH521696

1. Start your walk from the reception and follow the path that leads down to the house.

2. As you follow the path, stop by the cricket pavilion and look over to the old stable block, which is now run by the Conway Centre. This was the Marquess's garage and was where members of the family would put on plays they had written themselves. One of the plays was called *The Pink Shirts*, which was captured on film in the 1930s.

3. Follow along the path and as you turn the corner prepare for fantastic views of the Menai Strait and the house. (During winter opening hours, turn right here and continue down the dock road, rejoining the route at point 5.)

4. Continue down the path until you reach the courtyard, where you follow the path that goes off to your right. Notice the sloping lawn to your right; this is where the Marquess and his sister used to play 'roly poly' down the hill with their dog Cheeky.

5. Follow the tarmac path that goes down to your left, then take the path on your right. To the left you will be able to see the old swimming pool where the family used to go sailing and swimming. It's now privately run by the Conway Centre.

6. Continue along the tarmac path. If you want to take a break at this point, there's a bench on your left with glorious views. Or you may like to explore the Camellia Dell on your right.

7. Come back to the path and continue forwards, then go uphill off the path and onto the grass and look for a gap in the trees. See if you can spot one of the oldest trees in Plas Newydd. Continue going uphill until you reach the tarmac path.

8. Now it is time to explore the area that the Marquess's children named the 'West Indies'. Can you think why they gave it this name? Meander through the grassy area and look out for the new tree house.

9. Stay on the grassy area and head up to the woods, where children can enjoy the adventure playground. From here, retrace your steps past the cricket pavilion and make your way back to your starting point.

Children playing among the 140-year-old Monterey cypress trees at Plas Newydd.

Make the Most of Your Day

Be sure to visit the house while you're here. Set on the shores of the Menai Strait amidst breathtakingly beautiful scenery, this elegant house was redesigned by James Wyatt in the eighteenth century. Restyled in the 1930s, the interior is famous for its association with Rex Whistler and contains an exquisite mural and the largest exhibition of his works. A military museum contains relics from the 1st Marquess of Anglesey's tenure, who commanded the cavalry at the Battle of Waterloo.

Food and Facilities

When you've finished your walk, why not visit Whistler's Restaurant for a bite to eat? Or pop into the coffee shop by the house, where you can enjoy the subtropical Menai Courtyard (note: the coffee shop is not open during winter). Toilets are available near the car park.

Northern Ireland

93. Crom Ghost Walk

Crom
Upper Lough Erne
Newtownbutler
County Fermanagh
BT92 8AP
028 6773 8118
crom@nationaltrust.org.uk
www.nationaltrust.org.uk/
crom

About this walk
A loughside walk

Good for spotting bats
and fungi

Dogs welcome on a lead

Distance 3.5 miles (5.6km)

Time 1 hour 30 minutes

With its ancient woodland, picturesque islands and historic ruins, the tranquil landscape of the Crom Estate has given rise to a number of ghostly tales and unexplained spectral sightings. This easy walk takes you around the edges of Upper Lough Erne, which is home to many rare species. Look out for wildflowers, fungi and bats along the way.

Above: A misty view across Upper Lough Erne at Crom, in County Fermanagh.

Things to see

Woodland
The ancient yews in the Old Castle Garden have been named among the '50 greatest British trees'. In the nineteenth century, parties of 200 people are said to have dined beneath their branches. The Crom Estate is one of the largest areas of semi-natural woodland in Northern Ireland, with a rich variety of uncommon lichens and wildflowers such as dog violet and wood anemone. Many different species of fungi can be found here, including waxcaps – bright toadstools that emerge in autumn in short grassland.

Spectral lights
From the early eighteenth century until the 1960s, locals spoke of eerie lights that appeared above the waters of Upper Lough Erne. The lake doesn't produce the right settings for marsh gas, which is the usual explanation for these occurrences. Some believe them to be ghostly 'fianna', the fair-headed people who resided here long ago. Others have sought for a more down-to-earth explanation, believing they might relate to the area's smuggling history, lights being used to keep law-abiding locals away from illicit activities.

Ghostly visions
In 1992 a man had a disturbing experience while on Inishfendra, a small island in Upper Lough Erne. Having fallen asleep on a rock jutting out into the water, he woke suddenly to find himself surrounded by a group of bare-chested, heavily armed men who disappeared moments later. When he described his experience to a local volunteer at the visitor centre, detailing the strange archaic clothing the figures had worn, the volunteer realised that the rock was in fact a votive stone, a sacred place where pre-Christian Celts used to make sacrifices to their gods.

How to Get There

By Boat Ferry from Derrymore church (book 24 hours in advance)

By Car 3 miles (4.8km) west of Newtownbutler on Newtownbutler to Crom road

OS Map OSNI Discoverer Map 27

Start / End Crom visitor centre, **OS grid ref: H332244**

Upper Lough Erne

WC

Lough Nalughoge

White Bridge

The Boathouse

Walled Garden

Old Castle

Visitor Centre

Jetty

N

200 m

---

1. Start at the Crom visitor centre, an old stone estate yard overlooking Upper Lough Erne. The barns provide a roosting site for bats, of which there are seven different species in this area. Look at the walls to see the little holes that act as their doorways. (Please note: the visitor centre is closed from October onwards, but you can still see the roosting bats if they are out and about.) Turn left as you leave the yard and walk along the old carriageway towards Crom Castle for a short while, before turning left again through a gate into the parkland.

2. Follow the path to the Old Castle. Here you'll encounter one of the oldest yew trees in Ireland. Estimates of its age vary between 400 and 1,000 years. Be careful not to stand on its roots as they're quite delicate.

3. Continue along the loughside, past a pretty boathouse, before crossing the White Bridge onto Inisherk Island.

4. Make a little loop of the island, passing a walled garden.

5. Cross back over the bridge and turn left, taking a path through the trees, with Upper Lough Erne on your left and the grounds of Crom Castle to your right.

6. Reach the castle's main drive and continue walking until a path breaks off to your right near the small inland Lough Nalughoge. Rejoin your first path and turn left, returning to the visitor centre and car park.

Make the Most of Your Day
To truely experience Crom, take a boat trip on Lough Erne. There is no feeling quite like sailing down the lough, stopping off at an island or two, and seeing the estate from the exceptional vantage of the water. The National Trust also organises some fantastic events, including cruises on the lough in a 100-year-old traditional craft and Jazz by the Lake (check property website for details).

Food and Facilities
Light refreshments are available in the visitor centre. Toilets can also be found on site.

94. Murlough Nature Trail

Murlough National
Nature Reserve
Keel Point
Dundrum
County Down BT33 0NQ
028 4375 1467
murlough@nationaltrust.
org.uk
www.nationaltrust.org.uk/
murlough

About this walk
Wonderful mountain views

Please keep to paths to avoid
disturbing wildlife

Dogs welcome on a lead

Distance 2.5 miles (4km)

Time 1 hour 15 minutes

Explore Murlough National Nature Reserve, a fragile 6,000-year-old sand-dune system that is home to a wide range of habitats, including heathland, species-rich grassland, woodland and scrub. Along the way, you'll get fabulous mountain views, walk along one of the finest beaches in County Down, and discover the site of the rare marsh fritillary.

Above: View across Murlough nature reserve, County Down.

Things to see

Scenery
This walk offers some great sights and beautiful scenery. You can look out over the mountains Slieve Donard and Slieve Commedagh, both cared for by the National Trust. In the opposite direction you can see Dundrum Castle, a fortress built by John de Courcy that dates back to the late twelfth century.

Marsh Fritillary
This beautiful little fritillary can be seen in flight from late May and June. Sadly, its numbers are declining all over Europe; the UK is considered a stronghold for this butterfly and it's a priority species in Northern Ireland. The caterpillar

feeds on devil's-bit scabious, a tall purple-flowered plant in full bloom in late August and September. This flower also provides valuable nectar for other butterflies, particularly in late summer.

Heathland habitat
August is the best month to appreciate the Murlough heathland in its full glory. Look for the two species of heather: bell heather and common heather, or ling. Bell heather's flowerheads are purple and flower slightly earlier than the pink ling heather, making for an attractive contrast. Thousands of years of rain have washed out the

calcium from the sand, allowing for more acid-loving plants to flourish. Bell and ling heather both grow on the older dunes, creating an unusual dune heathland.

Common heather, or ling.

1. Start at the main Murlough car park at the Cottage Café. Enter the reserve through the pedestrian gate in the centre of the car park. Turn left and follow the boardwalk.

2. Continue along the boardwalk to spaghetti junction, where the boardwalks meet.

3. Continue down the boardwalk until you reach a gap in the dunes to the south, where you get great view of the Mournes Mountains.

4. This path brings you out onto Murlough Beach. Go onto the beach and turn left. Follow on past a black waymark post until you reach the next yellow post.

5. Turn left back onto the reserve from the beach.

6. You are now on the aptly named Archaeology Path. Follow this path until you reach the next yellow post.

7. Point 7 on the map marks the area that is home to colonies of the endangered marsh fritillary butterfly.

8. When you reach the yellow waymark 8, you'll find 'Tomorrow's Heathland Heritage' site with its array of bell and ling heather.

9. Turn left and follow the path to get good views of Dundrum Castle.

10. Continue on the path that curves to the right to bring you to the Exmoor Kraal. On reaching the gravel lane, turn left (south) and return to the car park.

Make the Most of Your Day

Visit the Mournes, the most famous mountains in the country, immortalised in the 1896 song 'Mountains o' Mourne', and famously sung by Don McLean. Here you can explore Bloody Bridge, the site of a massacre during the 1641 rebellion, where the bodies of slain prisoners were thrown over the bridge into the river, turning the water red.

Food and Facilities

Refreshments can be found at the Beach Café at Murlough. Toilets are located in the car parks at Murlough and Bloody Bridge.

95. Mount Stewart Winter Walk

Treat yourself to a gentle stroll around the beautiful lake and world-famous gardens at Mount Stewart, where the landscape brilliantly reflects the seasonal changes through its wide variety of flora and fauna. The gardens are testament to the great planting artistry and rich tapestry of design that was the hallmark of Edith, Lady Londonderry.

Mount Stewart
Portaferry Road
Newtownards
County Down BT22 2AD
028 4278 8387
mountstewart@nationaltrust.
org.uk
www.nationaltrust.org.uk/
mount-stewart

About this walk
A walk through world-famous gardens

Option of a shorter route

Distance 2 miles (3.2km) or shorter 0.75-mile (1.2km) walk

Time 1 hour (or shorter 15 minutes)

Above: Autumn colours reflected in the lake at Mount Stewart, County Down.

Things to see

Tir Nan Og
This is the private burial ground and resting place of Lord and Lady Londonderry, protected by a turreted wall, ornamental gates and statues of Irish saints. The White Stag statue placed at the entrance to the family burial ground hints at Lady Londonderry's interest in Celtic myths. It is seen as a guide to heaven and represents the near proximity of the other world.

The lake
This expansive 7-acre (2.8ha) lake was created in the 1840s by Charles, 3rd Marquess of Londonderry, and subsequently landscaped in the 1920s by Lady Londonderry, wife to the 7th Marquess. In autumn, the lake at Mount Stewart provides a perfect surface to reflect the changing hues of the surrounding trees and shrubs. Take a closer look at these plants around the lakeside and you'll find that they are teeming with beautiful green lichens.

Formal gardens
In winter the formal gardens at Mount Stewart seem to take on a more subtle appearance, with the statues and columns contrasting against the evergreens and bare branches of the trees and shrubs.

An Irish harp in clipped yew is one of the many Irish symbols to be found in the Shamrock Garden at Mount Stewart.

The topiary Irish harp.

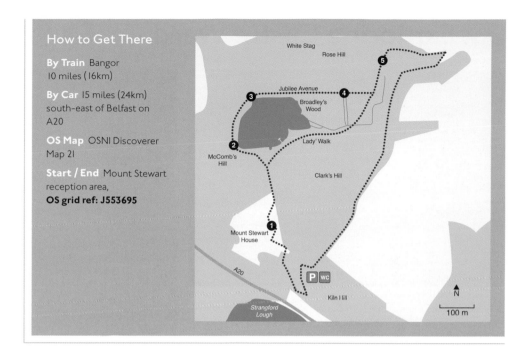

How to Get There

By Train Bangor
10 miles (16km)

By Car 15 miles (24km)
south-east of Belfast on
A20

OS Map OSNI Discoverer
Map 21

Start / End Mount Stewart
reception area,
OS grid ref: J553695

---

1. Starting your walk from the main reception area at Mount Stewart, make your way round to the north front of the mansion, where you'll find tree species such as monkey puzzle, Californian redwood and Australian cordylines. Join the wide gravelled path that meanders left towards the lake.

2. After passing a little wooden jetty you come to a bank with a seat set into the wall. You are now at the site of the private burial ground, Tir Nan Og, meaning 'Land of the Ever Young' in Gaelic.

3. On reaching the bottom of the hill you can either follow the Rock Walk or the Gravel Walk alongside Jubilee Avenue, where you can spot the White Stag statue.

4. If you cross the little stone bridge over the stream you come to Lady's Walk; following this will shorten your walk and set you on the path back to the mansion house. (Note: for the full walk go to point 5 below.) In the 18th century, ladies used the original path here to take their outdoor exercise. Spend a few minutes on

the tiny tranquil island with a lovely view of Tir Nan Og opposite, before heading back to the house.

5. Alternatively, walk past the bridge and Lady's Walk and continue forwards from Jubilee Avenue onto Rhododendron Hill, which rises up to the left. There are several flower- and tree-lined tracks here. Follow these round until you get a good view of the house before the path descends steeply to the north lawns and eventually back to the mansion house.

Make the Most of Your Day

At the time of going to press, the house is undergoing an exciting restoration programme, giving visitors the opportunity to see conservation in action. A special restoration tour is replacing the house tour.

Food and Facilities

End your walk with a visit to the cosy Bay Restaurant; there is also an ice-cream shop between the reception and the gardens. Toilets can be found by the reception.

96. Exploring Castle Ward

Castle Ward
Strangford
Downpatrick
County Down BT30 7LS
028 4488 1204
castleward@nationaltrust.org.uk
www.nationaltrust.org.uk/castle-ward

About this walk

An easy stroll in an Area of Outstanding Natural Beauty

Several short steep sections

Optional extension to Audley's Castle

Distance 2.5 miles (4km)

Time 50 minutes to 1 hour

Overlooking the shores of Strangford Lough, Castle Ward is one of Northern Ireland's finest country estates. At its heart lies an unusual Georgian mansion, famed for its mixture of architectural styles: classical on one side, Gothic on the other. This walk explores the waterside, a ruined castle, woodland, an ornamental lake and follies. Visit in winter for a chance to see a fantastic range of migrating birds and the resident seals.

Above: The 'classical side' of Castle Ward, with Srangford Lough beyond.

Things to see

Strangford Lough

Strangford Lough is the United Kingdom's largest sea inlet, covering 60 square miles (155km²) with over 350 islands. Millions of gallons of water flow in and out twice daily, bringing vast quantities of plankton and nutrients for wildlife to feed on. Underwater reefs and kelp forests provide a habitat for 2,000 marine species such as anemones, sea-squirts, starfish, sponges and urchins. Mussel beds are also an important habitat here, although in recent years trawling has done real damage to them.

Audley's Castle and Castle Ward

Audley's Castle, now a ruin, was home of the Audley family from the 1550s. Nearby is the site of Audley's Town, cleared in the Georgian era by the owners of Castle Ward to improve the views from their newly landscaped park. Viscount Bangor spent a lot of money in the eighteenth century on perfecting his country seat at Castle Ward and, to keep up with the latest aristocratic fashions, he wanted a large mansion with sweeping views down to Strangford Lough.

Birds

Winter is an excellent time to watch wading birds such as oystercatcher, dunlin, curlew and knot in Castle Ward Bay. Some species perform spectacular aerial displays in the evening as they prepare to roost. As many as 75,000 wildfowl and waders spend the autumn and winter at Strangford Lough, including 75 per cent of the worlds light-bellied brent goose. The Ards-Peninsula side of the lough is the best place to spot them.

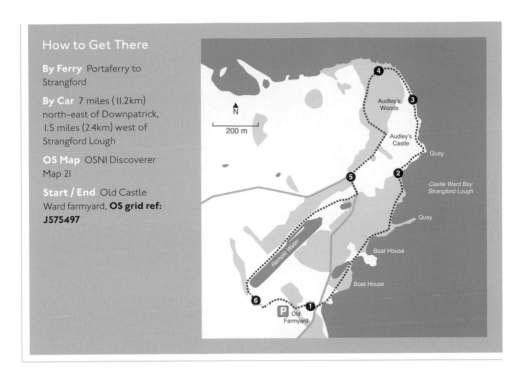

How to Get There

By Ferry Portaferry to Strangford

By Car 7 miles (11.2km) north-east of Downpatrick, 1.5 miles (2.4km) west of Strangford Lough

OS Map OSNI Discoverer Map 21

Start / End Old Castle Ward farmyard, **OS grid ref: J575497**

1. Start your walk at Old Castle Ward farmyard. Note the tower house, a fortified home built in 1610. It was Castle Ward Estate's main residence before the mansion was built in the eighteenth century. Follow the blue trail down through a large stone gateway towards the water and boathouse. The name Strangford comes from the Old Norse for 'strong fjord' and probably describes the powerful currents where the Irish Sea enters the lough.

View down Strangford Lough from Castle Ward Bay.

View through the gateway at Old Castle Ward.

4. After your detour, continue walking along the loughside, then turn left away from the water and through Audley's Wood, home to badgers and lots of small birds.

5. Where the path exits the woodland, head right on a track that soon leads to a gate in a stone wall. Emerge through this gate into the parkland surrounding Temple Water, which is an important piece of garden history. Although canals of this sort became fashionable among landowners in Ireland at this time it is now one of the very few to survive. The temple itself is perched up on your right. You soon pass a Victorian walled garden, currently used to grow wildflowers.

6. Follow the path away from the lake along a tree-lined avenue back to the farmyard. In summer, note the wildflower meadow on your left. A series of paths leads to the mansion house, woodland and playgrounds. To find out more about wildlife on the estate and lough, visit the Strangford Lough Wildlife Centre, adjacent to the farmyard.

Make the Most of Your Day

Take time to visit the eighteenth-century mansion, built in two contrasting architectural styles: the classical facade to the lawn and the Gothic facing Strangford Lough. Or stroll through the sunken garden, where vivid reds, yellows, greens and pinks from flowers and subtropical plants create a blaze of colour in this four-tier Victorian design. The adventure and woodland playground is sure to provide lots of fun for the kids, as will the Victorian Past Times Centre where children can enjoy dressing up as a Victorian boy or girl.

Food and Facilities

Enjoy freshly made scones, cakes and soups at the Coach House tea-room. Hot tea and coffee, as well as the recently installed wood burning stove, will help keep you warm during winter visits to the property. Toilets can also be found on site.

2. Follow the path along the waterfront, passing boathouses and small quays before reaching Audley's Wood. Enjoy the beautiful views across to Portaferry along the way. You may see seals bobbing about in the water and, in autumn and winter, birds such as redshank and oystercatcher.

3. At the edge of the wood, a path on the left takes you on a short, optional detour up to the sixteenth-century Audley's Castle, now a picturesque ruin. Climb to the top for a great panoramic view across the estate and Castle Ward Bay. Look out for pine marten and a long-eared owl that are sometimes seen here at dusk. Close to the castle is a Neolithic cairn where around 30 skeletons were found.

97. Minnowburn: Belfast's Green Oasis

A green oasis situated on the southern edge of Belfast, Minnowburn is the perfect place for a gentle stroll. Starting alongside the Lagan River, the trail soon heads south, taking you through deciduous woodland and farmland before looping back to the river once more. Along the way you'll find a Neolithic monument and a magical garden, and may even spot spawning salmon or sea trout.

Edenderry Road
Belfast
County Down BT8 8LE
02890 647787
minnowburn@nationaltrust.
org.uk
www.nationaltrust.org.uk/
minnowburn

About this walk
A picturesque walk close to
the heart of Belfast

Site of archaeological interest

Some stiles

Dogs welcome under control
near grazing animals

Distance 3 miles (4.8km)

Time 1 hour 20 minutes

Above: The River Lagan at Minnowburn, in County Down, is a popular recreational site.

Things to see

River Lagan
The Lagan is the main river that flows through Belfast. It was used as a canal for more than two centuries, linking the city with Lough Neagh until the navigations' closure in 1958. Today, the Lagan towpath forms the spine of the Lagan Valley Regional Park and is an important walking and cycling facility. This stretch of the river is a wonderful wildlife haven where wetland birds such as little grebe, moorhens and tufted duck can be seen. You might even see one of the seals that commonly make their way upriver from the port.

The Giant's Ring
This massive earthwork circle, roughly 600ft (183m) across and 13ft (4m) high, is a beautiful example of a henge monument. It was built around 2700BC, during the Neolithic period. In the middle is a passage tomb made up of five upright stones and a large capstone. The site has always been a popular attraction and has been in some sort of public use since the time it was first built.

Terrace Hill Garden
This garden was built by the famous linen merchant Edward (Ned) Robinson in the mid-1930s. This is one of the best viewpoints in the Lagan Valley, but it became very overgrown until 2001 when the National Trust began to restore the garden back to something resembling its former glory. The location of many an after-dinner stroll in its heyday between the 1930s and 1950s, this site commands superb views across the Lagan Valley to Malone House and the Belfast hills beyond.

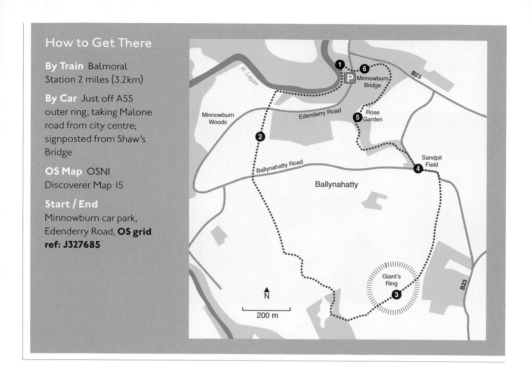

How to Get There

By Train Balmoral Station 2 miles (3.2km)

By Car Just off A55 outer ring, taking Malone road from city centre; signposted from Shaw's Bridge

OS Map OSNI Discoverer Map 15

Start / End Minnowburn car park, Edenderry Road, **OS grid ref: J327685**

1. From the car park, follow the Lagan riverbank path upstream. After about 200 yards (180m), take the first path on the left-hand side.

2. Follow this path, crossing the Edenderry Road with care. Continue on with the mature woodland on your left and you'll soon enter young broadleaved woodland. The woods at Minnowburn are mostly fairly young. Mainly beech, much of it dates from the early 1960s. The more recently planted woods tend to be native broadleaves such as oak, ash and hazel. Carry on until you reach the Ballynahatty Road. Cross the road with care and take the path opposite.

3. Follow the path, which has fields on either side, for about half a mile (0.8km), until you reach the Giant's Ring. After exploring this ancient monument, make your way out through the gate at the opposite side from which you arrived. Pass through the car park and carry on down the avenue until you reach the road.

4. Cross the road, taking care to watch out for traffic, and climb over the stile opposite. You're now in the Sandpit Field, a marvellous natural amphitheatre that was carved by retreating glaciers during the last Ice Age. Follow the track around the top of the big pit until you come to a stile beside a road.

The picturesque Minnowburn Bridge, much loved by artists and photographers.

Children at Rowallane Garden in October.

5. Climb over the stile and cross the road. Go through the pedestrian gate opposite, follow the path through a second gate and continue on the old tarmac path up Terrace Hill. This path used to be the main avenue to Terrace Hill House; in spring the bank on the left is covered in daffodils and bluebells. Carry on until you reach Terrace Hill Garden. Once you've explored this magical place go back the way you came and take the path on the left, leading downhill through the young woodland.

6. Follow the path to Minnowburn River, then walk along the banks of the river downstream until you reach Minnowburn Bridge. The bridge probably dates from the late seventeenth or early eighteenth century and is famed as a romantic spot where courting couples would meet before strolling together along the river. It's also a favourite with artists and photographers who can often be seen capturing an image of the iconic scene. From here, continue back to the car park.

Make the Most of Your Day
After your walk, head south to Rowallane Garden, one of the most beautiful gardens in Northern Ireland. A mix of formal and informal spaces, with many unusual vistas and unique plants from across the world, this is a place where you can leave the outside world behind and immerse yourself in nature's beauty.

Food and Facilities
Refreshments are available in Malone House, across the River Lagan via Shaw's bridge (owned and managed by Belfast City Council). You'll find the nearest toilets here, too.

98. Across the Black Mountain

The Black Mountain sits in the heart of the Belfast Hills, which provide the backdrop to the city's skyline. This bracing walk takes you through a rich and varied terrain, along tarmac tracks and boardwalks, and across heathland and blanket bog. From the summit of the Black Mountain you'll be rewarded with spectacular views across Northern Ireland and Belfast.

Divis and the Black Mountain
Divis Road
Hannahstown
Belfast BT 17 0NG
028 9082 5434
divis@nationaltrust.org.uk
www.nationaltrust.org.uk/divis-and-black-mountain

About this walk
Affords wonderful views from the summit

Some stiles

Tends to get boggy towards end of walk

Dogs welcome on a lead around livestock

Distance 5 miles (8km)

Time 3 hours

Things to see

The Long Barn
The Long Barn visitor centre was formerly a cattle barn, converted in 2008. Here you can enjoy a warm beverage while learning about the history and archaeological heritage of this unique site.

Black Mountain summit
Enjoy uninterrupted views of Belfast, out across the mouth of the lough and on towards the Scottish shoreline. On a clear day you can see the Isle of Man, the Lake District in Cumbria and Holyhead in Wales.

Opposite: Red grouse.

The Gamekeeper's Cottage
The old Gamekeeper's Cottage that you cross at point 6 on your walk was once home to Sammy Lyttle,

gamekeeper for the Milne and Barbour families who used to hold the hunting rights to the mountains.

Top: Looking across the rugged terrain towards the Belfast Hills.
Above: A skylark in flight.

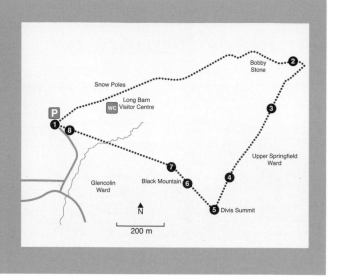

How to Get There

By Train Great Victoria Street Railway Station, Belfast 7 miles (11.2km)

By Car Minor road off B38 Upper Springfield Road, off A55 Outer Ring

OS Map OSNI Discoverer Map 15

Start / End Divis Road car park, **OS grid ref: J740266**

1. From the car park, head towards the Divis transmitter mast. Follow the wooden boardwalk to the right onto the summit of the Black Mountain, marked by a trigonometry pillar. Take a while to admire the stunning views across Belfast and Northern Ireland.

2. Walk straight down from the summit, heading in the direction of Belfast. When you reach the fence line, turn right and head for the summit of Black Hill in front of you.

3. Negotiate the stile beside the field gate and continue with the fence line on your left.

4. Continue until you reach the telegraph poles and the fence takes a sharp left turn. Head left to the trigonometry pillar on the summit of the Black Hill.

5. With the trigonometry pillar to your back (so you are facing away from the city), head straight down the hill.

6. Pass over the walled remains of the old Gamekeeper's Cottage.

7. Carrying onwards, cross the fence line at the stile beside the old mill dam. This dam was one of two feeder dams on the Collin River that provided a steady water source for McCance's Mill in the townland of Suffolk, near Belfast. Turn left (facing 10 o'clock) and continue.

8. Pass through the kissing gate to enter the main car park, finishing this circular route.

Make the Most of Your Day

After your walk, why not do something completely different and head north to the Patterson's Spade Mill in Templepatrick? This is the last working water-driven spade mill in daily use in the British Isles, where you can hear the hammers, smell the grit and feel the heat of traditional spade-making. Guided tours vividly capture life during the Industrial Revolution and reveal the fascinating history and culture of the humble spade.

Food and Facilities

Refreshments can be found at the Long Barn visitor centre, where toilets are also available.

99. Across the Giant's Causeway

Flanked by the wild North Atlantic Ocean on one side and a landscape of dramatic cliffs on the other, for centuries the Giant's Causeway has inspired artists, stirred scientific debate and captured the imagination of all those who see it. This walk follows the Blue Trail, which leads directly from the award-winning visitor centre to the world-famous stones.

Giant's Causeway
60 Causeway Road
Bushmills
County Antrim BT57 8SU
028 2073 1855
giantscauseway@
nationaltrust.org.uk
www.nationaltrust.org.uk/
giants-causeway

About this walk
Site of geological interest

Dramatic views

Steep gradients in places

Distance 1.5 miles
(2.4km) return

Time 50 minutes return trip
plus time spent at the stones

Above: View across the Giant's
Causeway, County Antrim.

Things to see

Humphrey the Camel
At the viewing point before Windy Gap, pause to look out over Portnaboe Bay. The bay's most famous resident is Humphrey the Camel, who is lying asleep. See if you can spot him.

Giant's Causeway
The Giant's Causeway provides a glimpse into the Earth's most ancient past. For this reason, it's been designated a World Heritage Site by UNESCO. Made up of over 40,000 interlocking basalt columns, the causeway is the result of intense volcanic activity millions of years ago.

Weird but wonderful
Take a look behind you when you are on the Giant's Causeway and see if you can see the aptly named dog's vomit fungus creeping towards you! National Trust rangers recently found this weird fungus at the causeway. It's not actually a fungus, but a so-called slime mould that is capable at moving at a snail's pace. It starts life as a single-celled organism but when feeding conditions are good, and it encounters a suitable mate, the two coalesce into a plasmodium stage, at which point it starts to move, oozing over its feeding material.

The basalt columns of the
Giant's Causeway.

How to Get There

By Train Coleraine 11 miles (17.6km)

By Car On B147, 2 miles (3.2km) from Bushmills, 11 miles (17.6km) from Coleraine

OS Map OSNI Discoverer Map 4 and Map 5

Start / End Giant's Causeway visitor centre car park 1, **OS grid ref: NW2918297863**

Grand Causeway
Port Noffer
Wishing Chair
Great Stookan
Port Ganny
Windy Gap
Aird Snout
Weir's Snout
Portnaboe
Visitor Centre
B146
N
200 m

A curiously shaped rock at the Giant's Causeway.

> **Stay Safe** The causeway stones can be slippery and dangerous when wet – take care and always heed the advice of the rangers.

1. Park in car park 1 and take time to explore the wonderful new visitor centre. Here you can pick up an audio guide, which will highlight points of interest along your walk. While you're here, look up to see people tentatively stepping over the glass panels in the ceiling. When you're ready to start your walk, go to the back of the centre and exit through the rear doors. Alternatively, you can walk up the incline and over the grass roof, descending the steps to come out at the rear of the visitor centre.

2. Follow the kerb-stone footpath eastwards. On your right is the sheer dramatic cliff face, and on your left the wild North Atlantic Ocean.

3. Continue to follow the kerb-stone footpath heading eastwards. Look out for a curiously shaped rock feature, known as Humphrey the Camel, along the way. Shortly the path turns a sharp corner called Windy Gap. From here the causeway stone outcrop is visible in the distance, beyond the bay.

4. The formal kerb-stone path becomes a hard-core gravel surface just before the causeway stone outcrop. Look for a gap in the rocks beyond the tarmac bus drop-off point and follow this path, continuing to walk in an easterly direction until you reach the causeway. Spend as much time as you like exploring this famous landmark, then retrace your steps back to the visitor centre and car park.

Make the Most of Your Day

Unlock the mystery of the landscape by exploring the exhibition area of the visitor centre. Officially opened in July 2012, the building was the result of an international architecture competition. Since opening, it has won many prestigious awards for design innovation and sustainability. Take an official tour to find out more, or join one of the special family events, such as a face-painting day or activities in celebration of St Patrick's Day. See the website for more details.

Food and Facilities

Enjoy a selection of local tasty food and refreshments in the visitor centre café. Whether you fancy a quick cappuccino or a wholesome bowl of traditional Irish stew, the menu is sure to have something to tempt you. Toilet facilities are also located in the visitor centre, as well as outside at the group entrance.

The award-winning visitor centre at the Giant's Causeway is an attraction in its own right.

100. Portstewart Sand Dune Trail

Many walkers and families enjoy the 2-mile (3.2km) stretch of magnificent golden sands at Portstewart Strand. Fewer are aware of this lovely trail that meanders through the 6,000-year-old dunes to the river's edge at the Bann Estuary. Here you'll find a different world, rich in wildflowers and butterflies in spring and summer, and a haven for birds throughout the year.

Portstewart Strand
118 Strand Road
Portstewart BT55 7PG
028 7083 6396
portstewart@
nationaltrust.org.uk
www.nationaltrust.org.uk/
portstewart-strand

About this walk
A lovely walk across ancient sand dunes

Good for bird and butterfly spotting

Some steep sandy paths

Distance 3.5 miles (5.6km)

Time 2 hours

Things to see

Wildlife
As you pass through the sand dunes, look out for rabbits nibbling at the marram grass, and a carpet of bird's-foot trefoil, wild pansy and thyme, teeming with butterflies and bees. In the estuary you'll see wintering wildfowl and waders feeding on the mudflats, and a wide range of migratory species in the spring and autumn. Look out for species such as shelduck, curlew, redshank and mallard along the river's edge. If you like bird watching, after your walk you could visit the Barmouth bird hide, located just across the river in a nearby wildlife reserve. Keys to the hide are available at the visitor centre.

Orchids
There are at least four different types of wild orchid in the dunes during the summer months. Look out for pyramidal orchids with their slender stems crowned with a tall stack of pink petals. Probably the most exciting is the bee orchid, with its large pale pink or white sepals on either side of the velvety labellum, which looks like a bee with its brownish red and yellow markings – hence the name.

Maintaining the habitat
Portstewart Strand and the Bann Estuary are designated an Area of Special Scientific Interest (ASSI). In order to protect the area's biodiversity, cattle are left to graze the sand dunes in a fenced-off area from late summer to early spring.

Top: The dunes at Portstewart Strand, County Derry.
Above: A bee orchid.

Their job is to keep the sward height short, which allows wildflowers such as bird's-foot trefoil, wild thyme and pyramidal orchid to flourish. These in turn attract bees, butterflies and moths.

How to Get There

By Train Coleraine
12 miles (19km)

By Car Take A2 to
Portstewart and follow
signs to The Strand
Sat nav: BT55 7PG

OS Map OSNI
Discoverer Map 4

Start / End Portstewart
Strand visitor centre,
OS grid ref: C811366

1. Start your walk at the visitor centre and make your way to lifebuoy station 10, about 1 mile (1.6km) from the visitor centre.

2. Climb the sand ladder at lifebuoy 10 to leave the beach behind. Soon you will enjoy the tranquility of the dunes.

3. You now have the choice of two different paths. The one on the right leads you through the kissing gate inside a fenced area where cattle graze between September and March. Small waymark posts will guide you across to the Bann Estuary. Alternatively, if you choose the other path, just follow it along the fence line until you reach the Bann Estuary.

4. No matter which path you have chosen, turn right when you come to the River Bann. You are now walking through an area of salt-marsh. Be aware that cattle may be grazing on the salt-marsh, too.

5. Follow the path through the salt-marsh and you will come to a kissing gate leading into Crab Bay. Follow the path around the edge of the dunes.

6. This path brings you back to the beach at lifebuoy 14. From here it is about 2 miles (3.2km) back to the visitor centre.

Make the Most of Your Day

A few miles to the west of Portstewart you'll come to the Downhill Domesne and Hezlett House. Here you can discover the striking eighteenth-century mansion of the eccentric Earl Bishop, which now lies in ruin, then explore Mussenden Temple, perched on the cliff edge. As an extra treat you can learn about the reality of life in the rural seventeenth-century cottage of Hezlett House, told through people who once lived there in one of Northern Ireland's oldest buildings.

Food and Facilities

The Portstewart Strand visitor centre serves ice cream and hot and cold drinks, while Aunt Sandra's Candy Factory will delight children with its selection of lollies, marshmallow sandwiches, honeycomb and much more. Tea and coffee facilities are also on offer at the reception of Hezlett House. Toilets can be found by Portstewart Strand.

Index

Picture Credits